10699332

Studies in
Cross-cultural
Psychology

Studies in Cross-cultural Psychology

Volume 1

Edited by

NEIL WARREN

School of African and Asian Studies,
University of Sussex, Brighton, England

1977

ACADEMIC PRESS

London   New York   San Francisco

A Subsidiary of Harcourt Brace Jovanovich, Publishers

ACADEMIC PRESS INC. (LONDON) LTD
24-28 Oval Road,
London NW1

U.S. Edition published by
ACADEMIC PRESS INC.
111 Fifth Avenue,
New York, New York 10003

Copyright © 1977 By ACADEMIC PRESS INC. (LONDON) LTD

All Rights Reserved

No part of this book may be reproduced in any form by photostat, microfilm, or
any other means without written permission from the publishers

Library of Congress Catalog Card Number: 7648386

ISBN: 0-12-609201X

PROPERTY OF
NATIONAL UNIVERSITY
LIBRARY

PRINTED IN GREAT BRITAIN BY
T. & A. CONSTABLE LTD, EDINBURGH

To Michael Ogbolu Okonji

Contributors

P. R. DASEN, *Faculté de Psychologie et des Sciences de l'Education, Université de Genève, 1211 Geneva 4, Switzerland.*

P. L. ENGLE, *Division of Human Development, Institute of Nutrition of Central America and Panama, Carretera Roosevelt Zona 11, Guatemala City, Guatemala, Central America.*

M. IRWIN, *Division of Human Development, Institute of Nutrition of Central America and Panama, Carretera Roosevelt Zona 11, Guatemala City, Guatemala, Central America.*

R. E. KLEIN, *Division of Human Development, Institute of Nutrition of Central America and Panama, Carretera Roosevelt Zona 11, Guatemala City, Guatemala, Central America.*

P. KLINE, *Department of Psychology, University of Exeter, Exeter, EX4 4QG, England.*

E. ROSCH, *Department of Psychology, University of California, Berkeley, California 94720, USA.*

R. TAFT, *Faculty of Education, Monash University, Clayton, Victoria, Australia.*

C. YARBROUGH, *Division of Human Development, Institute of Nutrition of Central America and Panama, Carretera Roosevelt Zona 11, Guatemala City, Guatemala, Central America.*

Foreword

A decade ago, it may have been possible for a diligent psychologist interested in cross-cultural studies to survey and sift all the relevant literature at first hand. That soon ceased to be a realistic possibility; and one came instead to rely on one's judgement and hunches and on reviews, citations and gossip in trying to pinpoint the important developments and promising trends. Now, we begin to be swamped. Certain textbooks and sets of readings have helped for teaching purposes; but the need for detailed, high-level presentations and evaluations of particular areas of enquiry in cross-cultural psychology has not yet been met. This and subsequent volumes are intended to remedy that deficiency. The authors address themselves to those who are already involved with psychology's cross-cultural dimension: to their professional peers, to the relevant graduate students and to some advanced undergraduates. It is also my expectation that some who do not consider themselves cross-cultural psychologists will find here material worth their while – notably certain anthropologists and those psychologists concerned with processes partly open to cross-cultural elucidation.

The book is somewhat shorter than was planned, for two contributions eventually had to be held over for publication in the second volume. For this and other reasons tiresome to relate, the publication of this volume has been somewhat delayed; my apologies are thus due to those authors who produced their chapters in good time. I am grateful to the Commonwealth Foundation, to Academic Press, to the University of Sussex and to the Australian National University for financial provision relating to the preparation of this volume; to Elizabeth Mandeville, Marie Jahoda and Gün Semin for their continuous stimulation and support.

Brighton,
October 1976   NEIL WARREN

Contents

Contributors vii
Foreword ix
Introduction xiii

1 | Human Categorization
E. ROSCH

I. The categorization of attribute domains 3
  A. Colour 3
  B. Prototypes in other attribute domains 15
II. The nature of categories 18
  A. Some digital representations of categories 18
  B. Analog representations of categories: prototypes 20
III. Classifications of concrete objects 27
  A. Basic objects in natural categories 30
  B. The origins of noun category prototypes 35
  C. Implications for other fields in psychology 37
  D. Implications for cross-cultural research 40
IV. General summary 45
Acknowledgement 46
References 47

2 | Cross-cultural Studies and Freudian Theory
P. KLINE

I. Introduction 51
II. Methodological problems in cross-cultural research 56
III. Categories of cross-cultural research 56
IV. Results of hologeistic studies ' 72
V. Cross-cultural psychological studies 82
VI. Conclusions 85
References 86

3 | Malnutrition and Mental Development in Rural Guatemala
R. E. KLEIN, M. IRWIN, P. L. ENGLE and C. YARBROUGH

I. A selective review of the literature 92
  A. Definitions of malnutrition 92
  B. Timing of malnutrition 93
  C. Definitions and measurement of mental development . . . 94
  D. Age of measurement of mental development 96
  E. Attribution of causality 97

II.   The INCAP study   98
      A. Design   98
      B. Definition of the independent variable   99
      C. Definition of the dependent variable   100
      D. Intervening variables   103
      E. Results to date   103
III. Discussion   115
Acknowledgements   117
References   117

4 | Coping with Unfamiliar Cultures
    R. TAFT

  I.   Introduction   121
 II.   The varieties of culture coping situations   122
      A. Variations in the difficulty of the coping task   .   .   .   124
      B. Factors determining the difficulty of culture coping   .   .   .   124
III.   Learning to become a member of society   127
      A. Socialization and resocialization   127
      B. Enculturation and reculturation as psychological processes   130
IV.   Culture shock   139
 V.   Multi-culturalism   143
VI.   A multi-facet framework for analysing long-term adaptation to new
      cultures and societies   146
Acknowledgements   151
References   151

5 | Are Cognitive Processes Universal? A Contribution to Cross-
    cultural Piagetian Psychology
    P. R. DASEN

  I.   Introduction   155
 II.   The stages of sensori-motor intelligence in the African baby   .   .   157
      A. Method   158
      B. Results and discussion   160
      C. Conclusion   163
III.   The stage of concrete operations   166
      A. Qualitative aspects: the sequence of stages   166
      B. Quantitative aspect: cross-cultural comparison of rates of develop-
          ment   168
      C. The performance/competence distinction   172
      D. The influence of acculturation   178
      E. The influence of ecological demands   184
      F. Method   187
      G. Results   190
      H. Discussion   195
IV.   Conclusion   196
References   198

Author Index   203
Subject Index   211

Introduction

NEIL WARREN

Only in the last decade have cross-cultural studies become a going concern in psychology. The recognition that psychology is to be advanced by comparisons which cross cultural boundaries was slow to mature. A different assumption used to prevail, and may still be observed: that it is the study of culture, or of primitive people, which is to be informed by the application to it of psychological knowledge and theory. Not many years ago a British degree syllabus included a course entitled "The Psychology of Primitive Peoples". The corresponding course today would overlap little in its issues and sources with the earlier course; and it would very probably be called "Cross-Cultural Psychology".

This composite term, awkward at first meeting, is of recent coinage — possibly dating from no earlier than the nineteen-sixties. The term has quickly become established, however. It appears, for instance, in the titles of a journal and of an international association. It subsumes studies whose specific rationales tend to vary somewhat; but cross-cultural psychologists would easily agree on the general aim of extending psychology beyond its Western, and possibly ethnocentric, base. It is a common complaint that psychologists have too readily found their subjects at hand: students, patients, schoolchildren, and certain convenient laboratory animals. The day is now past when the psychology of human beings was thought to be in principle deducible from the behaviour of rats. The next recognition has to be that the humans of certain countries — roughly Europe and North America — are liable to be an unrepresentative minority of mankind. Psychology's subject matter, its very research issues, may be similarly limited; this is obviously true of "applied" work and research with practical ends. Cross-cultural psychology is, among other things, an attempt to correct this tilted balance.

Cross-cultural psychology obviously has no real history; but it does have a longish past. Antecedent figures from that past actually include a few very famous names — for example, Darwin, Galton, Rivers, Freud, Jung,

Bartlett. But, unless perhaps one be a fully committed Freudian or Jungian, there are no works of any truly classic status. The relevant past also includes the "culture and personality" school, based in American cultural anthropology and drawing heavily on psychoanalytic psychology. That movement, however, is more or less discontinuous with today's cross-cultural psychology: this is primarily because of the seemingly inappropriate theoretical manoeuvre involved. The "culture and personality" approach in general took psychodynamic theory as validly given and proceeded to employ its concepts and insights to interpret and explain aspects of culture. In this volume Paul Kline gives an account of "culture and personality" in reviewing cross-cultural studies in relation to Freudian theory. But Kline's review brings the appropriate scientific attitude to bear on the possibility of testing psychoanalytic theory. Far from drawing on supposedly established theory for interpretive purposes, the tenor of cross-cultural psychology includes a strong emphasis on the development and extension and above all on the testing and validation of theory. It is thus much nearer than anything from its sporadic past to the scientific and academic centre of contemporary psychology. Comparisons across cultures are seen to be too important for psychology to be left to the anthropologist.

Is cross-cultural psychology a *branch* or an *area* or a *field* of psychology? These metaphors are certainly used, and one may be at a loss for alternative terms; but they are a little misleading. Consider first subject matter. The "cross-cultural" category cuts directly across the usual categories (areas, fields) of subject matter. It may in principle take its problems from anywhere within the complete range of psychological phenomena — from physiological psychology and perception on the one hand to social psychology and personality on the other. Nothing is by its nature excluded. Of course, what actually happens is that only *certain* research issues appear amenable to fruitful elucidation by cross-cultural comparisons; for example, those which are difficult or impossible to study experimentally and for which cultural variation provides a critical range in independent and dependent variables. These nodal points are thought of as exemplifying the subject matter of cross-cultural psychology. The range of their content is nonetheless extremely broad. Next consider methods or techniques. Does cross-cultural psychology boast its own ways of gathering data and collecting information? The answer must in general be no. Researchers who work with foreign languages and in alien cultures do have their own peculiar difficulties. They have developed some ways of systematically dealing with these — a good example is the use of back-translation. Measuring techniques in use in Western countries often have to be adapted and re-validated. Some methods in which Western students, with their conception of an "experiment" or "test", will readily engage by the adoption of an "as if" attitude simply bemuse non-Western illiterates, and have to be avoided or greatly modified. None of these, however, are special techniques for cross-cultural psychology to boast of. They are rather attempts to draw on the available stock of methods as far as and as adequately as possible. And they are sometimes ways of doing the best one can in the circumstances.

What remains, to provide distinctiveness and commonality, is the cross-cultural element itself — an aspect of design rather than of method, substance or theory. Cross-cultural psychology extends across cultures, and that is its mainstay. It is thus best thought of as resulting not from logic or illogic but from a division of labour within psychology; so that we now have a loose coalition of psychologists who are concerned that the cross-cultural element should not be neglected and quite naturally take an interest in each other's work. The characterization of cross-cultural psychology must, in this spirit, be a liberal one, not unnecessarily stringent or exclusive, and I have deliberately aimed at a broad-minded policy in selecting contributions for these volumes.

A feature of this policy which deserves special mention concerns research of an "applied" or practical nature. I hope to be able to include in each volume one major contribution that deals with the psychological dimension of a third-world problem with whose solution or alleviation psychologists may usefully assist. Instances of such problems would be protein–calorie malnutrition and its psychological effects, education and literacy, national development and rapid acculturation, and family planning and population control. Not many psychologists specialize in these fields, though their number is increasing. I have not conducted the head count, but it seems likely to be true that many more psychologists conduct encounter groups for Western business-men and housewives than are engaged in work on malnutrition. If half the world's children are malnourished, as is frequently estimated, then there is the balance to be redressed again. It is appropriate that cross-cultural psychology encompass such work as that of Robert Klein and his colleagues, of INCAP in Guatemala, on the methodologically hazardous problem of identifying the lasting psychological effects of protein–calorie malnutrition. Their painstaking longitudinal study is not yet complete, but I am pleased to be able to include a detailed progress report in this volume.

It also happens that Ronald Taft began with a research interest in a practical issue, that of the cultural adjustment of immigrants to Australia. In his chapter for this volume, however, he has broadened this focus into what amounts to a social psychology of culture coping in a wide range of situations. In this case it is Taft's subjects, of course, who cross cultures; and by this token his chapter brings together material which is unique to, and within, cross-cultural psychology. Another research question which seems uniquely to belong to cross-cultural psychology but yet has clear and important implications for psychology in general is whether there are psychological universals. To use an old phrase for it, in what sense and in what degree may the psychic unity of mankind be said to obtain? Paul Kline points out the importance of taking this issue seriously for psychoanalytic theory, whose apparent claim or assumption is of generalizability to all mankind. Given great impetus by the arguments of linguists such as Chomsky and Labov, and then in psychology by the work of Cole *et al.* (1971), the question of psychic unity has become at least a background issue of much cross-cultural work in recent years. It is hard to answer definitely, obviously in part because the next study from some new location may always turn up something which does not fit and which therefore becomes a major problem for explanation. But also, as Eleanor Rosch makes clear in her contribution, the good answer to the question will usually not be a tally but a theory. It is the same psychological *processes* which will be universal, if at all, and thus it is successful theoretical comprehension of these processes which will be able to specify the limiting cultural conditions for commonality and variation. No-one need be so rash as to claim that we are all exactly alike in order to endorse unity or universality. All the same it begins to look as if we are all more alike in certain fundamental ways than used to be thought in the days when researchers were looking for and stressing cultural differences and the plasticity of man, not to speak of those who have linked surface differences with race.

Both Eleanor Rosch's and Pierre Dasen's chapters, being explicitly and strategically addressed to the possibility of psychological universals, are major contributions to the issue. Both demonstrate the testing of fundamental psychological theory by cross-cultural comparison. But at the same time both exemplify something else, that for such theory-testing the cross-cultural dimension is likely to be one dimension among others in the overall strategy of research. Cross-cultural comparison may be indispensable for certain aspects of the theory, but other aspects may properly be elucidated experimentally or developmentally at other times or by other researchers. Rosch's extensive programme of research, reported in her chapter, combines these various approaches by remarkable good judgement. She has developed and consolidated a general theory of human categorization, initially and in part by cross-cultural research, and indicates that its cross-cultural cycle is by no means complete. Piaget's theory of cognitive development was first elaborated in very great detail in total innocence of any cross-cultural comparisons. The situation is now greatly changed. This is in no small part due to Dasen, who has reviewed the cross-cultural Piagetian literature elsewhere (1972) and here presents some of his own recent work and examines the relevant work of others. His recurrent question is whether the developmental stages and processes posited by Piaget's theory are or are not universal. This comes to involve Dasen in conceptual distinctions between "strong" and "weak" universals, and between "competence" and "performance".

This volume is dedicated to the memory of Ogbolu Okonji. A chapter by him was to have been included in this volume, on the cross-cultural evidence pertinent to Witkin's theory and measures of cognitive style or field dependence. He died before the chapter could be finished. Okonji's death at a ridiculously early age is an awful loss for cross-cultural psychology; and also, to cut psychology another way, for the profession of psychology in Africa. Okonji had shown himself outstanding among the small but rapidly growing number of African psychologists. An exile from Nigeria during the civil war, he had worked in Uganda and Zambia, quickly commanding respect and affection in both countries. Subsequently he returned to Nigeria, to the University of Lagos, where he died. His work in all three countries, and in Scotland, steadily contributed to the literature that his chapter was to take stock of. Okonji, too, would perhaps have touched on the issue of psychological universals, at least implicitly. I remember in particular a nicely ironic complaint of his, that a certain theoretical position does not seem able to take account of Western man, and that cross-cultural psychology's mission could take it absurdly far from its Western base. Ogbolu Okonji would point out too that, after Piaget's, no theory has generated more cross-cultural research than Witkin's. It would be inappropriate to omit consideration of this work. I hope to include a completed version of Okonji's chapter in the second volume of this series.

Subsequent volumes will inevitably take different samples of cross-cultural psychology. This first sample, even without Okonji, may appear somewhat skewed towards cognitive processes, developmental psychology, and the issue of universals. I believe, however, that the emphases of much recent work are well reflected in this volume. And this in turn reflects — and of course contributes to — the recent vigorous advances in the study of cognition and child development in general. Cross-cultural psychology may be as yet too young for it to be otherwise.

REFERENCES

Cole, M., Gay, J., Click, J. and Sharp, D. W. (1971). "The Cultural Context of Learning and Thinking." Basic Books, New York.
Dasen, P. R. (1972). *J. Cross-Cult. Psych.* **3**, 23–39.

1 | Human Categorization

ELEANOR ROSCH

In so far as psychology is to be a science whose statements are of some interest and some beauty, it must attempt to formulate principles of the mental and behavioural functions of humans which are general and universal. That is not to say that theory must focus only on the ways in which humans are the same; rather, the universality of theory comes from its ability to encompass and predict differences as well as universals in human thought and behaviour. Robin Horton, in a comparison of traditional and scientific explanation (Horton, 1967), succinctly describes all explanatory theory as "the quest for unity underlying apparent diversity; for simplicity underlying apparent complexity; for order underlying apparent disorder; for regularity underlying apparent anomaly" (p. 51).

Such an ideal can be better approached, I believe, if cross-cultural investigations and general experimental psychology become more closely integrated. Without the guidance of general psychological theory, cross-cultural psychology can only continue to amass miscellaneous facts or pursue its own autonomously developed research traditions — such as the inherently inconclusive comparison of the performance of Western and traditional peoples on standard psychometric measures. Equally strong is the need for experimental psychology to take into account cross-cultural diversity. Laboratory studies can also evolve into autonomous research traditions in which specialized and atypical sets of stimuli become the exclusive domain of investigation and the problem-solving strategies of particular subject populations are taken for general psychological laws.

Human categorization was chosen as the topic of the present chapter both for substantive and methodological reasons. Not only is categorization a content area of major importance, but, in addition, research in this area illustrates the possibilities of a progressively increasing interplay between theory and cross-cultural research.

Categorization is a content area of major importance because the world consists of a virtually infinite number of discriminably different stimuli. Since no organism can cope with infinite diversity, one of the most basic functions of all organisms is the cutting up of the environment into classifications by which non-identical stimuli can be treated as equivalent. This important function would, thus, seem to be a prime target for theoretical accounts — by what principles do humans divide up the world in the way that they do? Why do we, for example, have "red" and "orange" which are considered two different colours and "cats" and "dogs" which are considered two different animals while other cultures may cut up these domains in different ways?

Surprisingly, until quite recently, such questions have received virtually no attention from the social sciences. Linguistics, psychology, anthropology, and cross-cultural psychology have commonly avoided the issue by means of the assumption that segmentation of the world is originally arbitrary. For example, ". . . the physical and social environment of a young child is perceived as a continuum. It does not contain any intrinsically separate 'things'. The child, in due course, is taught to impose upon this environment a kind of discriminating grid which serves to distinguish the world as being composed of a large number of separate things, each labelled with a name" (Leach, 1964, p. 34). Much of the research reported in the present chapter has been devoted to showing that, contrary to this viewpoint, the world *does*, in a sense, contain "intrinsically separate things".

The chapter is divided into three major sections which delineate the development of theories of human categorization of two quite different types of categories. The first section treats the categories into which the most general attribute domains such as colour and form are segmented. For such domains, it will be argued that categories form around perceptually salient points in the domain and that such points form cognitive "prototypes" for the categories. This is an example of the type of argument which both offers a framework for cross-cultural comparison and has implications for psychological theory. Because the prototypes are probably physiologically determined, for such categories, the content as well as the form of categories should be universal, and only the category boundaries are expected to vary with culture. The assumption that categories were arbitrary, with the resultant cataloguing of such cultural differences as exist in the segmentation of attribute domains, until recently obscured what is probably the basic structure of those domains.

Implications for psychological theory go beyond categorizations of attribute domains and involve the logic of category structure in general. The arguments in Section I of this chapter that attribute categories could be analog in nature challenge the prevalent assumption in psychology that all categories must consist of discrete criterial features. The second section of the chapter shows the manner in which a model of the structure of categories derived from cross-culturally based research on attribute domains could be generalized to categories of concrete objects. For these categories, the content of categories is assumed to vary with culture but the nature of structure to be universal; that is, evidence is presented that common semantic noun categories (such as "furniture" and "bird") are structured in an analog manner in terms of more and less prototypical members just as attribute categories are structured.

The central issue of this research on categorization is the question of why cultures categorize the world in the ways that they do; that is, it is a request for a theoretical explanation of human categorization. Noun category prototypes, unlike the attribute domains dealt with in Section I, are neither physiologically determined nor cross-culturally universal; thus, the question of the origins of categories of concrete objects and the origins of the prototypes of such categories is a central one. The third section of this chapter offers a theory for categorization of physical objects which attempts to answer such questions. In the first place, it is argued that categories of objects become organized so as to maximize the correlation of attributes and, hence, predictability of attributes, within categories. Therefore, the basic category cuts in the environment should be those which follow the structure of co-occurrence of attributes in the real world. In the second place, it is argued that for object categories, prototypes are the objects which most strongly reflect the attribute structure of the category as a whole; thus, by means of prototypes, categories can be made to appear simpler, more clear-cut, and more different from each other than they are in reality. As implied in the second section, for categories of objects, the content of categories and the nature of the prototypes of categories can be expected to vary across cultures but the principles of category formation and of the development of prototypes can be expected to be universal.

Both in the study of attribute domains and in the study of physical objects, development of a theory of the psychological principles underlying the formation of categories was previously inhibited by the assumption that categories were arbitrary. Although the primary evidence for principles of category formation for objects presently comes from studies within Western culture, these studies offer an explicit outline for the programme of research needed to verify the universal nature of such principles.

I. THE CATEGORIZATION OF ATTRIBUTE DOMAINS

A. Colour

The earliest cross-cultural discussions of colour were reports by travellers, missionaries, and anthropologists of the ways in which colour terminology in the strange culture visited was different from the terminology of the home culture (see, for example, Berlin and Kay, 1969, for a history of colour term reports). In this fact lies a first lesson in the effects of an atheoretical comparison between cultures. The facts about a new culture which are most likely to be observed and noted by a naïve observer are the ways in which the strange culture differs from the familiar. Thus, we do not find reports of other cultures which tell us that the people chew their food, or that they smile, or that it was possible to learn their words for familiar objects or for colours. All such facts are taken for granted and, in the absence of a theory which directs the field-worker's attention to the phenomenon, they tend to be overlooked. Thus, the initial knowledge of colour terminology gleaned from anthropological study appeared to support the idea that the colour space, like all domains, could be segmented arbitrarily into different colour categories.

The first use of colour terminology by modern psychological theory was as a domain of study in which empirical support for the concept of linguistic relativity could most readily be obtained. Linguistic relativity, in its "strong form" in which the assertion is made that differences in language in different cultures cause differences in thought, had been movingly argued in relation to the metaphysics of grammar by linguists such as Whorf (1956). However, in the effort to turn this assertion into an empirical hypothesis which could be tested, psychologists were reduced to the study of the overt classifications made by the vocabulary items of languages (Rosch, 1974). Colour appeared to be an ideal domain in which the necessary controls for such a study existed: it was a domain which could be measured independently of the way it was encoded by language (for example, in physical units such as wave-length); it was a domain for which measures of specific cognitive operations such as perception and memory could be obtained which were independent of, rather than simply assumed from, the language under study; the domain itself did not differ greatly between cultures — as, for example, man-made objects do — and it was a domain for which anthropologists reported great differences among languages.

A seminal study of the effects of language on cognition was performed by Brown and Lenneberg (1954). Brown and Lenneberg found that the codability of a colour (a composite measure of agreement in naming, length of name, and response latency in naming) correlated with memory accuracy (the accuracy with which a colour could be remembered in a recognition task). The standard interpretation (see Krauss, 1968) has been that the more codable colours were better remembered, particularly under conditions of delayed recognition, specifically because of the greater ease with which they could be linguistically coded and stored in memory. The Brown and Lenneberg study was correlational in its design; it used only speakers of a single language. The logic of its argument, however, was covertly cross-cultural. Which particular colours are most codable could be expected to vary between languages, but the lawful relationship between memory and codability should remain true — whatever colours are most codable, they should be better remembered by speakers of that language than the less codable. That this would be the case seemed so obviously true that it was not tested for many years.

A challenge to this entire view of colours came from Berlin and Kay (1969), two anthropologists to whom it first occurred to look at that which was taken for granted in colour terminology. Considering the hundreds of reports of differences in colour terminology between cultures, Berlin and Kay wondered at the ease with which they were able to learn to use correctly the colour terms of the cultures they had studied. They first looked at the reported diversity of colour names linguistically, and they found that there was actually a very limited number of basic — as opposed to secondary — colour terms in any language. "Basic" was defined by a list of linguistic criteria; for example, that a term be composed of only a single unit of meaning ("red" as opposed to "dark red") and that it name only colour and not objects ("purple" as opposed to "wine"). Using these criteria, Berlin and Kay reported that no language contained more than 11 basic colour names; three achromatic (in English, "black", "white", and "grey") and eight chromatic (in English, "red", "yellow", "green", "blue", "pink", "orange", "brown", and "purple" — a possible ninth chromatic term is a term for "light blue" in Russian and Hungarian).

Berlin and Kay next asked speakers of different languages to identify the colours to which the basic colour names in their language referred. Their initial group of subjects were 20 foreign students whose native language was not English. Subjects saw a two-dimensional array of coloured chips — all of the hues at all levels of brightness (all at maximum saturation) available in the "Munsell Book of Color" (Munsell Color Company, 1966). The students performed two tasks: (a) traced the boundaries of each of their native language's basic colour terms; (b) pointed to the chip which was the best example of each basic term. As might have been partially expected from the anthropological literature, there was a great deal of variation in the placement of boundaries of the terms; however, surprisingly, the choice of best examples of the terms was quite similar for the speakers of the 20 different languages. Berlin and Kay called the points in the colour space where choices of best examples of basic terms clustered "focal points", and argued that the previous anthropological emphasis on cross-cultural differences in colour names was derived from looking at boundaries of colour names rather than at colour-name focal points.

Berlin and Kay's work represents an empirical generalization which ran directly counter to the accepted anthropological and psychological assumptions about colour language diversity. It did not, of itself, constitute a psychological theory. Psychological implications, however, can be derived from the work. Brown and Lenneberg's results had been interpreted as a demonstration of the effect of codability on memory. On the lowest theoretical level, the discovery of colour focal points suggests an alternative explanation for those results — that there are areas of the colour space which are perceptually more salient to all peoples and that these areas both become more codable and can be better remembered as the direct result of their salience. If such salience can be documented, a higher level of theory is made possible, namely an account of the manner in which salient focal colours determine the development of the partitioning of the colour space into colour name categories. And such an account of the nature of colour categories has implication for the logic of semantic categories in general.

Even at the lowest theoretical level, the hypothesis of the relationship between saliency, codability, and memory is an inherently cross-linguistic and cross-cultural hypothesis. If codability (a linguistic variable) is the result of salience, the same colours should be the most codable in all languages; specifically, focal colours should be universally more codable than non-focal colours. And if memory (a psychological variable) were the direct result of salience, rather than codability, focal colours should be better remembered than non-focal even by speakers of a language in which these colours were not more codable. The second of these hypotheses is inherently cross-cultural as well as cross-linguistic for it not only requires native speakers of a language for whom not all focal colours are named but also requires that those speakers not know any other language which could supply them with additional colour names. Such a requirement raises two general points of method which must be discussed before the content of the research is further described.

Both points concern the way in which cross-cultural research which is aimed at casting light on general psychological processes might generally use strategies different from those of research derived from anthropological or practical concerns which are centred on an entire culture. The more trivial of the issues concerns choice of the culture or cultures in which to work. If a cross-cultural test of a hypothesis is needed, then the culture(s) to be used for the test should be chosen specifically to provide the necessary conditions required for such a test.

The important and complex issue of method concerns the logic of what may be learned from cross-cultural comparison. Because anthropology has traditionally studied the interrelated aspects of entire cultures and because workers in practical fields, such as educators, wish to achieve objectives with the people of the culture as a whole (such as educating them), cross-cultural questions have typically been phrased in terms of a comparison between the performance of two cultures. Such comparisons can, unfortunately, easily fall into the logic of a psychometric "deficit model". Hypotheses are stated in terms of "how well" entire cultures perform on a particular test. For example, a hypothesis might state that "members of traditional cultures cannot think creatively" or that "the more words a language has for colours, the better speakers can remember colours". The investigator might administer a test of "creative thinking" to Americans (not a traditional culture) and to the Yemenites (a traditional culture) or administer a colour memory test to Americans (many colour terms) and to the Dani (few colour terms). When the Yemenites performed poorly on the creativity test and the Dani poorly on the colour memory test, the investigator would conclude that his causal hypothesis was supported. However, it should be obvious that innumerable other factors besides those in which the investigator is explicitly interested vary between "us" and "them". Motivations, cultural meaningfulness of the materials, general familiarity with, or even previous explicit training with, the kind of task used are some obvious examples. In fact, any pre-literate culture will probably perform "less well" than a Western culture given almost any Western "test". But if Dani can be expected to perform below Americans in *any* memory test, how may we conclude that it was the number of colour terms which determined their poor performance in the colour memory test? In short, positive results are assured the investigator who frames hypotheses such that a single Western and single non-Western culture are compared with a prediction in the direction of the non-Western culture giving poorer performance than the Western — but such results will be uninterpretable.

Are there remedies for the impasse? One trend has been to try to invent tasks which are as culturally relevant in content and form of administration to a particular pre-literate culture as Western tests are to Western cultures. The format of the research is typically this: stage 1 — an investigator demonstrates that the people of culture X fail to exhibit some ability (for example, "abstract thinking") on a standard Western test. Stage 2 — the same or a different investigator manipulates the content and context of the test until he has demonstrated that, under the right circumstances (for example, if asked to reason about a court case in their own culture rather than about coloured geometric forms), the people of X do exhibit "abstract thinking". At its best, such a series of steps can cast light not only on the thought processes of the people of X but also on the nature of the ability under study and, thereby, the nature of the components of the Western tests traditionally used to measure that ability. For examples of this method used particularly fruitfully, see Cole (1975) and Scribner (1974). Unfortunately, such research can also easily fall into a circular dialectic in which the two stages simply cancel each other and make little contribution to our understanding of basic human thought processes. What is particularly distressing about this method is that it really ought to go without saying that all tasks in cross-cultural research should be as appropriate for the people taking them as possible. Indeed, without some level of appropriateness, meaningful data cannot be collected at all. However, culturally meaningful tasks do not of themselves produce well conceived research. In fact, hypotheses need not necessarily be framed in terms of differences in absolute level of performance between "us" and "them" at all.

A second approach to the impasse uses a model based on epidemiological methods in the health sciences. Epidemiology can be used both as an atheoretical means for the generation of hypotheses (e.g. the incidence of typhus can be examined to gain clues to its origin) or epidemiology can be used to test a hypothesis. In anthropology, such an approach means that *many* cultures which differ in both the dependent variable of interest and the many suspected independent variables must be studied, as must groups within a single culture. (For a more detailed discussion of the epidemiological model see Levine, 1970; and for an interesting example of its use, see Segall *et al.*, 1966). Unfortunately, owing to practical considerations, the epidemiological method has seldom been applied to the study of cognitive factors.

Perhaps the simplest and most direct way of circumventing the problem of measuring cognitive variables cross-culturally, is to abandon research designs whose emphasis is on "main effects" of culture *per se*. Hypotheses may be formed, not in terms of absolute differences between cultures, but in terms of interactions between variables within and between cultures. Take, for example, the hypothesis that number of colour terms affects colour memory. Instead of comparing speakers of two languages one of which has more colour terms than the other, we might search for cases where it is possible to compare relative performance for different areas of the colour space for languages which differed in the relative number of terms they had for these areas. Perhaps one language has many terms for blue and green colours but few terms for the yellow-brown colour area, another language just the opposite. Our prediction could then be that speakers of the first language would show relatively better memory for the blue-green than for the yellow-brown area; whereas, speakers of the second language would be relatively more proficient with yellow-brown colours than with blue-green. With research so designed, it would not matter how well either culture remembered in total. Such an approach may be a key to meaningful comparisons, even between quite different cultures.

To return to the substantive issue in question — that of the relation of the Whorfian hypothesis to the domain of colours; two hypotheses were in need of test. The first was that the codability of colours was the result of colour salience and should, thus, be universal. The second was that memory for colours is the result of colour salience, rather than the result of codability, and should, thus, remain a function of salience whenever codability and salience differed.

If codability is the result of salience, focal colours should be universally more codable than non-focal colours. The author (Heider, 1972b) tested this possibility using native speakers of 23 diverse languages drawn from seven of the major language families of the world. A focal colour representing each of the eight basic chromatic terms was chosen from the centre of each of the best-example clusters produced by Berlin and Kay's subjects; non-focal colours were chosen from the "internominal" areas of the colour space, areas which were never picked as the best example of any basic colour name. The chips were mounted on cards and shown, one at a time, in scrambled order, individually, to 23 people whose native language was not English. A subject's task was to write down what he would call each colour in his language. The results of the study were clear; the focal colours were given shorter names and named more rapidly than were the non-focal colours. Thus, in this quite varied language sample, it was the same colours that were most codable in different languages.

If memory for colours is the direct result of their salience, rather than their codability, focal colours should be better remembered than non-focal even by speakers of a language in which these colours were not more codable. The first methodological point comes into play in the choice of a culture in which to work. Berlin and Kay's claim about the number of basic colour terms was that there were never more than but could be fewer than 11 terms; in fact, they argued that colour terms enter languages in a specific evolutionary order. The Dani of West Irian (Indonesian New Guinea) are a Stone-Age, agricultural people who have a basically two-term colour language (Heider, 1970; Heider, 1972a, 1972b; Heider and Olivier, 1972). Colour systems of that character have been reported for other cultures as well and form Stage I, the first and simplest stage, of Berlin and Kay's proposed evolutionary ordering of colour systems. For Dani, the eight chromatic focal chips were not more codable than the internominal chips (established by having 40 Dani name all of the colour chips in the Berlin and Kay array).

Since the Dani fulfil the criteria for a people on which to test the hypothesis, the second point of method becomes relevant. The research question is: would Dani better remember focal than non-focal colours even without names for the focal colours? To find out, Heider (1972b) administered, to a sample of Dani and a sample of Americans, a colour memory test very similar to Brown and Lenneberg's. Subjects were shown focal and non-focal colours, individually, in random order, for 5 seconds, and after a 30-second wait, were asked to recognize the colour they had seen from an array of many colours. The mean number of errors that each culture made to each kind of chip are shown in Table 1. The main results were clear: Dani, as well as Americans, recognized the focal colours better than the non-focal.

The way in which this study illustrates the point of method is this: a striking aspect of Table 1 is that Dani memory performance as a whole was poorer than American. If the hypothesis had been in terms of absolute differences between cultures, we would have noted that Dani both had fewer colour terms and poorer memory for colours than Americans, and might have claimed that linguistic relativity was thereby supported. However, it must be remembered that the Dani are a pre-literate people, living in face-to-face communities, probably without need for or training in techniques for coping with the kind of overloads of information which this

Table 1
Accuracy of colour memory

Culture	Stimulus colours	
	Focal	Internominal
United States	5·25	3·25
Dani	2·05	0·47

unfamiliar memory test required. All of those extraneous factors undoubt-edly affected Dani memory as a whole. Our hypothesis, however, con-cerned differential memory for different types of colours within culture, and, therefore, was not negated by general cultural differences in "test taking".

Colour initially appeared to be an ideal domain in which to demonstrate the effects of lexical differences on thought; instead, it now appears to be a domain particularly suited to an examination of the influence of underlying perceptual factors on the formation and reference of linguistic categories. Certain colours appear to be universally salient. There are also universals in some aspects of colour naming. How (by what mechanism) might the salience be related to the naming?

Once this question is asked, we are looking at another step of generality of implication of the initial psychological hypothesis. What we are asking for is an account of the development (both in the sense of individual learning and the evolution of languages) of colour names which will specify the precise nature of the role played by focal colours in that development.

Rosch (1973, 1975a) proposed the following account of the development of colour names: there are perceptually salient colours which more readily attract attention (even of young children — Heider, 1971) and are more easily remembered than other colours. When category names are learned, they tend to become attached first to the salient stimuli (only later generalizing to other, physically similar, instances), and by this means these natural prototype colours become the foci of organization for categories. How can this account be tested? In the first place, it implies that it is easier to learn names for focal than non-focal colours. That is, not only should focal colours be more easily retained than non-focal in recognition over short intervals (as has already been demonstrated); they should also be more readily remembered in conjunction with names in long-term memory. In the second place, since a colour category is learned first as a named focal colour and second as the focal colour plus other physically similar stimuli, colour categories in which focal colours are physically central stimuli (central in terms of some physical attribute, such as wave-length) should be easier to learn than categories structured in some other manner (for example, focal colours physically peripheral or internominal colours central and no focal colours at all).

A test of these hypotheses obviously could not be performed with subjects who already knew a set of basic chromatic colour terms provided by their language. This brings us to another important possible method for cross-cultural research which has seldom been applied — a learning paradigm. Many cultures lack codes (or a full elaboration of codes) for some domain. If an investigator has theories about that domain, instead of framing his hypotheses in terms of deficits in performance resulting from the lack of codes (with attendant problems in interpreting absolute differences between cultures), he can frame hypotheses in terms of *learning* the codes for the domain. Codes can then be taught — the input stimuli precisely specified and controlled within the context of the experiment in accordance with the relevant hypotheses. Since the variations are within culture, any general difficulty which the people may have with the learning task *per se* will not influence the conclusions. The Dani, with their two-term colour language, provided an ideal opportunity to teach colour names.

Three basic types of colour category were taught. In Type 1, the physically central (i.e. of intermediate wave-length or brightness) chip of each category was the focal colour, and the flanking chips were drawn from the periphery of that basic name area. In Type 2, central chips lay in the internominal areas between Berlin and Kay's best-example clusters; flanking chips, thus, tended to be drawn from the basic colour name areas on either side. Since two different basic colour name chips were included in the same Type 2 categories, these categories violated the presumed natural organization of the colour space. Type 3 categories were located in the same spaces as Type 1; however, instead of occupying a central position, the focal colour was now to one side or the other of the three-chip category.

Subjects learned the colour names as a paired associate task, a standard learning task in which subjects learn to give a specific response to each of a list of stimuli. In the present case, colours were the stimuli, and the same Dani word was the correct response for the three colours in a category. Finding suitable names at first seemed a serious obstacle to the study since Dani would not learn nonsense words, even those constructed according to the rules of the Dani language. Here is an example of a case in which it was necessary to make the task culturally meaningful if it was to be performed at all. Eventually, it was found that there was a set of kin groups called "sibs" (something like clans) whose names were all well known to the Dani and which the Dani could readily learn as names for the colour categories ("sibs" did not have particular colours associated with them in Dani culture). The task was described to each subject as learning a new language which the experimenter would teach him. The subject was told the names for all of the colour chips; then presented with each chip and required to respond with a name. Chips were shown in a different random order each run, five runs a day, with feedback after each response, until the criterion of one perfect run was achieved.

The results of the learning supported Rosch's account of the role of focal colours in the learning of colour names. In the first place, the focal colours were learned with fewer errors than other colours even when they were peripheral members of the categories. In the second place, the Type 1 categories in which focal colours were physically central were learned as a set faster than either of the other types. The Type 2 categories, which violated the presumed natural organization of the colour space, were the most difficult of all to learn. Thus, the idea of perceptually salient focal colours as natural prototypes (rather like Platonic forms) for the development and learning of colour names was supported.

We have been speaking of focal colours as "perceptually" salient. Is this just a metaphor, or is there an actual mechanism of colour vision which could be responsible for the salience? The answer is "both". There is a theory of colour perception (Hering, 1964) supported by both psychophysical and physiological data (De Valois and Jacobs, 1968; Hering, 1964), which claims that the primary colours red, green, yellow, and blue correspond to physiologically "unique hues". To get some notion of the meaning of unique hues, imagine that there are two opponent colour coding systems in the primate nervous system (in actual fact, in the lateral geniculate), each of which can respond positively or negatively. One system is responsive to red and green wave-lengths of light, the other to yellow and blue wave-lengths. Think of the probabilities of stimulation of each system distributed over wave-length. There will be four points (particular wave-lengths) at which one system responds uniquely; that is, a point at which the yellow-blue system is neutral and the red-green system positive, a point at which yellow-blue is neutral and red-green negative, and points at which red-green is neutral and yellow-blue positive and negative.

Do the wave-lengths of the proposed four unique hue points correspond to focal colours? They cannot correspond exactly because physiological and psychophysical visual research tends to be performed with monochromatic light (radiant light of a single wave-length) whereas Munsell chips are "broad band" light (reflected light containing many wave-lengths). However, the dominant wave-length of each Munsell chip has been calculated (Munsell Color Company, 1970). It is, in fact, the case that the dominant wave-lengths of focal red, yellow, green, and blue correspond reasonably well to the proposed unique hue points. Evidence of an even more direct match of focal yellow, green, and blue to unique hue points is provided in McDaniel (1972). While unique hue points are not presently an unchallenged physiological theory and while the theory fails to account for the other four proposed basic chromatic colour terms (pink, orange, brown and purple), it does lend considerable concreteness to the supposition that focal colours are physiologically, rather than mysteriously, salient.

One of the characteristics of cross-cultural research which is addressed to questions of psychological theory is that it should easily articulate with research designs testing the same hypotheses within Western cultures. One obvious parallel to the cross-cultural learning studies is developmental research. Rosch's account of the role of focal colours in the learning of colour names not only has implications for adult learning of colour categories in a culture which lacks the basic colour names, but also has implications for a child's learning of colour names in a culture whose language possesses the full complement of basic colour names. In the first place, focal colours should prove salient to children prior to their learning of colour names just as they are to adult Dani. Rosch (Heider, 1971) showed that three-year-old American children prefer to show an adult focal rather than non-focal colours and that four-year-olds perform better on a colour-matching task with focal colours than with non-focal colours. In the second place, when variation in colour naming is studied developmentally, foci for colour categories should become established and be stabilized earlier than category boundaries and judgments of focal colours should always be more stable than boundary judgments. Mervis et al. (1975) tested these hypotheses. American kindergartners, third graders, and adults designated the best example and outlined the boundaries for each of 11 basic colour names for the array of colours used by Berlin and Kay (1969). Results showed that mean focal choices for the youngest children tested were the same as those for adults; whereas, the boundary judgments obtained from the children differed on hue, brightness, and saturation from adult boundary judgments. Furthermore, as assessed by variance measures, focal judgments were generally more stable than boundary judgments. Thus, the developmental data are complementary to the cross-cultural data.

In all of the research reported so far, a prototype structure of colour categories has been inferred from linguistic judgments, development, memory, learning, or physiology. Do humans actually use the prototype structure in the cognitive processing of colour categories? Do mental representations of colour categories reflect colour category prototype structure? Such a question is difficult to define operationally, and is more readily first investigated within a known Western culture than cross-culturally.

Two series of studies have been performed which indicate that the prototype structure of colour categories is a cognitive reality. The first group of studies were derived from Wertheimer's (1938) suggestion that among perceptual stimuli, there are certain "Ideal types" which act as the anchoring points for perception. The hypothesis was that focal colours (and similar stimuli from other domains such as vertical and horizontal lines from the domain of line orientations) act as reference points in relation to which other stimuli of the domain are judged. The first experiment used the logic of natural language "hedge" terms. Subjects placed pairs of stimuli into sentence frames consisting of linguistic hedges such as "— is essentially —". Results were that the supposed reference stimuli (focal colours, vertical and horizontal lines, etc.) were placed in the second (reference) slot more often than stimuli slightly deviant from the reference points. In the second experiment, judgments of physical distance were used. A subject placed a stimulus in physical space to represent his feeling of the psychological distance of that stimulus from another spatially fixed stimulus. Results showed that, when supposed reference stimuli were fixed, other stimuli were placed closer to them than vice versa. The results indicated that focal colours do appear to act as cognitive reference points in relation to which other colours in a colour category are judged (Rosch, 1975b).

Of more interest and greater delicacy is the question of whether mental representations of colour categories reflect the prototype structure of the category. A task which appears to offer considerable potential for investigation of the precise nature of representations (and, in so doing, provide an operational meaning for representation) is that of priming (Beller, 1971) in the type of matching paradigm described by Posner and Mitchell (1967). In the original matching research, subjects were required to decide as rapidly as possible whether two simultaneously presented visual letters were the same or different; under some conditions "same" was defined as physical identity (e.g. AA), and under others as possession of the same name (e.g. Aa). If a subject is provided with some of the information which he needs to make the match in advance of presentation of the pair, matching speed should be facilitated. Beller (1971) primed subjects with a letter, A (presented the letter two seconds in advance of the pair) and found that physically identical, AA, as well as same-name, Aa, pairs improved — even when physically identical pairs were in the opposite case from the case presented in the primed. Beller (1971) and Posner (1969) argued that this showed that subjects were not simply retaining a literal representation of the presented letter but were generating an abstract expectation or representation which did not depend on case.

A similar logic was applied to the study of the representation generated by colour names. Each of the eight basic hue categories was represented by pairs of good examples of the category (focal colours) and pairs of poor examples of the category. Chips representing the poor example colours were determined by a pilot study in which subjects sorted chips into colour name categories; the poor example chips chosen were those furthest in saturation or brightness from the focal chips but which 90% of the subjects still labelled with the basic colour name. In the experiments, in primed trials, the name of a basic colour category, and in unprimed trials, the word "blank" was presented to subjects in advance of a pair of colours. It was found that for responses of "same" to physically identical colours, a prime presented in advance of a colour pair facilitated responses to good and actually impeded responses to poor members of the category — under conditions when "same" was defined as physically identical as well as when "same" was defined as belonging to the same category. It was conluded that the cognitive representation of colour categories contains information used in the perception of physical colour stimuli (is like a concrete image of the colour) and that the representation (image) is more like good than poor members of colour categories. That subjects could not overcome the advantage of priming to focal over non-focal colours, even after two weeks of practice with a small sets of colours, further confirmed the non-arbitrary nature of the structure of colour categories (see Rosch, 1975d, for further clarification of this series of experiments). In short, the results of the priming studies indicate that mental representations of colour categories do reflect the prototype structure which has been inferred from other evidence. Thus, colour appears to be one domain in which all evidence — physiology, language, memory, learning, child development, and information processing experiments — converge in supporting the assertion that the categories possess an analog prototype structure.

B. Prototypes in Other Attribute Domains

Colour is not the only domain in which perceptually salient, natural prototypes appear to determine categories; there is evidence that geometric forms and facial expressions of emotion become structured in a similar manner. That there is something particularly "well formed" about certain forms, such as circles and squares, was proposed long ago by the Gestalt psychologists. Rosch (1973, 1974) tested the hypothesis that such forms act as natural prototypes in the formation of form categories just as focal colours do for colour categories. The Dani also do not have a terminology for two-dimensional geometric forms, and some pilot studies showed that they neither possessed usable circumlocutions for referring to forms in a communication task nor did they tend to sort forms by form type. Thus, it was reasonable to teach Dani form concepts just as they had been taught colour concepts. The logic of the form learning experiment was the same as that of the colour learning. Circle, square, and equilateral triangle were taken as the presumed natural prototypes of three form categories. In the naturally structured categories, these good forms were physically central to a set of distortions (such as gaps in the form or lines changed to curves). In other categories, a distorted form was the central member, the good form peripheral. The results mirrored those for colour. The good forms themselves were learned faster than the distorted forms, and the sets of forms in which the good forms were central were learned faster than sets in which they were peripheral. Furthermore, for the forms (though not for the colours), Dani were willing at the conclusion of learning to point to which stimulus they considered the best example of the name they had just learned. The good forms tended to be designated as the best examples even when they were actually peripheral to the set; it was as though subjects were trying to structure the categories around the good forms even when the actual sets were structured otherwise.

Facial expressions of emotion are a surprising addition to the class of natural categories. Not only were they once not considered universal, but there was considerable doubt that, even within one culture, emotion could be judged better than chance from the human face (Bruner and Tagiuri, 1954). As had been the case with colours, such judgments seemed to stem from the unsystematic employment of miscellaneous facial expressions in judgment experiments. Ekman (1972) claimed that there were six basic human emotions (happiness, sadness, anger, fear, surprise, and disgust) and that each was associated with a quite limited range of facial muscle movements constituting a pure expression of that emotion; other expressions tended to be blends of emotions, or ambiguous or non-emotional expressions which could not be expected to receive reliable judgments. When Ekman put together sets of pictures of pure expressions of the proposed basic emotions, he found that these pictures were judged correctly by Americans, Japanese, Brazilians, Chileans, and Argentinians. Furthermore, two pre-literate New Guinea groups with minimal contact with

Caucasian facial expression, the Fore and the Dani, were able to distinguish which of the expressions was meant on the basis of stories embodying the appropriate emotion. Like colour, universality was discovered in facial expressions of emotion only when an investigator thought to ask, not about all possible stimuli, but about the prototypes (best examples) of categories.

Although the content and the process of category formation of colour, form, and facial expression of emotion categories may be universal, some aspects of categories, even in these domains, probably differ between cultures. The extent of elaboration of language codes for the categories, conceptual levels of categorization (are the basic categories divided into subordinate and/or combined into superordinate categories?), category boundaries, treatment of inter-category stimuli (such as blends of emotions), rules for use of the categories (such as aesthetic rules for colours and display and suppression rules for expressions of emotion) — all leave room for the development of cultural differences. What are those differences and how do they develop? At present, we have virtually no usable data for an explanation of such questions. What the present chapter wishes to emphasize is that questions about cultural specifics in these domains can be reasonably asked and answered only in relation to the basic universal aspects of the categories.

Let us trace the development of the argument to this point. We are concerned with encouraging fruitful interrelations between psychological theory and cross-cultural research. The issue of colour categories has been the primary focus. Cross-cultural colour research began with the observations of naïve observers placed in cross-cultural contexts who reported what they noticed — differences in colour names between cultures. However, such unlimited relativism violated another cross-cultural observation, namely that it appeared possible to communicate cross-culturally about colour regardless of differences in naming. Berlin and Kay formulated a systematic empirical description of universals in the referents of basic colour names and in the evolution of colour terminology.

Given an empirical description of possible universals in colour naming, Rosch sought psychological principles which might underly the universals. Principles of increasingly broader import were tested both developmentally and cross-culturally. Cross-cultural tests were always of hypotheses which predicted differences within, not between cultures, thereby avoiding the pitfalls of uncontrolled variables in performance on tests between cultures. In the first stage, perceptual saliency was argued to underly universals in both colour naming and memory. When the implications of this hypothesis were verified, salient colours were proposed to be the foci around which the colour space becomes structured into categories. Broader implications still were that colour was not the only domain so structured but that other domains with a possible physiological basis, such as form and expressions of emotion, might be structured in the same way.

The broadest implications, however, concern the general logic of categorization. Categories have tended to be treated in philosophy, psychology, linguistics, and anthropology as "Aristotelian" and digital, that is, as logical, bounded entities, membership in which is defined by an item's possession of a simple set of criterial features. The work on colour, just reviewed, shows one clear case in which the categories of a domain appear to be analog. Can other categories, even those not physiologically based, be considered as also structured in an analog manner? Section II of this chapter shows the way in which, by analogy with the colour research, the structure of other types of categories came to be examined.

II. THE NATURE OF CATEGORIES

Any study of category learning and use within a culture as well as any cross-cultural comparison of categories will be conceived and carried out by methods which depend upon the investigator's prior concept of what a category is. The overwhelming preponderance of American studies, in attempting to treat categories scientifically, have defined and treated them as though they were digital, that is, as though they were composed of discrete units which are either/or in nature. Thus, most studies carry the unexamined assumption that categories are arbitrary logical conjunctions of criterial attributes which have definite boundaries and within which all instances possessing the criterial attributes have a full and equal degree of membership.

A. Some Digital Representations of Categories

The best example of such a treatment is the class of experiments known as concept formation or concept identification. Typically in such experiments (see the summary by Bourne, 1968), the subject sees an array of artificial stimuli: for example, squares, circles and triangles, each form occurring once as red, once blue and once green, each colour of each form occurring once with one border and once with two, etc. The subject must learn which of these stimuli are and which are not members of the "concept" which the experimenter has in mind. The concept may consist of any combination of attributes: for example, "all the red things," or "red and square things," or "square or two borders or both," etc. Note that stimuli for such experiments consist of discrete attributes (such as red versus green, square versus circle); the categories to which these attributes themselves belong are generally already well known to the subject (e.g. American college sophomores have learned the concepts "red" and "square" long before); and the sub-set of attribute combinations which comprise the to-be-learned concepts can be formed arbitrarily out of any logically possible combinations of attributes. For such concepts, once the subject has learned the rule(s) defining the positive subset, boundaries of the concept can only be "well defined" (Neisser, 1967), and the concept has no rational basis for internal structure. That is, any one stimulus which fits the rule is as good an exemplar of the concept as any other — for example, if the positive sub-set consists of the conjunction "red square" with size as an irrelevant attribute, it makes no logical sense to ask the subject whether the small or large red square was a better example of the concept "red square". While the limited and controlled nature of the stimuli in concept formation tasks has made possible the collection of a large body of precise information about learning and problem solving, such tasks may not be representative of the majority of natural concepts. For example, as the research in Section I has demonstrated, colour categories violate all of the characteristics of concepts in the concept formation paradigm: the physical properties of light, such as wave-length are not discrete (e.g. "long" and "short") but composed of continuous variation; a colour name such as "red" does not refer to a logical combination of simpler, already learned attributes (in fact, perceived colours are not "analysable" into combinations of discrete dimensions: Garner, 1970; Shepard, 1964); boundaries between colour categories are not well defined; and, as previously discussed, there are focal colours which are better members of particular colour categories than other colours.

In quite a number of fields, the semantic categories of natural languages are treated in a manner quite similar to the concept formation paradigm. A major trend in linguistics (see Katz and Postal, 1964) is to treat semantic categories as bundles of discrete features which determine how the words can be used in sentences. Features, loosely speaking, are those characteristics of nouns which we can describe with adjectives. In these terms, the meaning of "girl" might be represented by such features as +animate, +human, +young, −male. These features clearly differentiate the category from all others and also render each category instance logically comparable to all others, in that instances are alike in possessing the defining combination of features. Studies of the nature of semantic representation in memory (both computer models and empirical studies of retrieval from memory — see the articles in Section II of Tulving and Donaldson, 1972) usually demonstrate indirectly by their choice of stimuli and testing methods that categories are assumed to be clearly bounded entities all of whose members are equivalent.

Developmental studies have either treated concepts as equivalent to those of concept learning research (see virtually any concept identification study in a developmental psychology journal), or, within the Genevan tradition (see Inhelder and Piaget, 1958), have not been concerned with the internal structure of categories but rather with the development of deductive logical relations between classes.

It is not surprising, with the heavy emphasis on digital models of categories provided by linguistics and psychology, that anthropological studies of folk classifications (Tyler, 1969) have tended to use a feature analysis of categories. Methods, such as componential analysis, seek to find the minimum basic criterial attributes by which folk use of the terms of a domain can be formally ordered. Thus, reports have tended to concentrate on a limited number of domains such as kinship; perhaps, because the domain on which kin terms are mapped does contain discrete attributes (e.g. sex, generational steps distant from speaker) which may be logically combined to give the formal meaning of the terms — in much the same way that attributes are combined in the concept formation study. (That such formal meaning is not sufficient for a full exposition of the meaning even of kinship terms has been argued in several recent papers, see Kay, 1972.)

Undoubtedly, some categories and some kinds of processing of categories do involve digital codes. The technical criteria for membership in those categories that do have technical criteria are probably a case in point. However, the model of categories provided by artificial concept identification research may be pernicious in that researchers have, thereby, tended to neglect other types of categories and category codes which may be more appropriate to the way natural categories are formed and coded in cognition and more appropriate for cross-cultural comparisons.

B. Analog Representations of Categories: Prototypes

In fact, there is a small body of research which has attempted to treat categories and the process of categorization as analog functions ("non-Aristotelian" in the Cassirer sense of Aristotelian). Such attempts are important, not only in terms of impact on a conceptualization of categories but in terms of the long-range possibility of developing theories which attempt to embody, rather than get around, the probably essentially analog nature of many mental processes.

Research dealing with analog categories has generally fallen under the heading of schema or prototype research. The term "schema" has been used to stand for a number of proposed codes or abstract mental representations by which people might be enabled to store and recognize members of categories given the infinite variations in the instances of the categories encountered. In its simplest form a schema could consist of the elements common to all instances of a category along with notation about departures of individual instances (Oldfield, 1954). In this form, a schema is digital and no different from a list of criterial attributes such as a subject might learn in a concept identification task; for example, the verbalized code ("anything red, form varies") might be the schema in a concept identification study for the concept "red." However, research on schemas has largely been concerned with more complex stimuli in which concepts cannot be identified by means of easily coded common elements or in which the mental representation, even of simple concepts, is proposed to be in a form other than a verbal list of elements, for example, in the form of an image. (Note that Berkeley's claim was not that we could not verbalize that a triangle was a plane figure consisting of three straight joined lines; his claim was that we could not form an abstract image of a generalized triangle.)

There is considerable evidence that subjects can form mental schemas for types of artificial categories which do not lend themselves to a feature description. Most work on schema formation was performed on random visual patterns such as nonsense polygons (Attneave, 1957) and dot patterns (Posner et al., 1967). Such stimulus materials are used both because they can be carefully controlled and produced to order for the purpose of the experiment and because they are completely novel to the subject — thereby eliminating the prior history of learning of the actual concepts with which subjects come into the experiment. To produce categories from such materials, a set of patterns is generated by applying distortions to an initial random pattern; for example, by a random walk of the points forming the pattern. The initial pattern is, thus, the central tendency of a family of patterns. The work of most relevance to the present purposes is that which (using such measures as speed and accuracy of classification) indicates that, during learning and/or classification, subjects actually generate a mental representation of the schema pattern even when that specific pattern was never actually presented to them (Bransford and Franks, 1971; Franks and Bransford, 1971; Posner, 1969, 1973; Posner and Keele, 1968; Reed, 1972).

Such prototype research demonstrates dramatically the capacity of the human mind for coping with analog categories; however. the categories used are still artificial and arbitrary. The schema patterns chosen and the rules for distortion of the schema are created at the will of the experimenter. One of the major claims which can be derived from Section I of this chapter is that natural categories can also be characterized in terms of prototypes and deviations from prototypes.

As previously argued, the colour space is probably the real world domain most obviously different from the kinds of attribute combinations used in digital artificial concept formation studies. Section I of the chapter presented evidence that an analog prototype conception of colour categories is supported by converging operations from widely different types of experiments in child development, learning, memory, and information processing. However, colour and similar categories such as form are a special type of category; they are general attributes of all concrete things and they appear to have biologically determined salient stimuli around which the domains can become structured.

Not all categories have an obvious perceptual basis, and many categories may be culturally relative. It is unreasonable to expect that humans come equipped with natural prototypes, for example, for dogs, vegetables, and Volkswagens. For colours and forms, internal structure and the concept of focal and non-focal category members have a relatively concrete meaning; are such concepts more generally applicable to noun categories of other types? Applicability actually refers to two issues: can subjects make consistent, meaningful judgments about internal structure — the degree to which instances are focal members of categories — and can a reasonable case be made that internal structure affects cognition with respect to categories?

1. Subjects' Judgments about Internal Structure

With respect to the first issue, several studies have demonstrated that subjects reliably rate best examples of common semantic categories. In two studies (Rosch, 1973, 1975c), a total of 322 subjects were asked to rate, on a 7-point scale, the extent to which instances of common superordinate categories (such as furniture and vehicle) represented their "idea or image" of the meaning of the category name. The results showed high agreement between subjects, especially in rating the best examples of the categories. Correlations within categories between ranks received in different orders of presentation of instances was high, the lowest being 0·87. Although conditions of presentation differed between the studies (in one case six items per category were rated, in the other 50–60 items per category), the rank orders of all items which occurred in both studies were identical. In an additional study (Rips et al., 1973), subjects ranked, on a 4-point scale, the extent to which instances of semantic categories were associated with the category name. These ratings were consistent and were correlated with the Rosch (1975c) norms. A final study (Rosch and Mervis, 1975) dealt with semantic categories (such as chair and car) at a lower level of abstraction than the superordinate (see Section III for a discussion of levels of abstraction). The goodness of example of 15 pictures in each of six categories were rated; agreement in rating was equivalent to that obtained for the superordinate categories. In short, it appears that prototypes and reliable gradients of category membership do exist for semantic categories in the sense that subjects consider it a meaningful task to rate members of such categories according to how well they fit the subjects' idea or image of the meaning of the category name and that there is high agreement between subjects concerning these rankings.

2. Evidence that the Internal Structure of Natural Categories Affects Cognition

Although subjects agree on the goodness of example of instances of a category, such knowledge might be irrelevant for the ways in which subjects process the category. If the "real meaning" of categories lies in a list of common attributes which a thing must have to belong to the category, it is quite possible that processes such as recognizing instances, judging category membership, searching categories, and the logic of the use of category terms in linguistic contexts are all derived from the common criterial attributes. We are engaged in a series of programmatic studies using diverse operations to determine the nature of the codes for categories; below is presented some of the evidence that natural categories are processed in terms of the prototype and distance from the prototype.

(a) Judging statements about category membership. Many studies of retrieval from semantic memory have used tasks which required subjects to respond "true" or "false" to statements of the form: "A (member) is a (category)", where the dependent variable of interest was reaction time. In such tasks, responses of "true" are invariably faster for the items that had been rated more prototypical, even with other factors controlled (Rips *et al.*, 1973; Rosch, 1973; Rosch *et al.*, 1976a; Smith *et al.*, 1974a; Smith *et al.*, 1974b). Although the theoretical interpretation of such findings is presently an issue of debate (the data can be predicted by alternate theories of semantic memory — see Collins and Loftus, 1975; Smith *et al.*, 1974a), at the very least, the findings demonstrate that the internal structure of categories has an effect on cognition — the extent to which a category member represents the core meaning of the category affects the time needed for subjects to judge that the member belongs to the category.

(b) Order and probability of item output. Battig and Montague (1969) provided a normative study of the probability with which college students listed instances of superordinate semantic categories. This order is

24   E. ROSCH

correlated with the Rosch (1975c) norms for ratings of prototypicality.
Using artificial categories in which frequency of experience with all items
was controlled, Rosch *et al.* (1976a) demonstrated that the most
prototypical items were the first and most frequently produced items when
subjects were asked to list the members of the category. Thus, the internal
structure of categories appears to affect the way in which categories are
searched and items retrieved.

(c) The nature of the mental representation generated by a category
name. In Section I of the present chapter, the question was raised of whether
the prototype structure of colour categories was a part of the mental
representation generated from colour names. The logic of the technique of
priming was described as was a series of priming studies which indicated that
mental representations of colour categories appeared to be at the level of
physical features and more like prototype than non-prototype colours. An
analogous series of studies was performed upon the members of semantic
categories. Semantic category members were taken from the previously
described norms for goodness of membership for 10 semantic categories;
items were chosen to represent high, medium, and low ratings (for example,
for fruit, an example of high is apple, medium is grapefruit, low is
watermelon; for birds, an example of high is sparrow, medium is owl, low is
penguin). Procedures were similar to those described for priming of colour
categories. The results showed that, as had been the case for colours, for
physically identical pairs of items, advance presentation of the category
name facilitated (speeded) responses of "same" to the high good example
members and depressed performance (slowed "same" responses) for the
low members. Such results confirm that the representations generated by
semantic category names, like those generated by colour category names,
affect perception of the stimuli and are more like the good than poor
examples of the category. Unlike colours, however, there was no effect of
priming for semantic categories when instructions were to define "same" as
physical identity rather than as membership in the same category. Thus, the
representations of these superordinate semantic categories do not appear to
occur on the level of physical features as do colours, but are of a more
abstract nature (see Rosch, 1975c, for greater detail and see Section III for a
comparison with representations generated by less abstract semantic
categories).

(d) The logic of natural language use of category terms: substitutability
into sentences. The meaning of words is intimately tied to their possible uses
in sentences; in fact, there have been many attempts to define meaning,
synonymy and semantic contrast in terms of substitutability of words into the
same sentences without and with changes in the truth value of the sentences
(see Fodor and Katz, 1964, for summaries). Certainly, judged similarity

between words appears to be highly correlated with substitutability into linguistic frames (Stefflre *et al.*, 1971). The claim of the present theory, that categories are processed in terms of the prototype and distance from the prototype, means that the better examples of the category should be closer to the core meaning of the superordinate term than the poorer examples. If this is the case, ratings of goodness of example should predict substitutability of category member terms for their superordinates and vice versa. On the other hand, if the core meaning of the superordinate terms consists of a list of criterial attributes common to all category members, substitutability should be equivalent for all members of the category. To test this, subjects were asked to generate sentences using the category names for some of the categories for which ratings of members had already been obtained (e.g. fruit, bird, weapon, vehicle). The superordinate terms were then replaced by member terms at five levels of goodness of example and other subjects rated the sentences as to their degree of naturalness–peculiarity. The ratings showed a strong linear relationship between rated goodness of membership and substitutability. For example, in the sentence "Twenty or so birds often perch on the telephone wires outside my window and twitter in the morning," the term "sparrow" may readily be substituted for "bird" but the result turns ludicrous by substitution of "turkey". Similarly in "A bowl of fruit makes a nice centre-piece," the substitution of "apples" but not "watermelon" produced a sentence which retains its naturalness and truth value. (That this is not simply a matter of the frequency of the events is demonstrated in Rosch, 1975a).

(e) The logic of natural-language use of category terms: hedges. Although logic and psychology may treat categories as though membership is either/or and all members have a full and equal degree of membership, natural languages themselves possess linguistic mechanisms for coding and coping with gradients of category membership. In English there are qualifying terms and phrases which Lakoff (1972) calls "hedges" (terms such as "almost", "virtually"). Lakoff pointed out that even people who insist that statements such as "A robin is a bird" and "A penguin is a bird" are equally true, would have to admit that different hedges were applicable to statements of category membership for the two birds. Thus, it is correct to say that a penguin is "technically" a bird but not that a robin is "technically" a bird because a robin is more than just technically a bird — it is a "real" bird, a bird *par excellence*. Systematic study of some properties of hedges (one example, see Rosch, 1975b) is now in progress.

(f) Development of semantic categories. In Dani learning of colour categories, focal colours were learned before non-focal. It is possible that even with semantic categories in which the prototypes are culturally defined, prototype structure of categories is apparent developmentally. Children may initially define a category by means of its concrete clear cases rather than in terms of abstract criterial attributes. Anglin (1976) obtained evidence that young children learn category membership of good examples of categories before that of poor examples. In the category membership verification study described earlier, Rosch (1973) found that the differences in reaction time to verifying good and poor members were far more extreme for 10-year-old children than for adults, again indicating that the children had learned the category membership of the prototypical members earlier than that of other members.

In summary, the first part of the present chapter reviewed the evidence, largely obtained from cross-cultural research, that colour and some other attribute domains are structured in an analog manner around perceptually salient prototypes. Section II has explored one implication of such an argument, that non-physiologically based categories of concrete objects are also structured in an analog manner. Evidence produced by widely converging experimental techniques was presented to show that noun categories can be viewed as coded and used in terms of prototypes and distance from the prototypes. Such a finding is even more impressive when it is realized that these experiments have been performed on educated Americans, probably one of the populations most likely to have available explicit, verbalizable lists of attributes and formal technical criteria for category membership.

The concept of prototype structure of categories has two types of implication for cross-cultural research. In the first place, the claim that semantic as well as perceptual categories are analog must be verified cross-culturally. The experiments outlined in this section provide a variety of techniques by which this issue may be investigated. Referents of superordinate categories and goodness of example norms should be expected to vary between cultures. But given the structure of superordinate noun categories in any culture, reaction time studies, the logic of natural language treatment of categories, and development of knowledge of category membership should provide data consistent with that obtained in American culture. In the second place, given that semantic categories are universally analog, the concept of a category as a prototype and distance from the prototype may be even more helpful in studying categories of other populations and other cultures than it is in understanding Western categorizations. Most field-workers have probably experienced the frustration of an informant who seemed unable or unwilling to understand and comply with questions about why he was calling something an X; it may be that explicit formal criteria for membership are not available at all for some categories and/or some cultures. Asking which Xs are the most X-like may be a more universally fruitful way of approaching the issue. If people really code categories in an analog prototype manner, then we should be finding out about prototypes cross-culturally; that is, it is prototypes that may provide a cognitively real framework for cross-cultural comparison of categories.

III. CLASSIFICATIONS OF CONCRETE OBJECTS

This chapter began with the question of why cultures categorize the world in the ways that they do. The previous stance in social science was that categories were arbitrary, which is really an assertion that the question is not an appropriate one for scientific investigation. In the previous sections of this chapter, it has been shown that the question is a quite relevant one to ask about categorizations of general attribute domains such as colour and form which are categories referred to in English by adjectives. The concept of category structure derived from an investigation of those domains proved applicable to categories of concrete objects, those referred to by nouns in English. However, we have not investigated the question of the origins of such categories. It is the purpose of this section to present a general theory of the principles behind the formation of noun categories. It is a theory derived from general principles of modern cognitive psychology and from laboratory research in American culture. However, it is believed to be generally applicable to all cultures and to be potentially of great usefulness in understanding how cultures make sense of their environment.

A basic argument of the theory is that a view of categories as initially arbitrary would be reasonable only if the world were entirely unstructured: that is, using Garner's (1974) definition of "structure", if the world formed a set of stimuli in which all possible stimulus attributes occurred with equal probability combined with all other possible attributes. Thus, if the attributes were size (large, small), colour (red, green), and form (square, circle), the set would consist of a small red square, a small red circle, a small green square, a small green circle, a large red square, etc. In this example, to make the stimuli more of a continuum, we need only increase indefinitely the number of values for each attribute with a subsequent increase in possible combinations.

As explained in Section II, such stimulus arrays have been typically used in concept identification research (Bourne, 1968). In addition, these are the typical stimulus sets which are used when subjects are asked to free sort, that is, to sort stimuli into groupings of their choice. For free sorts of such stimuli, it has been repeatedly found that the overwhelming tendency is for subjects to sort on the basis of the levels of a single dimension (Handel and Imai,

1972; Handel and Preusser, 1969; Huang, 1945; Imai, 1966; Wing and Bevan, 1969). Thus, for the example given, subjects would typically sort into two groups based either on colour or form or size but not on combinations of attributes. Both individuals and groups tend to have consistent preferences for sorting on one dimension rather than another; usually the preference is for colour (Garner, 1966; Imai and Garner, 1965; Serpell, 1969; Suchman and Trabasso, 1966; Wing and Bevan, 1969). Such findings do not go far towards developing principles by which we may explain how the world is cut up; indeed, a striking quality of such classifications is that they do not seem to correspond to "things" or noun classes at all, since by the nature of the stimulus sets, groupings must be divided on the basis of one attribute and that one must be in conflict with divisions based on any other attribute.

Unfortunately, psychological cross-cultural studies of classification have tended to use just such sets of stimuli. Even in those studies in which not all attributes occur with all others, because the stimulus arrays are so arranged that the attributes are in conflict (see Cole and Scribner, 1974, for a review of the cross-cultural classification studies), subjects must typically choose to classify on the basis of a single attribute such as colour *or* form *or* function. Typically the question asked, both in developmental and cross-cultural studies of clasification, has concerned the concreteness or abstractness of the rule on which individuals or cultural groups base their sorts. This line of research has yielded few consistent findings: concrete–abstract has been defined in a number of ways, and the relative abstractness with which a people sort by any of these criteria is dependent upon a multitude of factors having to do with the particular form and content of the task (Cole and Scribner, 1974). Such a tradition of enquiry would seem to represent a very poor example of the use of psychological techniques for cross-cultural research. Since the stimulus arrays used tell us little about the nature of categories or the principles of categorization in our own culture, they can be expected to be equally uninformative when applied to the peoples of other cultures.

The psychological principles of categorization proposed in this chapter are based on the recognition that the real world is not an unstructured total set. The aim of the research was to show that the world does, in a sense, contain "intrinsically separate things". The world appears to be so structured because of three principles. In the first place, real-world attributes, unlike the sets often presented laboratory subjects, do not occur independently of each other. Creatures with feathers are more likely also to have wings than creatures with fur, and objects with the visual appearance of chairs are more likely to have functional sit-on-able-ness than objects with the appearance of cats.

In the second place, categories are determined because the world appears to be so structured that in taxonomies of concrete objects, there is generally one level of abstraction at which the most basic category cuts can be made. The basic level of abstraction can be described both in general terms of cognitive economy and in the specific language of probabilistic cue validity (Brunswik, 1956). With respect to general cognitive economy, the basic level is the level of abstraction at which the organism can obtain the most information with the least cognitive effort. That is, to categorize a stimulus means to consider it, for purposes of that categorization, not only equivalent to other stimuli in the same category but also different from stimuli not in that category. On the one hand, it would appear to the organism's advantage to have as many properties as possible predictable from knowing any one property (which, for humans, includes the important property of the category name), a principle which would lead to formation of large numbers of categories with the finest possible discriminations between categories. However, on the other hand, in so far as categorization occurs to reduce the infinite differences between stimuli to behaviourally and cognitively usable proportions, it is to the organism's advantage not to differentiate stimuli from other stimuli when that differentiation is irrelevant for the purposes at hand. The basic level of classification, the primary level at which cuts are made in the environment, appears to result from the combination of those two principles; it is the most general and inclusive level at which categories can delineate real-world correlational structures.

These intuitions about structure can be made more precise through the concept of *cue validity*. Cue validity is a probabilistic concept; the validity of a given cue x as a predictor of a given category y (the conditional probability of y/x) increases as the frequency with which cue x is associated with category y increases and decreases as the frequency with which cue x is associated with categories other than y increases (Beach, 1964a, b; Reed, 1972). The cue validity of an entire category may be defined as the summation of the cue validities for that category of each of the attributes of the category. A category with high cue validity is, by definition, more differentiated from other categories than one of lower cue validity. A working assumption of the present research has been that, in the domain of both man-made and biological objects, there occur information-rich bundles of perceptual and functional attributes that form natural discontinuities. If basic objects (e.g. chair, car) are the most inclusive level of categorization at which there can be many attributes common to all or more members of the category, basic objects will, thereby, be categories at the level of abstraction for which cue validities are maximized. That is, categories at higher levels of abstraction than the basic (e.g. furniture, vehicle) possess few attributes common to members of the category; categories subordinate to the basic (e.g. kitchen chair) share most attributes with contrasting subordinate categories. Thus, basic level categorizations should contain the distinctions between stimuli which will be required and will be satisfactory for most purposes. These concepts are explained further below in terms of the methods used to operationalize them.

In the third place, categories become definitively structured because, even when correlational structure in the world is only partial or when attributes are continuous, thus producing categories which might tend to blend with other categories at the same level of abstraction, categories are maintained as discrete by being coded in cognition in terms of prototypes of the most characteristic members of the category. As detailed in the first sections of the chapter, many experiments have shown that categories appear to be coded in the mind neither by means of lists of each individual member of the category nor by means of a list of formal criteria necessary and sufficient for category membership but, rather, in terms of a prototype of a typical category member. The most cognitively economical code for a category is, in fact, a concrete image of an average category member.

The first part of Section III will summarize some evidence that there are basic objects (categories at basic levels of abstraction) in the world determined by real-world correlational structure. The second part will show how coding in terms of prototypes and distance from prototypes is integrated with basic levels of abstraction. Some implications for perception, for developmental psychology and for psycholinguistics which have already been tested will be presented. Finally, the issue of the universality and cross-cultural implications of these theories will be discussed.

A. Basic Objects in Natural Categories

Real-world correlational structure of concrete objects itself consists of a number of inseparable aspects, any one of which could serve as the point of departure for the present analysis. The four aspects for which experimental evidence will be given below are attributes in common, motor movements in common, objective similarity in shape, and identifiability of averaged shapes.

1. Common Attributes

Basic level objects should be the most inclusive level of classification at which objects have numbers of attributes in common. Although in experimental psychology and in cultural anthropology as a whole, categories have generally been taken as arbitrary, a number of ethnobiologists have, for some time, asserted a claim somewhat similar to the claim of the present study — that there is a level of biological classification which corresponds to "natural groupings" of organisms which possess "bundles" of correlated features and which are "obviously" different from other organisms (Berlin, 1972; Bulmer, 1967; Bulmer and Tyler, 1968; Rosaldo, 1972). Berlin (1972) has gone considerably further and argued an evolutionary theory of plant names. He identified the natural grouping at the level of the genus (oak, maple) and has amassed considerable evidence in support of the claim that the first plant names refer to this level. The seminal work already done by ethnobiologists is limited for use in a general theory by a number of factors: it refers only to biological classes; the claims for natural groupings have tended to be supported only by the ethnographer's mention of a few correlated attributes (a tendency being corrected in Berlin's current ethnobotanical studies — see Berlin et al., 1966); and the location of natural groupings at a particular level of abstraction is defined by linguistic–taxonomic, rather than psychological, criteria (see Berlin et al., 1973). The purpose of the first experiment in the present research was to provide a systematic empirical study of the co-occurrence of attributes in the most common taxonomies of man-made and biological objects in our own culture.

The hypothesis that basic level objects are the most inclusive level of classification at which objects have numbers of attributes in common was tested (Rosch et al., 1976b) for categories at three levels of abstraction in the nine systematically chosen taxonomies shown in Table 2. Criteria for choice of these specific items were that the taxonomies contain the most common (defined by word frequency) categories of concrete nouns in English, that the levels of abstraction bear simple class inclusion relations to each other, and that those class inclusion relations be generally known to our subjects (be agreed upon by a sample of native English speakers). The middle level of abstraction was the hypothesized basic level: for non-biological taxonomies this corresponded to the intuition of the experimenters (which also turned out to be consistent with Berlin's linguistic–taxonomic criteria); for biological taxonomies it corresponded to the level of the genus, the basic level by Berlin's criteria (Berlin, 1972; Berlin et al., 1973).

Subjects received sets of words taken from the nine taxonomies shown in Table 2; the subject's task was to list all of the attributes he could think of which were true of the items included in the class of things designated by each object name. These attribute lists were tallied, and a cut-off point of six or more listings of an attribute was adopted as the criterion for inclusion of the attribute in the final tally. The veracity of attributes was rated by

Table 2
The nine taxonomies used as stimuli

Superordinate	Basic level	Subordinates	
		Non-biological taxonomies	
Musical	Guitar	Folk guitar	Classical guitar
Instrument	Piano	Grand piano	Upright piano
	Drum	Kettle drum	Base drum
Fruit[a]	Apple	Delicious apple	Mackintosh apple
	Peach	Freestone peach	Cling peach
	Grapes	Concord grapes	Green seedless grapes
Tool	Hammer	Ball-peen hammer	Claw hammer
	Saw	Hack hand saw	Cross-cutting hand saw
	Screwdriver	Phillips screwdriver	Regular screwdriver
Clothing	Pants	Levis	Double knit pants
	Socks	Knee socks	Ankle socks
	Shirt	Dress shirt	Knit shirt
Furniture	Table	Kitchen table	Dining-room table
	Lamp	Floor lamp	Desk lamp
	Chair	Kitchen chair	Living-room chair
Vehicle	Car	Sports car	Four door sedan car
	Bus	City bus	Cross country bus
	Truck	Pick-up truck	Tractor-trailer truck
		Biological Taxonomies	
Tree	Maple	Silver maple	Sugar maple
	Birch	River birch	White birch
	Oak	White oak	Red oak
Fish	Bass	Sea bass	Striped bass
	Trout	Rainbow trout	Steelhead trout
	Salmon	Blueback salmon	Chinook salmon
Bird	Cardinal	Easter cardinal	Grey tailed cardinal
	Eagle	Bald eagle	Golden eagle
	Sparrow	Song sparrow	Field sparrow

[a] Fruit is not considered a biological taxonomy by the criteria in Berlin (1972).

additional judges and a second tally, slightly amended by the judgments, was also computed.

Results showed that for both the raw and the judge-amended tallies, very few attributes were listed for the superordinate categories, and a significantly greater number of attributes were listed for the supposed basic level objects. Subordinate level objects did not receive significantly more attributes listed than basic level objects. The few additional attributes listed for subordinate object names tended to be adjective rather than noun or functional attributes. A check on the likeness of attributes listed for object names and for visually present objects showed that a single subject listing all attributes per item for 20 different actual objects (e.g. chairs) produced essentially identical attribute tallies to those produced by 20 subjects for a single object name (e.g. "chair"). The single unpredicted result was that for the three biological taxonomies shown in Table 2, the basic level, as defined by numbers of attributes in common, appeared to be the level we had originally expected to be superordinate, that is, one level higher in abstraction than predicted by Berlin (1972).

2. Motor Movements

Inseparable from the attributes of objects are the ways in which humans habitually use or interact with those objects. For example, when performing the action of sitting down on a chair, a sequence of body and muscle movements are typically made which are inseparable from the nature of the attributes of chairs — legs, seat, back, etc. This aspect of objects is particularly important in light of the role which sensory-motor interaction with the world appears to play in the development of thought (Piaget, 1952; Bruner et al., 1966; Nelson, 1974).

In our study of motor movements, each of the sets of words used in the previous experiment was administered to new subjects. Instructions were for the subject to describe, in as much finely analysed detail as possible, the sequences of muscle movements he makes when using or interacting with the object. Subjects' protocols were analysed as follows: the description was first divided into the major activities which appeared to be described (such as hammering in a nail or watching a bird). Each major activity was then divided into the part of the body used in each part of the sequence, and each body part for each part of the sequence was divided into the specific movement(s) made by that body part at that point. Tallies of four or more listings of these same movements of the same body part in the same part of the movement sequence formed the basic unit of analysis; these repeated movements were tallied and analysed as the attributes had been in the previous experiment.

Results were identical to those of the attribute listings: virtually no motor movements occurred in common for the supposed superordinates (supposed superordinates displaced upwards one level of abstraction for the three biological taxonomies); a large number of movements were made in common to basic level objects; and no more movements were made in common to subordinate than to basic level objects. For example, there are few motor programmes we carry out to items of furniture in general, several specific motor programmes carried out in regard to sitting down on chairs, but we sit on kitchen and living-room chairs using essentially the same motor programmes. As with the attributes, the results obtained from subject protocols based on introspection of motor movements were checked against subjects' descriptions of naïve models performing the dominant activity for four objects (sitting on a chair, eating grapes, putting on a sock, hammering in a nail). Essentially identical results were obtained from the introspective and live protocols (see Rosch *et al.*, 1976b, for additional detail).

3. Similarity in Shapes

Another aspect of the meaning of a class of objects is the way the objects of the class look. In order to be able to analyse real-world correlational structures by different but converging methods, it was necessary to find a method for analysing similarity in the visual aspects of objects which was not dependent upon subjects' descriptions (as the previous experiments had been), which was free from effects of the object's name (which would not have been the case for subjects' ratings of similarity), and which went beyond similarity of analysable, listable attributes which had already been used in the first experiment described. For this purpose, outlines of the shape of two-dimensional representations of objects were used, an integral aspect of natural forms.

Four superordinate categories were chosen for which it was possible to obtain a very large sample of pictures from books and/or from objects available in the immediate environment (furniture, clothing, vehicles, animals). Out of a pool of at least 100 pictures per object, four pictures of four basic level objects in each category were chosen by essentially random decision methods and were normalized for size (area within the outline of the object) and orientation. Similarity in shape was measured by the amount of overlap of the two outlines when the normalized outlines were juxtaposed.

Results showed that the ratio of overlapped to non-overlapped area when two objects from the same basic level category (e.g. two cars) were overlapped was far greater than when two objects from the same superordinate category were overlapped (e.g. a car and a motorcycle — recall that the pictures were normalized for size). While some gain in ratio of overlap to non-overlap also occurred for subordinate category objects (e.g. two sports cars), the gain obtained by shifting from basic level to subordinate objects was significantly less than the gain obtained by shifting from superordinate to basic level objects.

4. Identifiability of Averaged Shapes

If the basic level is the most inclusive level at which shapes of objects of a class are similar, a possible result of such similarity may be that the basic level is also the most inclusive level at which an average shape of an object can be recognized. To test this hypothesis, the same normalized overlaps of shapes used in the previous experiment were used to draw an average outline of the overlapped figures — that is, the central point of all non-adjacent points was taken and connected with lines. Subjects were then asked to identify both the superordinate category and the specific object depicted. Results showed that basic objects were the most general and inclusive categories at which the objects depicted could be identified. Furthermore, overlaps of subordinate objects were no more identifiable than objects at the basic level. This result was particularly important because it suggests that the basic level may be the most inclusive level at which it is possible to form a mental image which is isomorphic to an average member of the class and, thus, the most abstract level at which it is possible to have a relatively concrete image.

In summary: converging experiments have shown a basic level of abstraction in human classification of concrete objects. Basic objects were found to be the most inclusive categories whose members consisted of clusters of correlated attributes, were used by means of the same motor movements, had objectively similar shapes, and for which an averaged shape of members of the class was recognizable. It is the last finding which makes it possible to articulate this research with previous findings in regard to coding categories by means of prototypes.

B. The Origins of Noun Category Prototypes

The theme of the present chapter has been that division of the world into categories is not arbitrary. The formation of category prototypes appears to be determinate also and to be closely related to the initial formation of categories. For those categories which probably have a physiological basis such as colours, forms, and facial expressions of basic human emotions, prototypes appear to be stimuli which are salient prior to formation of the category, whose salience, at the outset, determines the categorical structuring of those domains. For categories of concrete objects, however, prototypes would appear to develop through the same principles, such as maximization of cue validity, as those governing the formation of the categories themselves.

In support of such a hypothesis, Rosch and Mervis (1975) have shown that the more prototypical of a category a member is rated, the more attributes it has in common with other members of the category and the fewer attributes in common with members of contrasting categories. This finding was demonstrated for natural language superordinate categories, for natural language basic level categories, and for artificial categories in which amount of experience with items could be strictly controlled. Other principles of prototype formation also appear related to the cue validity principle. Since the present theory is a structural theory, one aspect of it is that "centrality" shares the mathematical notions inherent in measures like the mean and mode. Prototypical category members have been found to represent the means of attributes which have a metric, such as size (Reed, 1972; Rosch, 1975a; Rosch et al., 1976a). Like items with most attributes in common with other members of a category, an item possessing the mean value of a category attribute is closer to other items in the category than is a member possessing an extreme value of the attribute. In addition, more highly correlated attributes are probably given greater weight in formation of the prototype than the same attributes not related contingently to each other — and contingency relations are the basic structures by which categories are formed. Frequency (repetition) of the same item is a special case of correlated attributes (Rosch, 1975a).

In short, it would appear that prototypes of many categories form by the same principles as basic categories themselves are formed. Prototypes appear to be just those members of a category which most reflect the redundancy structure of the category as a whole. That is, if categories form to maximize the information-rich clusters of attributes in the environment and, thus, the cue validity of the attributes of categories, prototypes of categories appear to form in such a manner as to maximize such clusters and such cue validity still further within categories.

The research reported in Section II of the present chapter argued that the prototype structure of categories is used in the cognitive processing of those categories. The structural principles by which categories and prototypes of categories are formed suggest functional reasons why this might occur. In the first place, prototypes would appear to enable a subject to make use of his knowledge of the contingency structure of the environment without his being forced to engage in the laborious cognitive process of contingently computing and summing the validities of individual cues. That is, by use of the efficient processing mechanism of matching to a prototype, humans need not sacrifice attention to the validity of cues.

In the second place, prototypes enable humans to make greater use of representational codes such as imagery, a type of code which (whatever its logical status as a variable, Pylyshyn, 1973) can be argued to be useful or necessary for the performance of many cognitive activities (Paivio, 1971; Cooper and Shepard, 1973). The fact that basic level objects were the most inclusive categories at which an averaged member of the category could be identified suggested that basic objects might be the most inclusive categories for which it was possible to form a mental image isomorphic to the appearance of members of the class as a whole. This hypothesis was tested by two additional experiments (Rosch *et al.*, 1976b): (a) using a signal detection paradigm, basic level classes were shown to be the most inclusive categories for which advance presentation of the category name aided detection of a picture of the object in visual noise; (b) using a priming paradigm, basic level categories were shown to be the most inclusive categories for which — as in the case of colour categories but not superordinate semantic categories — priming with the name of the object affected responses under instructions to define "same" as physical identity. These experiments demonstrated that basic level objects appear to be the most abstract categories for which an image can be reasonably representative of the class as a whole. Thus, it is through prototypes that the efficiency of basic level categories in providing the most information for the least cognitive effort can be translated into an actual cognitive code.

C. Implications for Other Fields in Psychology

The theory of categorization outlined above has implications for several fields which have already been tested. For perception, the evidence suggests that objects are first seen or recognized as members of their basic category, and only with the aid of additional processing can they be identified as members of their superordinate or subordinate category. Ethnographic support for this hypothesis comes from Hunn's (1972) interviews with experienced bird-watchers; such individuals (for whom the basic level for birds is, presumably, the generic level) reported that they recognized a class such as gulls directly from seeing the creature, whereas, to identify sub-divisions of gull, they consciously looked for and evaluated the distinguishing features. Experimental support was obtained by a study of category membership verification (Rosch *et al.*, 1976b). Subjects were presented with pictures of objects from Table 2 which could be named at all three levels of abstraction (for example, the same picture could be called "delicious apple", "apple", or "fruit") and were asked to verify whether or not each was a picture of an X, where X was either a basic level, superordinate, or subordinate name. Basic level names were responded to significantly faster than either superordinate or subordinate names. Thus, there is some evidence that the first and primary unit of identification for objects is the basic object category.

The present theory of categorizations has several implications for developmental psychology. Basic level objects should be the classifications first learned by means of visual perception and sensory motor interaction with the object; basic objects should be the classifications most differentiable from each other and, thus, the most generally useful distinctions to make in the world; and basic objects are the most general classifications which can be readily coded iconically by means of an image, a form of representation which may be the earliest used by children (Bruner *et al.*, 1966). Basic objects should, thus, be the first divisions of the world at which it might make sense to a child to put the "same type of things" together as a category. There is a long tradition of sorting research in the developmental literature which indicates that children, unlike adults, do not sort taxonomically, i.e., put together things of like category; rather, they tend to from *complexive classes* (Bruner *et al.*, 1966; Denney, 1974; Vygotsky, 1962). However, in all previous sorting tasks which have employed representational stimuli, possible taxonomic categories were invariably at the superordinate level; e.g., the child would have to put together a dog and cow rather than several dogs. We performed a study in which subjects, age three to adult, were divided into two groups, one of which was given an opportunity to sort sets of colour pictures of common objects into groups of basic level objects, another of which was given the same pictures but in sets cross-cutting the basic level so that taxonomic sorting would necessarily be at the usual superordinate level. At all age levels (in which a ceiling had not been reached), taxonomic grouping of basic level objects occurred far more frequently than of superordinate objects, an effect which was not dependent on language (Rosch *et al.*, 1976b). Thus, what had appeared to be entirely a difference in the structure of thought was shown to be partly due to the content of the usual tasks provided, an artifact which was caused by a lack of understanding of actual real-world structures and their reflection in psychological categories.

Other developmental implications concern the acquistion of language. Basic level objects should be those first named by the child. Furthermore, category membership of prototypical examples of objects should be learned before that of less good examples. Thus, basic level objects which are good representatives of their basic level category should be learned before any other concrete nouns. Using the protocols from Roger Brown's Sarah (Brown, 1974), we found that, for the nine taxonomies in Table 2, in all cases, the basic level names were learned and used before either superordinate or subordinate names (Rosch *et al.*, 1976b). Furthermore, using a mixture of category types, Anglin (1976) has shown that good examples of categories are learned before poor examples.

The third field to which this theory has direct implication is that of language use and language evolution. From all that has been said, we would expect the most useful and, thus, most used name for an item to be the basic level name. In fact, we found that adults almost invariably named pictures of the subordinate items of the taxonomies in Table 2 at the basic level, although they knew the correct superordinate and subordinate names for the objects (Rosch et al., 1976b).

On a more speculative level, in evolution of languages, one would expect names to evolve first for basic level objects, spreading both upwards and downwards as taxonomies increased in depth. Berlin (1972) claims such a pattern for the evolution of plant names, although that work is rendered somewhat equivocal by the difficulties in location of the basic level which we found for biological taxonomies. Of great relevance to this speculative evolutionary hypothesis is our finding that for the American sign language of the deaf, it was the basic level categories which were most often coded by single signs and super- and subordinate categories which were likely to be missing (Rosch et al., 1976b). An historical linguistic study of this hypothesis for domains other than botanical nomenclature is very much needed.

From the beginning of the discussion of basic objects, it has been implied that the study concerned universal principles of categorization of the concrete perceptual stimuli of the world. But what aspects of the theory are intended to be universals? The content of categories should not be universals. It has been argued that categories reflect real-world correlational structures. Since the structure of the environment, both the man-made objects and the flora and fauna of a region, should differ radically in different parts of the world, we would expect the categories of different cultures to differ.

At this point, it is necessary to clarify what is meant by categories reflecting real-world correlational structures. In the first place, we are not discussing the philosophical issue of a metaphysical real world which may exist apart from perceivers. We mean simply that, given an organism which can perceive attributes such as feathers, fur, and wings, it is an empirical fact "out there" that wings co-occur with feathers more than with fur. It is obvious that all cognitive categories are interactions between the correlational structures that exist in the world and the state of knowledge of the perceivers. However, the structures in the world place limitations on human knowledge: humans cannot perceive correlational structures where there are none; they can only be ignorant of structures which exist or exaggerate structures which exist by means of cognitive prototypes. Thus, in different cultures, not only available real-world structures may differ, but interest in attributes and their correlations for specific domains may differ — thereby, contributing to differences in the content of categories.

What is claimed to be universal in the present research are the principles of category formation. On the most general level, the assertion is that categories form so as to be maximally differentiable from each other. This is accomplished by categories which have maximum cue validity — that is, they have the most attributes common to members of the category and the least attributes shared with members of other categories.

For categories of concrete objects, this general principle leads to claims for a number of more specific principles which are asserted to be universal for concrete objects. For this domain, given that there are correlational structures which are known of and attended to by a culture and an individual, the claim is that the basic cuts in the environment are determined. Basic object categories will be the most inclusive categories which mirror the correlational structure of the environment, that is, the most inclusive categories which have many perceived attributes in common, very similar motor movement sequences made to objects of the category, are similar in their overall look, and can be represented by means of a concrete cognitive code. Universally, such categories should be the first classifications made during perception, the first learned and first named by children and the most codable, most coded, and most necessary in the language of any people.

D. Implications for Cross-cultural Research

The concept of real-world structure and its reflection in basic level objects is both a concept which may provide a helpful framework within which cross-cultural work may be carried out, and it is a concept which requires cross-cultural testing for its verification and extension. In terms of its effect on cross-cultural work, the concept of structure and basic level organization can provide a framework which anthropologists and psychologists can use as a first approximation for organizing questions and data concerning the classification systems of other cultures. As was pointed out at the beginning of this section, previous psychologically oriented cross-cultural studies of classification have tended to use arrays of objects like those used in artificial concept formation studies in Western culture. Research has focussed on the concreteness–abstractness of individual or cultural classifications. It should now be apparent why such tasks may be misleading. Real-world objects at the most basic levels of classification are not based on oppositions of single attributes but rather on correlated clusters of many attributes. The performance of a subject when faced with an artificial classification task may be quite task specific.

The confounding which has existed in cross-cultural studies of abstract and concrete modes of classification reveals an important point of method.

Because it is circular to infer the metaphysics of a people from the structure of their grammar (as Whorf, 1956, did), and because it is absurd to infer the logic of a people's everyday thinking from their religious thought (as Levy Bruhl, 1923, has been interpreted as doing), does *not* mean that a people's principles of classification cannot be inferred from the classifications which they make in everyday life. Thus, the psychologist should be quite suspicious whenever the modes of classification that people of a culture use consistently on his tests differ markedly from the modes they use in language and in everyday behaviour.

A case in point is the use of colour as a dominant principle of sorting in laboratory tests. Colour is a relatively useless attribute for classifications of objects since it is little predictive of other attributes. Of the basic level objects in the nine taxonomies which we studied experimentally, colour was not once listed as an attribute of the basic level objects by more than an occasional subject. Yet when faced with unstructured artificial arrays of stimuli in which all attributes combine with equal probability with all other attributes, even adult American subjects are likely to use colour as a principle of sorting (Wing and Bevan, 1969).

A further anomaly of this type occurs in developmental and cross-cultural comparisons of preferred sorting principles. Around the world, the younger the subject and/or the less Western the schooling he has received, the more likely he is to prefer colour as the basis of classification in a triads test in which classification must be made on the basis of colour, form, or size (see Serpell, 1969, for a review of studies). However, it is just young children and non-Western peoples who appear to be the populations least likely to classify by colour in more naturalistic contexts. It is the technologically less advanced cultures which appear to have smaller colour vocabularies and less cultural concern with colour distinctions and coordinations (see Berlin and Kay, 1969). Young children in Western cultures only come to use colour terms correctly and consistently at about the age when they begin to prefer form classification in the colour–form preference triads (Heider, 1971; Istomina, 1963). Further evidence comes from a study of the published diaries of the language development of individual children. Clark (1973) has examined all of the diary examples of young children's over-generalizations of words; that is, of cases where a child applies a newly learned word to a variety of things to which that word does not actually apply in the adult language (e.g. calling all animals "dogs"). Clark was interested in finding out the attributes by which children generalize meaning. What is relevant to the present issue is that, in all of the diary literature, there is not one single instance reported in which a child seemed to over-generalize a word on the basis of colour.

As Cole and Scribner (1974) point out, a Kpelle does not treat a brown cow, mud, and a brown hat as though they were the same sort of thing in the real world because they are the same colour. In fact, the present theory suggests that it is not particular attributes which are important bases of real-world classification so much as the structure of attribute sets. We recommend turning to the study of such a structure.

The previous discussion focussed on use of the present theory of classification as a framework for studying classifications cross-culturally. However, the theory itself is incomplete without the addition of cross-cultural data. Cross-cultural data is essential to the theory in a number of ways:

1. It is needed to verify the universality of the principles which have been suggested. It is also needed to clarify these principles. For example, we have argued that attributes, functions (motor movements), and the shape of objects are aspects of the same real-world structure. However, with further clarification, some of these aspects may be seen to take precedence over others. For example, attributes may tend to be defined in languages in terms of specific functions (e.g. "seat" refers to a functional aspect of a chair). It is absolutely necessary to have a broader data base than Western culture in order to assert that the principles of classification of concrete objects outlined in this chapter are universals.

2. A cross-cultural approach can help clarify the relationship of cultural knowledge and individual expertise to classifications. Expertise is a particularly important area of study since more than the traditional studies of memory (either episodic or semantic memory, see Tulving and Donaldson, 1972), gaining expertise is what learning and memory is about. In terms of classification, given that a human is capable of perceiving some set of attributes, and that those attributes possess a correlational structure in the world, the state of knowledge of the person may differ from the potential provided by the world in that the person may be ignorant of (or indifferent or inattentive to) the attributes, or he may know of the attributes but be ignorant concerning their correlational structure. Gaining expertise is gaining some of that knowledge. At present our ideas concerning the effects of greater knowledge on classification are derived from minimal and unsystematic evidence within American culture.

Let us take, as an example, the case of aeroplanes, a vehicle used in the experiments by which basic levels were verified. While "aeroplane" appeared to be the basic level for most of the subjects participating (i.e. the most inclusive level at which many attributes and motor movements were listed in common, etc.), for one former aeroplane mechanic, the taxonomy appeared to be quite different. The lists of attributes common to aeroplanes produced by most subjects were paltry compared to the lengthy lists of additional attributes which he could produce in common for different types of aeroplanes. Furthermore, his motor programmes as a mechanic were quite different for the different attributes of the engines of different types of planes. Finally, his visual view of aeroplanes was not the canonical top and side images of the public; his view concerned the undersides and engines of aeroplanes, for which, he assured us, we would have obtained quite different locations of the basic level in our shape experiments. However, his differentiation of aeroplanes was not infinite; he considered a single and twin engine Cessna quite similar and thought that they would probably constitute subordinates for him. Furthermore, he considered aeroplanes as a whole more similar to each other than vehicles, and he was able to take the role of an uninformed person and think of attributes, motor movements, and canonical shapes common to all aeroplanes. In short, aeroplanes appear to be an example of a category in which either one or two sets of correlational structures are available depending upon the degree of knowledge of the perceiver. A hypothetical taxonomy of this type and of a potential one-level

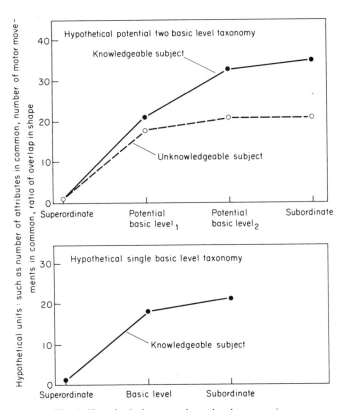

Fig. 1. Hypothetical one- and two-level taxonomies.

type are graphed in Fig. 1. In this figure, basic level objects are depicted as elbows in graphs of attributes in common, motor movements in common, similarity in shape, etc.

By reference to the two hypothetical taxonomies of Fig. 1, we can now clarify the possible reasons for the disparity between our findings in regard to the biological taxonomies and those previously predicted from linguistic and anthropological data (Berlin, 1972). The most probable explanation of the present data is that biological taxonomies are of the type in which two basic level groupings are possible but that our city-dwelling subjects were ignorant of the attributes in common, potential movements to be made in interaction with the objects, and the similarities in shape which were characteristic of the genus level biological categories in their environment.

The effects of expertise on classification is an issue for which systematic study is needed. We suspect that for all taxonomies, there is a level below which further differentiations cannot form basic level categories because, no matter how great the frequency of use of the objects or degree of expertise, there simply are not a sufficient number of attributes, movements, etc. which differentiate objects below that level. Thus, for any taxonomy, there should be a level at which the attributes, motor movements, and other information common to objects which is added by further distinction(s) will be out-weighed by the attributes which the newly distinguished classes share with each other. When a further distinction reduces, rather than increases, the cue validity of categories at the new level of classification, that distinction can be said to result in subordinate categories rather than new basic level categories. Both further theoretical formulation of change in knowledge structures with learning and further empirical (hopefully cross-cultural) study of experts are needed before this question can be discussed intelligently.

People with expertise are not only unable to differentiate categories indefinitely, but the effect of expertise is probably often confined to specific parts of a taxonomy, thereby creating unevenness in the expert's categorization of that taxonomy. One can easily imagine a poultry farmer for whom chickens and turkeys (and/or their subordinates) are basic objects but for whom the rest of the bird class remains undifferentiated, and one can imagine an antique furniture dealer for whom Chippendale and Hepplewhite chairs are basic objects but for whom kitchen and living-room chairs, in the average house, are as undifferentiated as they were for our subjects. Indeed, differentiation of mammals (but not birds, fish, and other major divisions of animals) into basic level objects can be observed at the present time in our own culture which is more knowledgeable about mammals than other animal classes. This may, in fact, be the reason behind lack of use of the word "mammal" by English speakers; mammals are thought of as members of their basic level classes and called by their basic names — and such names are one level in the taxonomy lower than are the basic level classes and names for other major animal classifications. Until studied further, the effects of expertise on classification remain largely speculative.

3. A cross-cultural approach is also needed in order to explore one of the intriguing possibilities of the concept of basic level objects. Due to the existence of some universals in human functions, there may be some universals in the content, as well as the principles of formation, of categories. For example, it is possible that the need of humans to sleep in a prone and extended body position leads to universals in the category beds, that is, to certain invarying attributes, motor movements, and shapes which define beds in any culture.

4. Given the framework of the concept of basic level objects, it may be possible to answer specific questions concerning why classification systems in languages are formed at all. We have already found that in American Sign Language of the Deaf, in certain domains, superordinates and subordinates were not essential. By study of when taxonomic depth does and does not occur, and by study of the evolution and degeneration of taxonomic depth, we may gain a great deal of knowledge of the functions and development of languages.

5. Finally the present theory offers a framework from which to study changes in categorization. What is the effect of having categories with prototypes of a given sort on category change given a change in environment? On human efforts to change the environment? On conservatism and change in cases of culture contact?

In short, the present theory is only a first step toward an understanding of human categorization of concrete objects. It requires cross-cultural work for its verification and further extension. It may also prove useful for the understanding of other issues in cross-cultural studies. The techniques and research designs described in work on American subjects can provide the framework and basic techniques for cross-cultural studies of these same issues.

IV. GENERAL SUMMARY

The present chapter has used the topic of human categorization to demonstrate possibilities for interplay between theory and cross-cultural research when the object of the theory and research is to formulate universal laws of psychological functioning. In Section I, categories of attribute domains were investigated. An initial cross-linguistic and cross-cultural empirical generalization about regularities in basic colour terms led to the formulation of psychological generalizations — that colour, and possibly form, categories appear around perceptually salient points in the domain and that such points form cognitive prototypes for the categories of those domains. Research done within the framework of this theory led to verification of universals in a domain in which unsystematic observation had observed only the existing cultural differences.

In turn, such research led to a more general psychological theory — it was proposed that other types of categories are structured, not in terms of clearly delineated criterial attributes, but in a manner analogous to the structure of colour and form categories. This hypothesis was tested using experimental techniques on adults within our own culture. Related developmental hypotheses within our own culture were also tested. The results suggest a programme for further research.

In Section III, categories of concrete objects were investigated. A theory of categorization based on the ecological structure of real-world attributes was formulated, and some implications were tested on adults and children within our own culture. The existing cross-cultural studies with which this work is in closest agreement are those in ethnobiology. This theory can only be verified and extended by means of a programme of further cross-cultural work.

Experimental psychology, developmental psychology, and cross-cultural psychology are often treated as separate fields of study. Any theory with explanatory power, however, should have implications for all of these fields. Categorization is a topic which lends itself to a demonstration of such interplay because the basic theoretical position on which the present research on this topic is based is that categorization, like other human psychological activities, makes sense at any age and in any culture. This chapter has reviewed part of the programme of research by which the author has searched for that sense.

ACKNOWLEDGEMENT

The research reported in this chapter was supported by grants to the author (under her former name Eleanor Rosch Heider) from the Foundations Fund for Research in Psychiatry G67-392, the National Science Foundation GB-38245X, The Grant Foundation, and the National Institutes of Mental Health 1 RO1 MH24316-01.

REFERENCES

Anglin, J. (1976). *In* "La mémoire sémantique" (Eds S. Ehrlich and E. Tulving). Bulletin de Psychologie, Paris.
Attneave, F. (1957). *J. exp. Psychol.* **54**, 81–88.
Battig, W. F. and Montague, W. E. (1969). *J. exp. Psych.* **80** (Monog. Suppl. 3, Part 2).
Beach, L. R. (1964a). *Psychol. Monogr.* **78**, Whole No. 582.
Beach, L. R. (1964b). *Psychol. Monogr.* **78**, Whole No. 583.
Beller, H. K. (1971). *J. exp. Psychol.* **87**, 176–182.
Berlin, B. (1972). *Lang. in Soc.* **1**, 51–86.
Berlin, B. and Kay, P. (1969). "Basic color terms: their universality and evolution." University of California Press, Berkeley.
Berlin, B., Breedlove, D. E. and Raven, P. H. (1966). *Science* **154**, 273–275.
Berlin, B., Breedlove, D. E. and Raven, P. H. (1973). *Am. Anthrop.* **75**, 214–242.
Bourne, L. E. (1968). "Human conceptual behaviour." Allyn and Bacon, Boston.
Bransford, J. D. and Franks, J. J. (1971). *Cogn. Psychol.* **2**, 331–350.
Brown, R. (1974). "A first language." Harvard University Press, Cambridge, Mass.
Brown, R. and Lenneberg, E. (1954). *J. abnorm. soc. Psychol.* **49**, 454–462.
Bruner, J. S. and Tagiuri, R. (1954). *In* "Handbook of Social Psychology" (Ed. G. Lindzey, Vol. 2), 634–654. Addison-Wesley, Cambridge.
Bruner, J. S., Olver, R. R. and Greenfield, P. M. (1966). "Studies in cognitive growth." Wiley, New York and Chichester.
Brunswik, E. (1956). "Perception and the representative design of experiments." University of California Press, Berkeley.
Bulmer, R. (1967). *Man* **2**, 5–25.
Bulmer, R. and Tyler, M. J. (1968). *J. Polynes. Soc.* **77**, 333–385.
Clark, E. V. (1973). *In* "Cognitive development and the acquisition of language" (Ed. T. E. Moore), 66–110. Academic Press, New York and London.
Cole, M. (1975). *In* "Cross-cultural perspectives on learning" (Eds R. Brislin, S. Bochner and W. Lonner), 157–175. Halstead Press, New York.
Cole, M. and Scribner, S. (1974). "Culture and thought." Wiley, New York and London.
Collins, A. M. and Loftus, E. F. (1975). *Psychol. Rev.* **82**, 407–428.
Cooper, L. A. and Shepard, R. N. (1973). *In* "Visual Information Processing" (Ed. W. G. Chase), 75–176. Academic Press, New York and London.
Denney, N. W. (1974). *Hum. Devel.* **17**, 41–53.
De Valois, R. L. and Jacobs, G. H. (1968). *Science* **162**, 533–540.
Ekman, P. (1972). *In* "Nebraska Symposium on Motivation" (Ed. J. K. Cole), 207–283. University of Nebraska Press, Lincoln, Nebraska.
Fodor, J. A. and Katz, J. J. (1964). "The structure of language." Prentice–Hall, Englewood Cliffs, New Jersey.
Frake, C. O. (1969). *In* "Cognitive Anthropology" (Ed. S. A. Tyler), 28–41. Holt, New York.
Franks, J. J. and Bransford, J. D. (1971). *J. exp. Psychol.* **90**, 65–74.
Garner, W. R. (1966). *Am. Psychol.* **21**, 11–19.
Garner, W. R. (1970). *Am. Psychol.* **25**, 350–358.
Garner, W. R. (1974). "The processing of information and structure." Halstead Press, New York.

48   E. ROSCH

Handel, S. and Imai, S. (1972). *Perc. Psychophysics* **12**, 108–116.
Handel, S. and Preusser, D. (1969). *Perc. Psychophysics* **6**, 69–72.
Heider, E. R. (1971). *Devel. Psychol.* **4**, 447–455.
Heider, E. R. (1972a). *Man* **7**, 448–466.
Heider, E. R. (1972b). *J. exp. Psychol.* **93**, 10–20.
Heider, E. R. and Olivier, D. C. (1972). *Cogn. Psychol.* **3**, 337–354.
Heider, K. G. (1970). "The Dugum Dani: a Papuan culture in the Highlands of West New Guinea." Aldine, Chicago.
Hering, E. (1964). "Outlines of a theory of the light sense." (Trans. L. M. Hurvich and D. Jameson). Harvard University Press, Cambridge, Mass.
Horton, R. (1967). *Africa* **37**, 50–71.
Huang, I. (1945). *J. genet. Psychol.* **66**, 59-62.
Hunn, E. (1972). Unpublished MS, Language-Behaviour Research Laboratory, University of California, Berkeley.
Imai, S. (1966). *Perc. Psychophysics* **1**, 48–54.
Imai, S. and Garner, W. R. (1965). *J. exp. Psychol.* **69**, 596–608.
Inhelder, B. and Piaget, J. (1958). "The growth of logical thinking from childhood to adolescence." Basic Books, New York.
Istomina, Z. M. (1963). *Soviet Psych. Psychiat.* **1**, 37–46.
Katz, J. J. and Postal, P. M. (1964). "An integrated theory of linguistic descriptions." MIT Press, Cambridge.
Kay, P. (1972). "On the form of dictionary entries: English kinship semantics." Paper presented at the SECOL VIII Conference, October. Georgetown University.
Krauss, R. M. (1968). *Am. Scient.* **56**, 265–278.
Lakoff, G. (1972). *In* "Papers from the Eighth Regional Meeting, Chicago Linguistics Society." University of Chicago Linguistics Department.
Leach, E. (1964). *In* "New directions in the study of language" (Ed. E. H. Lenneberg), 23–64. MIT Press, Cambridge.
Levine, R. A. (1970). *In* "Carmichael's manual of child psychology" (Ed. P. H. Mussen), 559–612. Wiley, New York.
Levy-Bruhl, L. (1923). "Primitive mentality." Beacon Press, Boston.
McDaniel, C. K. (1972). Unpublished Honours thesis, Harvard College.
Mervis, C. B., Catlin, J. and Rosch, E. (1975). *Devel. Psychol.* **11**, 54–60.
Munsell Color Company (1966). "The Munsell book of color" (glossy finish collection). Munsell Color Company, Baltimore.
Munsell Color Company (1970). "Dominant wavelength and excitation purity for designated Munsell color notation." Munsell Color Company, Baltimore.
Neisser, U. (1967). "Cognitive psychology." Appleton, New York.
Nelson, K. (1974). *Psychol. Rev.* **81**, 267–285.
Oldfield, R. C. (1954). *Br. J. Psychol.* **45**, 14–23.
Paivio, A. (1971). "Imagery and verbal processes." Holt, New York.
Piaget, J. (1952). "The origins of intelligence in children." International University Press, New York.
Posner, M. I. (1969). *In* "The psychology of learning and motivation" (Ed. G. H. Bower), Vol. 3, 44–100. Academic Press, New York and London.
Posner, M. I. (1973). "Cognition: an introduction." Scott Foresman, Glencoe, Illinois.
Posner, M. I. and Keele, S. W. (1968). *J. exp. Psychol.* **77**, 353–363.
Posner, M. I. and Mitchell, R. F. (1967). *Psychol. Rev.* **74**, 392–409.

Posner, M. I., Goldsmith, R. and Welton, K. E. (1967). *J. exp. Psychol.* **73**, 28–38.
Pylyshyn, Z. W. (1973). *Psychol. Bull.* **80**, 1–24.
Reed, S. K. (1972). *Cogn. Psychol.* **3**, 382–407.
Rips, L. J., Shoben, E. J. and Smith, E. E. (1973). *J. Verb. Learning Verb. Beh.* **12**, 1–20.
Rosaldo, M. Z. (1972). *Southwest. J. Anthrop.* **28**, 83–99.
Rosch, E. (1973). *In* "Cognitive development and the acquisition of language" (Ed. T. E. Moore), 111–144. Academic Press, New York and London.
Rosch, E. (1974). *In* "Human communication: theoretical perspectives" (Ed. A. Silverstein), 95–121. Halstead Press, New York.
Rosch, E. (1975a). *In* "Cross-cultural perspectives on learning" (Eds R. Brislin, S. Boschner and W. Lonner), 177–206. Halstead Press, New York.
Rosch, E. (1975b). *Cogn. Psychol.* **7**, 532–547.
Rosch, E. (1975c). *J. exp. Psychol. General.* **104**, 192–233.
Rosch, E. (1975d). *J. exp. Psychol. Hum. Perc. Perf.* **1**, 303–322.
Rosch, E. (1976). *In* "La mémoire sémantique" (Eds S. Ehrlich and E. Tulving). Bulletin de Psychologie, Paris.
Rosch, E. and Mervis, C. B. (1975). *Cogn. Psychol.* **7**, 573–605.
Rosch, E., Simpson, C. and Miller, R. S. (1976a). *J. exp. Psychol. Hum. Perc. Perf.* **2**, 491–502.
Rosch, E., Mervis, C. B., Gray, W., Johnson, D. and Boyes-Braem, P. (1976b). *Cogn. Psychol.* **8**, 382–439.
Scribner, S. (1974). *Cogn. Psychol.* **6**, 475–494.
Segall, M. H., Campbell, D. T. and Herskovitz, M. J. (1966). "The influence of culture on visual perception." Bobbs–Merrill, Indianapolis.
Serpell, R. (1969). *Int. J. Psychol.* **4**, 183–194.
Shepard, R. N. (1964). *J. Math. Psychol.* **1**, 34–87.
Smith, E. E., Rips, L. J. and Shoben, E. J. (1974a). *In* "The psychology of learning and motivation" (Ed. G. H. Bower), Vol. 8, 1–45. Academic Press, New York and London.
Smith, E. E., Shoben, E. J. and Rips, L. J. (1974b). *Psychol. Rev.* **81**, 214–241.
Stefflre, V., Reich, P. and McClaren-Stefflre, M. (1971). *In* "Explorations in mathematical anthropology" (Ed. P. Kay), 79–116. MIT Press. Cambridge.
Suchman, R. G. and Trabasso, T. (1966). *J. exp. Child Psychol.* **3**, 177–187.
Tulving, E. and Donaldson, W., Eds (1972). "Organisation of memory." Academic Press, New York and London.
Tyler, S. A., Ed. (1969). "Cognitive anthropology." Holt, New York.
Vygotsky, L. S. (1962). "Thought and language." Wiley, New York.
Wertheimer, M. (1938). *In* "A source book of Gestalt psychology" (Ed. W. D. Ellis), 265–273. Harcourt, New York and London.
Whorf, B. L. (1956). "Language, thought and reality: selected writings of Benjamin Lee Whorf" (Ed. J. B. Carroll). MIT Press, Cambridge.
Wing, H. and Bevan, W. (1969). *Perc. Psychophysics* **6**, 137–141.

2 | Cross-cultural studies and Freudian Theory

PAUL KLINE

I. INTRODUCTION

The impact of Freudian theory on the intellectual *Zeitgeist*, and its attraction for scholars in many diverse disciplines (anthropology, literary criticism and aesthetics, for example) other than psychology, derive from its explanatory power. There is almost no aspect of human behaviour which the theory is incapable of embracing. In this respect it contrasts well with most current psychological theories — of which information theory is a typical example — which apply mainly to highly limited and artificial laboratory data of little general interest beyond the confines of experimental psychology. However it is precisely this wide explanatory power that experimental psychology abhors, because it is antithetical to the scientific method as conceived, e.g., by Popper (1959). Thus, as the arch-critic of Freudian theory has succinctly put it, psychoanalysis is unscientific because it can explain everything but predict nothing (Eysenck, 1953), refutability of prediction being the essence of the scientific method.

We do not want to argue here the scientific merits or demerits of Freudian theory. We shall straight away admit that it is essentially unscientific because it lacks quantification, fails to distinguish between data and interpretation and employs hypotheses and constructs so vague as to make clear refutation impossible. In addition the theory is so constructed that at some points refutation is logically impossible, the notion of reaction formation being a notorious case in point. Furthermore the theory allows an implicit *ad hominem* argument which has particularly upset some scientists, of whom Medawar is an outstanding example. This argument is implied in the notion of resistance — that failure to admit the case is due to emotional barriers in the person observing rather than to the weakness of the case itself. Actually, of course, this assumes, with considerable psychological naïevete, the possibility of an objective observer, a notion which even experimental psychology has been forced to abandon and a fantasy with which psychoanalysis in its study of scientists is thoroughly at home (see Fairbairn, 1952).

Thus with Freudian theory we are faced with a dilemma. As experimental psychologists we are forced to admit its faults and weaknesses; but as students of human behaviour its explanatory power and its applicability to problems which have intrigued writers down the ages make it seem foolish to us to abandon it completely. Indeed, as Conant (1947) has pointed out theories are jettisoned not when certain uncomfortable facts fail to fit them but when better theories are proposed. Freudian theory, which relies on its explanatory power, still has no adequate replacement.

One solution to this difficulty has been advocated by Farrell (1964) and by the present writer (Kline, 1972, 1973). This necessitates restating Freudian theory as a large number of testable, refutable and hence scientifically respectable, hypotheses. This implies, of course, that Freudian theory is not one unified theory but a collection of theories such that it is possible for a number of them to be falsified without thereby refuting all of them. Now this is not to say that they are all unrelated in that it would be disappointing for Freudian theory as a whole if, for example, the notion of repression were found to be false. Nevertheless it does mean that it is idle to dismiss Freudian theory as a whole on the basis of a limited number of failures to support the theory in some particular.

Examples of restated hypotheses might be: within the content of every dream there lies a hidden wish; pointed, sharp objects symbolize male sexual organs, rounded, hollow objects represent the female sexual organs; there is a syndrome of oral character traits, dependency, optimism, talkativeness and generosity; this syndrome is related to early weaning. All these hypotheses are logically refutable and hence scientific, although it must be admitted that many such hypotheses, in practical terms, have so far defied adequate testing. At this point cross-cultural psychology has an important part to play — in the practical testing of Freudian hypotheses and thus in their scientific evaluation.

This brings us face to face with the problem of why we should study Freudian theory at all and this must now be briefly discussed. As we have mentioned it seems folly to ignore entirely on grounds of faulty methodology and inadequate data a theory so widely applicable and influential as psychoanalysis. It has to be admitted that this is simply a value judgment with which anyone can disagree. However, what is less controversial is the claim that, should large sections of psychoanalytic theory turn out to be correct, we should have remarkable and utilizable insights into human behaviour. Since there is no alternative theory it is surely not unreasonable to regard Freudian theories as useful working hypotheses to be put by appropriate methods on to a scientific basis. In other words, Freudian theory, because of its potential value if true, deserves to have its claims investigated, not rejected wholesale, as is usual in psychology, or accepted as by psychoanalysts.

With this justification for the scientific study of Freudian theory which assumes that the scientific method is the only sound basis for theory construction, we must now turn to the far more difficult question of how it is to be carried out. In our previous survey of research into the validity of Freudian theory (Kline, 1972) it was found that many experiments purporting to refute Freudian theory and some apparently supporting it were vitiated by poor methodology, a view shared by Eysenck and Wilson (1973). As is to be expected, the requirements for experiments into the validity of Freudian theory are no different from those in other branches of psychology. They may be summarized as: clear statement of the hypothesis to be examined; correct sampling and proper use of control groups, where necessary; adequate statistical analyses; consideration of alternative explanations of results. So that we can appreciate the place of cross-cultural studies in the scientific investigation of Freudian theory we must briefly discuss some of the problems associated with each of the four criteria.

An important logical difficulty associated with restating Freudian theories in testable form is the danger of thus changing them, as Martin (1964) points out. However with careful use of Freud's own words as much as possible, the worst excesses can be avoided. Perhaps more important is the risk of testing only relatively trivial aspects of the theory. As Rapaport and Gill (1959) have well argued there is effectively an hierarchical structure to Freudian theory in which at the base lie empirical propositions (e.g. at about the age of four girls desire a penis) while at the top are the metapsychological propositions exemplified by the conception of the polarity of Eros and Thanatos. What is interesting here is that many of the arguments concerning the impossibility of refuting psychoanalytic theory refer to the metapsychology for there can be no doubt that the empirical propositions are testable. Since this metapsychology was developed only to account for the propositions, until these have been shown to be true there is no need for it. Thus the fact that our approach to the validation of Freudian theory deals with the bottom rather than the top of the hierarchy is not necessarily a weakness. On the other hand it is true that many of the more profound concepts of psychoanalysis cannot be verified by this method. However this, in itself, is worthy of note in the light of the logical positivist position that meaningfulness implies refutability.

In the refutation of Freudian hypotheses, cross-cultural investigations can be powerful instruments. Let us take as an example the hypothesis that the oral character is linked to early weaning. There is far greater variation in time and in methods of weaning among different cultures than there is within any one culture. Hence a truly effective test of the oral aetiology of the oral character would look at oral character traits within various cultures where the weaning techniques were as diverse as possible. Furthermore if a culture be found where weaning is always exceptionally late it would be possible to argue as a test of the hypothesis that there should be no oral characters within the culture. An opposite hypothesis would test the theory in a culture, if any such there be, where weaning was always as early as possible. Our example here of the oral character merely highlights a powerful use of cross-cultural studies in the elucidation of Freudian theory. Thus wherever there is considerable stress on the importance of some environmental, familial factor in the theory cross-cultural studies are of the utmost value.

Apart from the fact that diverse cultures present a powerful means of putting large and important parts of Freudian theory to the test, being virtually real-life laboratory situations, cross-cultural investigations are valuable in another way with respect to Freudian theory. Cross-cultural studies are essential to test the generalizability of the theoretical claims of psychoanalysis. As we mentioned in our opening paragraph one of the attractions of Freudian theory lies in this wide applicability to diverse behaviours and to all mankind. At the same time, however, this relates to one of its major failings from the scientific viewpoint. More specifically the weakness lies in Freud's sampling procedures. It is now a standard textbook joke that Freud was prepared to make statements about "primitive" or "savage" behaviour based on his clinical work with well-to-do, middle-class, middle-aged, Jewish, Viennese, hysterical women, a clearly inadequate sample of the human race. It should be noted in parenthesis that this is a failing that seems to beset psychology in general since much psychology is based upon data derived from either white, middle-class, wealthy, presbyterian, intelligent, college majors or the hooded rat — neither sample much improvement, if any, on that of Freud. Actually as the biography of Freud (Jones, 1957) makes clear, it seems likely that a major source of Freud's theorizing was not even these clinical samples but his own self-analysis. Furthermore it has been pointed out that many of Freud's ideas seem to show the influence of the Jewish mystical tradition (Bakan, 1958). This is sufficient to show that Freud's statements, which almost always refer to men in general, have a totally inadequate sampling base. At best from the data of his own and his patients' analyses they could refer to a mid-European population.

It is interesting to speculate why it is that Freud's sampling is considered a fatal flaw to his theorizing whereas, as we have seen, much of psychology is not markedly superior in this respect but is not thus condemned. In our view the reason is not far to seek. Freud is quite explicit in his generalizations. For example in "Totem and Taboo" "primitive men" (1913, p. 159) are the subjects, Michelangelo and Da Vinci and even literary characters such as Hamlet and the brothers Karamazov have been analysed, together with, as we now know, Woodrow Wilson. Furthermore it might be possible to feel that the close family relationships of Freud's patients were capable of producing some of the feelings and affect attributed to them, if we were not implacably hostile to the theory. However it is not therefore obvious that similar feelings would be found in individuals reared in totally different family constellations — a point at least as old as Malinowski's (1929) observation on the matter. Other psychological theories, for example learning theory, imply generalizations at least as great but are quite unspecific. Thus reinforcement would be assumed to increase the probability of a response both in America and in the Trobriand Islands. However learning theorists have, very wisely, refrained from stating what such Trobriand reinforcements might be in the real life situation. It is clear from this example that learning theory is considerably more modest in its claims and entirely unspecific compared with Freudian theory.

From this discussion it can be seen that there are three distinct, albeit not entirely unrelated, objectives in the cross-cultural study of Freudian theory. In the first place cross-cultural investigations enable the generalizability of the hypotheses to be tested. If cultures are found where the hypotheses do not hold, the findings can enable us to work out the necessary and sufficient conditions. In this way cross-cultural studies provide a real life laboratory for elegant scientific testing of the theory. More than this, these studies can contribute to the development and precision of the theory. Perhaps gross generalizations can become accurately refined. Secondly, cross-cultural studies are the only means of testing those Freudian hypotheses which are directly anthropological. To take the familiar example of "Totem and Taboo", where it is claimed that totemism is the acting out of the Oedipus complex, we can put this to the test only in cross-cultural studies — in cultures where totemism still exists. It must be pointed out at this juncture that such investigations are not trivial to the theory. Thus it could be argued that totemism is not an important phenomenon in the context of the problems of modern society. While this is true the point of such investigations is not only the light they throw on the particular phenomena but also the evidence they provide — in this instance, on the pervasive influence of the Oedipus complex. If it turned out that the enormous explanatory power of psychoanalytic concepts was illusory and that they were as limited as might be expected from their derivation, then much of the attraction of psychoanalytic theory would disappear. The third objective of cross-cultural studies is related to the first. They again can provide a living laboratory for the investigation of the Freudian environmental hypotheses although detailed knowledge of cultures is essential.

These three objectives make it clear that cross-cultural studies are one important form of scientific research into the validity of Freudian theory, or, as we have argued, Freudian *theories.*

The remainder of this chapter will be taken up with an examination of the specific problems in the cross-cultural study of Freudian theory and with the assessment and discussion of some of the results achieved with this method. It will not be possible in a chapter of this length to review all such studies. Instead we shall concentrate on a few key investigations, notable for either the light they throw on the problems in this area or for the clarity of their results.

II. METHODOLOGICAL PROBLEMS IN CROSS-CULTURAL RESEARCH

One's position concerning the methodological problems of cross-cultural studies must depend, inevitably, on the purpose of the research. Since we have argued that the value of cross-cultural studies in relation to Freudian theory lies in the opportunity they present of putting the theories to a rigorous scientific test, it is essential that in such studies we do not abandon scientific methodology. In practice the major difficulty lies in the reliable quantification of the data. To give a simple example, it is relatively easy to obtain from a literate British sample a reliable measure of intelligence. Intelligence indeed, despite the sociological arguments, is probably the variable that in the West can be measured with the greatest reliability and validity. To attempt to measure intelligence among the Bushmen, say, would be a very different matter, not to mention the even more important point as to whether in non-Western cultures the concept is even meaningful. (Vernon, 1969).

Thus we shall discuss the problems of cross-cultural research method-ology from a rigorous, scientific position, because the purpose of the research is scientific validation. We may be forced to be critical of certain anthropological methods which are satisfactory for their purposes but deficient for ours. Similarly methods which are suited to the investigation of psychoanalytic theory may be defective for anthropology.

III. CATEGORIES OF CROSS-CULTURAL RESEARCH

It would appear useful to categorize cross-cultural research into four types, each with its own methodological problems and each of different value for the validation of Freudian theory. One group consists of the British social anthropologists and their followers. Radcliffe-Brown (e.g. 1952) and Gluckman (e.g. 1962) typify these researches, highly detailed studies of a society making deliberately little use of psychological or psychoanalytic concepts. Generally their work is not germane for our purposes. This is not to criticize anthropology of this type because it does not try to answer the questions that happen to be of interest to psychoanalysis but is concerned rather with questions of its own. However it does mean that the work of the social anthropologists is not especially relevant, as it stands, to Freudian theory. Sometimes, obviously, their descriptive data can be useful although again because they are attempting to answer different questions it is not always the kind of data that investigators of the validity of Freudian theory would want. Thus the school of social anthropology illustrates how differing objectives cause excellent work to be not highly useful for our purposes.

There is one further problem with this kind of social anthropology, a problem which we shall discuss below in connection with what have been called hologeistic studies (Campbell and Naroll, 1972), i.e., studies based on surveys of the ethnographic literature. This problem concerns the accuracy of the data collected by the observers. We do not intend to discuss this now in connection with social anthropology since it is obvious that their very different aims preclude their studies being of great concern to us as they stand, so that it is irrelevant to quibble over the quality of their data. It is sufficient for us to note that the reliability of their assessments is not without question.

We must now turn to the studies based on the ethnographic and anthropological data collected about various societies throughout the world, studies which comprise our second group of cross-cultural studies. This method makes use of descriptions from the kind of studies discussed above in our first group where each investigation is but one case in a sample. Perhaps the most celebrated example of this genre is Whiting and Child's (1953) investigation of "Child Training and Personality". Here the anthropological reports from 75 primitive societies were searched for data relating to child training and adult personality characteristics. The variables from this survey (ratings by independent observers) were then correlated. In this way it is possible to see whether late weaning is related to emotional disturbance or severe modesty training to low sexual activity, just for example. Obviously this is a method that can be used to test the world-wide generalizability of any theory involving the effects of child rearing, not only Freudian theory. As we have previously pointed out, this method has the obvious advantage for testing Freudian theory of increasing the variance of variables related to child-rearing procedures which by custom tend to be of low variability within any one culture, even a modern Western society, such as Great Britain (e.g. Newson and Newson, 1963). Since correlations are attenuated through homogeneity of variance this increase in variability allows relationships to show through more clearly than can studies in any one culture. The second advantage of the method lies in the fact that the relationships found are necessarily universal so that they must refer to human nature in general, which is particularly important in relation to Freudian theory. These are the two main advantages of the method claimed by Whiting (1968) and they are such that the present writer considers this to be a most powerful method of investigating the validity of Freudian theory. There is a further point which deserves mention which may also be regarded as an advantage of this hologeistic method. It may be possible in our own society to find a sample of mothers who wean their children extremely late or early or who do not bother to give them toilet training. However, such mothers are clearly deviant so that any apparent consequences in later behaviour would be contaminated by this fact of their deviance. This is not the case with the hologeistic method where the variables are the norms of the societies. This also means that the method holds constant individual variation whereas the usual psychological study of individuals in one society holds culture constant and makes individual variation the subject of study. Thus to this extent, as Whiting (1968) argues, the two methods are usefully complementary.

Nevertheless before we seize on the results of these researches to elucidate Freudian theory we must be aware of the considerable technical problems which, unless overcome, must considerably weaken the force of their results. Campbell and Naroll (1972) cite eleven problems in their excellent survey of this area and we shall discuss here the most salient points. The first difficulty concerns sampling societies. Thus there is no way of extracting a probability sample of existing societies simply because so many of them have not been described. Since there are in the region of 5,000 societies of which only one fifth have been sufficiently documented for study (and that not for all variables), sampling bias is obviously a factor in any investigation. However from the viewpoint of the validation of Freudian theory this problem is not important, because if Freudian hypotheses are or are not upheld in what at worst is a wider sample than that found in the consulting rooms of Vienna, the finding is significant. Thus if the hypotheses are confirmed, it is weak to argue that there are still societies of which we are ignorant. Similarly if the hypotheses are not supported it is unlikely that they would be in these other societies. However it remains true that complete generalization to all human beings is not possible. Another important problem related to that of sampling concerns the definition of a tribe or society. Although language, political organization and territorial occupancy have been used to define societal boundaries, there is no agreed definition among anthropologists. Nevertheless it is possible to draw up a world-wide cross-cultural sample of societies such that' there is no problem in discriminating any one society from any other. Since in such a sample of societies we can be sure that all the societies are different it makes sense to use this sample or draw from it in our cross-cultural studies of Freudian theory, as was done by Whiting *et al.* (1958) in their investigation of the Oedipus complex (see p. 73) where societies were chosen to represent as many as possible of the culture areas designated by this method (Murdock, 1957).

Data accuracy is the third point raised by Campbell and Naroll (1972) and is in our view the most critical of the problems. How accurate are anthropological data? Random errors tend to lower correlations so that the fact that significant correlations are obtained with these methods suggests that this is not an important feature. However there may be systematic sources of error which could produce artefactual correlations. While this could be the case it must be noticed that it must be a systematic tendency among anthropologists in general since Whiting and Child (1953) used 75 different societies involving a very large number of anthropologists. Bias among one or two would not have had this effect. Now this systematic biasing is very important in the elucidation of Freudian theory, because it is possible that the anthropologist was aware of Freudian theory so that critical Freudian variables, such as weaning and pot training and subsequent personality patterns might become the objects of subjective perception. In some cases of course the anthropologist may have been a committed Freudian, for example Roheim or Muensterberger, although as we have pointed out, one or two instances of bias in a large sample of reports should not grossly affect the results. Campbell and Naroll (1972) suggest that there are certain quality controls that can be used in the evaluation of anthropological reports — familiarity with the native language, length of stay among natives and the degree of participation in the culture. Related to these quality controls are such points as how many of the behaviours reported were actually observed. How many subjects actually responded in this way? How normal is such behaviour in the society — i.e., base-line rates need to be set up. How reliable, between observers, are these reports? However it should be noted that errors such as these are not systematic but random and would tend, therefore, to reduce the size of correlations. Our view of this problem of the reliability of the anthropological report is that it may be riddled with error especially where the information is obtained from informants. However it will be random error and the systematic sources of bias do not seem likely to be so important over a wide range of anthropologists. Thus we would argue that the fact that significant results can be obtained with this method, against all the possibilities of confounding error, means that the hologeistic method is still useful in the elucidation of Freudian theory.

Campbell and Naroll (1972) are, quite rightly, concerned over the interpretations of the correlations resulting from this approach, especially the problem of the causal analysis of correlations. They suggest, in view of the fact that there are often data on these societies which are relevant to cultural change, that cross-lagged correlations might be useful. However with reference to the notion of causality, if we can accept Cattell's (1973) concept of factors, when rotated to simple structure — an important proviso, which the majority of factor analytic researches fail to grasp (Cattell and Kline, 1976) — as causal agencies, the factor analysis of these correlation matrices is the obvious solution.

Another serious problem lies in the fact that there is a paucity of data relevant to certain problems in the published monographs which form the basis of these investigations. Obviously one solution is to attempt to collect the data specifically for the investigation but if a good sample of societies is to be included, then this is a lengthy procedure.

A final problem which Campbell and Naroll (1972) discuss is a general one with large matrices of correlations — namely that a number of correlations will be significant only by chance. However if we split the sample up into meaningful parts, for example, by region, this both tests the real significance of correlations (for true correlations will be significant in both samples), and looks at the interesting question of regional differences. Important here are the correlations that occur in both samples. If we have more than two samples failure to correlate in one of them may indicate genuine regional variation.

Galton raised a difficulty with this method — do cross-cultural correlations reflect functional association or cultural diffusion, owing to borrowing or migration? If the latter is the case then the problem of the independence of the samples arises and hence the statistical basis of the whole method. This problem is related to that of adequate sampling of cultures which we have already discussed. If however a sample is chosen such that no pair of the societies has contiguous borders, the effect of cultural diffusion is clearly minimized. But if our interest lies in the testing of particular hypotheses concerning child training and personality, as is the case in our concern for Freudian theory, the Galton problem is not serious since the personality patterns are unlikely to have spread via such cultural diffusion. For further discussion of this problem readers are referred to Naroll and Cohen (1970) and Whiting (1968).

These are the most important objections that have been raised to the quantitative cross-cultural method. As our discussion of these objections has shown, it is clear that important as some of them may be, for anthropological studies, in relation to the verification of psychoanalytic theory, they are not overwhelming. Thus we would still argue that this method can provide one of the most powerful means of putting psycho-analytic theory to the test.

So far we have discussed two of our categories of cross-cultural studies — the social anthropologists and the statistical cross-cultural surveys. The third group are the culture and personality proponents, many of whom have been overtly influenced by Freudian theory which has provided a framework for their investigations. A few of these anthropologists have been thorough-going Freudians who have tried to collect data almost of a clinical psychoanalytic type. Roheim exemplifies best this small group which could be regarded, as we shall see, as virtually a distinct sub-group. The results of some of the investigations of these anthropologists, in as much as they bear on the truth of Freudian theory, we shall discuss later in this chapter. Here we shall be restricted to a discussion of the problems involved in this approach.

First we must attempt to define the culture and personality school, which can be understood only in the context of the development of anthropology generally. As Spiro (1972) points out, anthropology during the first half of the twentieth century had been steadily collecting ethnographic facts, as a basis for the derivation of cultural laws, a descriptive task not unlike the pre-Linnaean description of species. It was avowedly atheoretical and so complex were the data that to many anthropologists it seemed unlikely that valid cultural laws could be found (e.g. Boas, 1938). Thus some kind of theoretical orientation seemed necessary to structure these data. Against this background two schools of anthropology arose: the British social anthropological school, interested in different forms of society, already discussed; and the culture and personality group whose interests were psychological, in the dynamics of behaviour. The culture and personality school was interested in culture as it influenced behaviour, i.e., personality. As Spiro (1972) succinctly puts it, for this school the question was what culture produced certain personality variables, not as with the social anthropologists, what historical or environmental variables produced a given culture. Thus culture and personality scholars were in effect the personality psychologists of "primitive" (living in small-scale societies, non-industrialized economies, kinship-based politics and non-literate cultures (Spiro, 1972)) societies. Thus the culture and personality school is one where the effects of culture on personality are studied. In this sense of course the hologeistic studies in our second group are really part of this third group but such a distinctive part that they are best treated separately, from the viewpoint of their value for the scientific study of Freudian theory.

The weakness of this type of culture and personality study is two-fold. First, typical anthropological reports do not meet the requirements of valid and reliable measurement necessary for the scientific study of psycho-analytic theory, where the lack of quantification is a serious objection. Of course there is no reason why studies of this sort should not attempt to obtain more precise data, for example test scores, but test-oriented cross-cultural psychology forms our fourth group of studies which we discuss below, a separate group because cross-cultural psychological testing contains its own problems over and above those of anthropological research. As an example of the difficulty over original data, the research into "primitive" Africans by Parin and Morgenthaler (1969) is a good case in point. Thus they admit that they were not able to master all the languages necessary to study the behaviour patterns of the different tribes and they did not want to confine their studies to published reports which were not always relevant to their objective — superego and ego development. Thus they were forced to rely on "information from local residents in English or French and interrogation with the help of local interpreters". We do not blame Parin and Morgenthaler for their use of this type of evidence for, as they point out, to master the languages would have required them to learn more than 100, a feat to strain even the talents of a Burton. Nevertheless interesting as their results are they cannot be used for the scientific elucidation or validation of Freudian theory. These data are of unknown validity and reliability, and are no better than the original clinical data of psychoanalysis. Although this is an extreme example, the data have to be taken on trust. This is yet another reason for supporting the hologeistic method because if the statistical analysis of such reports reveals significant relations then we may argue that despite individual deficiencies, overall there is some sense in the data.

This study by Parin and Morgenthaler (1969) also illustrates another flaw in this type of culture and personality research from the viewpoint of the scientific study of psychoanalysis. These authors simply interpret their findings in the light of Freudian theory. Certainly they modify the standard theory which they regard as for Europeans only and develop a new one for their African samples. But the new theory is within the psychoanalytic framework. Modifications to Freudian theory in the light of cross-cultural data of dubious validity cannot be considered as scientific. In essence this work is similar to clinical psychoanalysis but with data from different societies.

Some of the anthropological psychoanalysts who in some ways constitute a separate group from the culture and personality school, who perhaps are anthropologists influenced by Freudian theory, actually collect psychoanalytic data, e.g., dreams and their associations, as used by Roheim (1947) and the biographies of Du Bois (1944). Again however such data are an improvement on standard psychoanalytic observations only inasmuch as they are derived from societies widely disparate from those of Vienna. As data they still suffer from the same faults of being subjective and unquantified.

Thus we can conclude our discussion of the problems involved in the methods used by the culture and personality school by arguing that the inadequacy of the data and the fact of accepting psychoanalytic theory either as a framework or quite specifically means that their work is far from ideal in the scientific validation of Freudian theory.

Before we leave this branch of cross-cultural study there are a few more points worthy of mention because of their relevance to the study of Freudian theory. The most important of these concerns the fact that most of our discussion has centred around the investigation of the effect of culture on personality, which is a method of putting many aspects of Freudian theory to the test. Nevertheless this contrasts oddly with Freud's own work on culture. Thus in, for example, "Totem and Taboo" (Freud, 1913) the origins of the incest taboo and totemism are held to derive from the Oedipus complex. This is not the only example of how Freudian theory sees culture as reflecting personality. Roheim (1934) described Western society as a whole as anal, Menninger (1943) regarded pot training as crucial to the development of whole cultures and Freud considered much of the apparatus of civilization as but a defence mechanism against destructive and savage instinctual forces. Spiro (1968) indeed regards this as perhaps the main task of the culture and personality school — the elucidation of the effects of personality on culture. This failure to take into account the psychological nature of man he sees as the main weakness of the social anthropology group. The examples given by Spiro (1968) are highly interesting because they contrast the two groups of researchers so strongly and because they again show the weakness of the method (even inverted as a study of culture rather than personality) as a means of testing Freudian theory. Thus whereas a Freudian orientation means that post-partum fatherhood rituals are seen as cultural means of defence against Oedipal desires equivalent to a defence mechanism within an individual (Freud, 1913), Radcliffe-Brown (1952) regards them as symbolic expression of paternal concern. Now as Spiro (1968) points out the social anthropological hypothesis is implicitly psychological because it assumes that there is a necessity to symbolize certain human relationships, whereas the Freudian hypothesis is derived from "fairly well established empirically grounded principles of behaviour" (p. 600). While we can disagree with this description of psychoanalysis it is true that the hypotheses are derived from a theory and are testable to some extent although the predictions that can be made from an acceptance of this Oedipal cultural theory from "Totem and Taboo" are not strong and could almost certainly be understood in terms of other social theories. This again illustrates the problems with this culture and personality approach of adequately testing Freudian theory.

There was no necessity, of course, for the culture and personality school to use psychoanalytic theory as a basis for their work. However if we regard the development of their approach as a response to the apparently hopeless welter of evidence accruing about societies then the adoption of psychoanalytic theory can be considered to be a *faute de mieux* procedure, because for all its methodological imperfections it is about the only psychological theory capable of embracing these cultural phenomena. An alternative approach could be to search for the reinforcers operative in different societies but this would appear to be an even more hopeless task, in practice, than attempting to understand them in terms of psychoanalytic theory. It is unfortunate that accepting Freudian theory at the start makes it difficult to test.

Enough has now been said about the problems involved in the culture and personality school for us to leave them and turn instead to our fourth group of investigations — cross-cultural studies using psychological testing techniques and/or data collection and analysis of the type used in experimental psychology. The work of Lee (1958) on dreams and studies of the gender of symbolic words in different languages, which we discuss on pp. 82–84 and pp. 84–85 would exemplify investigations which are scientifically reputable but do not use tests. We must emphasize that our divisions are not intended to be mutually exclusive but are simply useful ways of looking at research in which the techniques and aims are broadly different. However culture and personality workers could easily use psychological tests and Malinowski was overtly interested in examining personality — the Oedipus complex. Nevertheless the use of psychological testing procedures does radically change the nature of the data to such an extent that the problems in methodology are totally different and, alas, in many cases, as we shall see, just as damaging to scientific validity, as the problems of the other types of cross-cultural study.

Since much has been written about the problems of test validity generally we shall assume familiarity with this work and concentrate on the specific cross-cultural difficulties. There are two methods of assessing personality — utilizing interviews or psychological tests. Personality tests are frequently categorized as psychometric or projective (e.g. Lindzey, 1961), although the latter category is somewhat old-fashioned and they are better regarded as but part of a larger group of performance (Cronbach, 1970) or objective tests (Cattell, 1973). This is not, in the context of cross-cultural testing, an academic or sterile distinction, as we shall see in our discussion of these tests. What we shall do is retain the projective test category, but simply for the convenience of discussing celebrated examples of the genre such as the Rorschach and the TAT.

The assessment of personality traits by interview in the cross-cultural situation is not a method which could be in any way recommended. Studies in the West have always shown that the interview is most unsatisfactory as regards reliability and inevitably validity (e.g. Vernon and Parry, 1949). Vernon (1964), who is by no means hostile to interviews, summarizes the position succinctly when he writes that the interview is at its best when it is used to amplify biographical information and paper qualifications and to assess the kind of qualities that *can* show themselves at interviews — verbal fluency would be a good example. However, it is at its worst when it is used to intuit or infer fundamental qualities of personality and character. Since it is precisely this last characteristic that is required of interviews in the cross-cultural study of personality, we can see that there can be little to support their use, unless of course there has been some fundamental change since the publication of Vernon's (1964) book. We can safely say that there has been no change, although publications on the skills of interviewing (e.g. Shouksmith, 1968) may have improved general interviewing competence. Furthermore there is nothing about the cross-cultural situation which is likely to improve the validity of the interview and make it a superior procedure *vis-à-vis* the West: on the contrary there are features of the cross-cultural context that are likely to make it worse. Thus there is the language difficulty, the artificial nature of the research interview, and, however long the investigator has lived in the society, the possible ignorance of or misinterpretation of normal non-verbal cues. To some extent these can be overcome by the use of native interviewers but even then there would be no reason to expect that the interview could be better than that in the West. A final objection to this procedure lies in the fact that there are undoubted differences in interviewing skill, a fundamental flaw in a scientific measuring instrument. Thus interview data do not seem a satisfactory basis for putting Freudian theory to the test.

Before turning from interviews there is a related procedure deserving of consideration. This is the rating scale as advocated by Cattell (1957, 1973), the source of his L or life-record data. It was found that such ratings could be reliable given ideal rating conditions and careful training of the raters. Although Cattell (1957) has a long list of criteria necessary to produce reliable and valid ratings the main essentials can be more briefly described. These entail that the rater live with the subjects whom he is rating so that they can be observed in as wide a variety of contexts as possible. In addition it is desirable that the descriptive trait words be exemplified by actual behaviour. Thus "very irritable" might be illustrated thus: shouts and flushes as soon as his desires are crossed; loses temper in an argument on almost every occasion; at committee meetings stamps out of the room. Such ratings are clearly difficult to make, particularly in an alien society and with possible linguistic difficulties. Nevertheless such careful rating methods have revealed in the West, at least, reliable and identifiable factors. Thus investigation could produce similar useful variables in other cultures, although as Spain (1972) points out, but with reference to projective tests, true cross-cultural study is not content to compare exotic with Western samples but is concerned with aspects of personality which are perhaps unique to each culture. It may be inappropriate therefore to attempt to measure traits and concepts derived from Western samples in non-Western samples. Although this is a sound argument, empirical research with tests that have been designed to sample the whole personality sphere (Cattell, 1973) suggests that there are source traits common to a number of cultures. Such results indicate that rating scales of the Cattell type could prove useful in the cross-cultural study of Freudian theory although the behavioural examples would, obviously, have to be relevant to the culture.

The use of psychological assessment techniques in cross-cultural investigations makes explicit a problem which is implicit (although no less serious for that) in the other types of research which we have discussed. This is the problem of sampling. If we test a hundred subjects how well does our sample reflect the population we hope we are studying? As we have had occasion to point out earlier in this chapter much Western psychology reflects the performance of students, often even more limitingly, students of psychology. Clearly the quality of a sample drawn from a single village or town depends upon the geographic distribution of the tribe or tribes represented in it. Nevertheless it is difficult to see how some of the cross-cultural studies to which we shall refer, which have used samples of less than 1,000 can represent Japanese, Ghanaians or Germans. There is no reason in a cross-cultural study to abandon the normal rules of sampling, despite the difficulty of obtaining adequate samples.

The problem of sampling has been raised at this point in the argument because it particularly bedevils rating scales of the type discussed above where it is obviously difficult for observers to rate more than a small number of subjects. Indeed it was the time consuming nature of these rating techniques and the associated sampling difficulties that led Cattell to turn to psychometric and other kinds of test in the measurement of personality.

Thus we can summarize our discussion of interviews and rating scales in the cross-cultural assessment of personality by dismissing the use of interviews as unlikely to produce either valid or reliable data; rating scales if tied to culturally relevant behaviours could yield adequate scientific data although it is unlikely, other than in large scale studies, that the sample thus measured would be satisfactory.

Cross-cultural psychometric testing of personality is beset with problems. First the items themselves may be culture-bound or culture-free (relatively, at least) (Cattell, 1957). Thus an item such as "Have you ever experienced headaches?" is presumably culture-free because this is an experience that is open to all men. This contrasts with an item such as "Taking part in a South Pole expedition" to which subjects have to indicate "Like" or "Dislike", which is clearly culture-bound. This problem means that in non-literate non-Western societies it it not always possible to use personality questionnaires. We have ignored the problem of language and translation, which compared with the meaningfulness or otherwise of items is trivial. However translation into the vernacular will do nothing to ease these itemetric problems. Where the items are meaningful, we have to ensure by item analysis and correlation of the translated and original versions that the two versions are in fact similar. Certainly research with the 16PF in different and varied cultures, such as Africa, India and Europe, but with highly educated and westernized samples, suggests that such translations can yield comparable and psychologically meaningful results (Cattell, 1973).

However, even if we eliminate items that are culture-bound in content, we cannot assume that the remaining culture-free items are valid. The same meaningful items could tap different personality traits in different cultures. Hence it is necessary to demonstrate that a test is both reliable and valid in the society where it is to be used. Vernon (1969) in the field of abilities showed striking changes in factor loadings of the same tests in different cultures.

As Cattell (1973) points out individual item variance is imperfectly accounted for, so that the selection of personality test items for use in non-Western cultures is difficult. For example in a comparative study of a personality test in Ghana and North India with highly educated samples Kline and Mohan (1974) found that items which had been successful in both Ghana and Great Britain failed in India, some without obvious reason. An additional problem in using psychometric tests in non-Western societies lies in test-taking attitudes. Such response sets as acquiescence and the tendency to put the socially desirable answer are particularly exacerbated (Cronbach, 1970) and these can create a spuriously high reliability.

If all the difficulties above have been overcome a critical problem with psychometric tests involves sampling, because they are suited only to literate samples. If we are forced to give the test individually as a series of questions, some of which will require explanation or further information, one of the main advantages of the questionnaire — the exclusion of variance due to examiner differences and interaction — will be lost. However to use literate samples in many societies is clearly highly restrictive in inverse relation to the literacy of the society. In practice it may mean that we restrict ourselves to student samples which are atypical. This necessity for literacy is a serious defect of the personality questionnaire in cross-cultural studies.

From the viewpoint of the scientific study of psychoanalytic theory there is another severe disadvantage of psychometric tests — the best known tests do not measure relevant variables, e.g. the MMPI, 16PF, EPI and Edward's Personal Preference measures. Kline (1973) has surveyed all the published psychological tests of any merit which are suitable for the verification of psychoanalytic theory. Of the psychometric examples the most used is the Dynamic Personality Inventory (Grygier, 1961). Although this has items of unusually simple format, it is almost certainly unsuited to cross-cultural studies: the items are culture-bound, e.g. hot milk, mixing paints, ballet dancing, flag poles, being a florist. Kline (1971) has developed a test of the anal or obsessional character — Ai3Q. This has been used both in Ghana (Kline, 1969) where it appeared to be valid and in India (Kline and Mohan, 1974) where it was almost certainly not. This test might be usable in some societies with highly educated samples but it is of course relevant only to one aspect of Freudian theory. There are almost no other psychometric tests of proven validity which are relevant to Freudian theory. Thus if we want to use such tests in our investigations not only have we to be able to suffer all the considerable disadvantages which we have so far listed; we have also to contruct them especially for our purposes. It becomes evident, therefore, that despite their attractions and despite the successful use of the 16PF (Cattell, 1973) in cross-cultural studies, for the purpose of investigating Freudian theory in a cross-cultural setting psychometric tests are hardly to be recommended.

We now arrive at our last category of personality tests, objective tests, which includes also that group of tests referred to as projective tests. Cattell (1957) has defined an objective test as a procedure for obtaining an individual difference score such that the import of the tests is unknown to the subjects and the nature of the response defies distortion in a desired direction. Eysenck (1960) refers to tests of this type as objective behaviour tests; Cronbach (1970) calls them performance tests. It is assumed that all responses can be scored reliably and objectively. Examples of such tests are: slow line-drawing, where subjects have to draw a line for a given time as slowly as possible; balloon blowing where subjects are instructed to inflate a balloon as large as they can. The score is the size of the balloon when the subject stops blowing, or the time taken till bursting. Cattell and his colleagues at Illinois have developed a huge number of such objective test devices which they regard as potentially the most fruitful approach to the measurement of personality and from which they derive T factors. Cattell and Warburton (1967) indeed list more than 200 such tests and over 800 variables that may be derived from them together with factor loadings and correlations where known. From this brief description of objective tests it should be obvious that as regards cross-cultural studies there are two huge advantages. It is easier to devise objective tests than to develop culture-free personality test items; and in so doing we eliminate the problems of literacy and response sets. Against this, however, it is difficult, even in the West, to demonstrate the validity of objective tests, and there are none at present which have been shown to be valid in non-Western cultures.

This implies that if objective tests are to be used in the cross-cultural validation of Freudian theory, an extensive research programme to develop and validate them would have to be first instituted. We must therefore conclude that such tests are of limited practical research value now. In the future they may turn out to be superior to other forms of assessment.

However under the heading of objective tests (if objectively scored) fall what are still called by many workers projective tests (e.g. Semeonoff, 1973), of which the most celebrated are the Rorschach and the TAT. Furthermore these tests because they are unstructured have been widely used in the anthropological study of personality. Cross-cultural comparison is apparently facilitated because the same materials can be used with all groups and such tests formed the data base for the search for the modal personality, the Eldorado of the culture and personality school (e.g. Du Bois, 1944).

Lindzey (1961) and Spain (1972) provide comprehensive reviews of the problems of using projective tests in the cross-cultural setting. Readers must be referred to these long discussions (each more lengthy than this chapter) for detailed treatment of all the possible problems and solutions. Here, however we shall concentrate on the points relevant to our task — the scientific validation of Freudian theory — and propose a possible solution to these difficulties which has had some success although it has not yet been used in a cross-cultural investigation.

The objections to projective tests on grounds of lack of scientific rigour have been made with such force by Eysenck (1959) (and more soberly by many other writers (e.g. Vernon, 1964)) that we can list them virtually without discussion in the knowledge that they are supported by a mass of incontrovertible evidence.

The scientific objections to projective tests are: poor reliability, both between occasions and between examiners; poor validity in the vast majority of cases, especially for the Rorschach Test; the fact that the test scores have been shown to reflect transitory moods of the subject although they are claimed to measure "deep" layers of the personality; and the fact that methods of test administration as well as how the subjects conceive the test also affect results as can response sets such as social desirability. This is why for the purposes of the scientific study of personality projective tests have been widely eschewed. Let us be clear that this condemnation by no means outlaws their use as one further means in addition to the interview and psychometric data for the clinician to gain valuable insight into a patient's problems. However, clinical intuition is different from scientific knowledge. Furthermore the cross-cultural use of projective tests does not nullify these disadvantages but adds yet further difficulties. For example the TAT pictures are culture-bound — to a middle-class America of the thirties. Lee (1953) produced an Africanized version but this would suit only certain tribes there, and would not be useful elsewhere. In addition cultural influences affect picture recognition and depth perception as shown in the work of Hudson (1960, 1967) in South Africa, Deregowski (1966) in Zambia and Kilbride and Robbins (1969) in Uganda. Kline (1975) indeed working with the Pinmen Test with Indian students found some similar perceptual problems. In fact Wober (1967) suggested that some cultures are not visually oriented but are keyed to other perceptual modes, a hypothesis that has profound implications for cross-cultural testing. From all this it must be concluded that the cross-cultural use of projective tests with visual stimuli is unlikely to yield data of high scientific integrity.

Of course it is possible to construct projective tests that do not employ visual stimuli, thus avoiding the special cross-cultural perceptual problems. Sentence completion techniques are well known non-visual tests and Phillips (1965) has produced an example which may be suitable in a wide variety of cultures. However, it demands literacy (if used as a group test), some familiarity with the conventions of test taking, and translation. Thus if used in a large number of different samples the similarity of one version to another is by no means obvious. Furthermore there is little evidence of validity so that at best it could be regarded as a measure worth further investigation.

Despite all these objections to the cross-cultural use of projective tests, which we regard as overwhelming, as the extensive bibliographies in Lindzey (1961) and Spain (1972) indicate, they have been widely used. Are we then to write off all this work as valueless? As scientific evidence, as we have argued, it is really unsatisfactory. However, the best of it provides marvellous insights into the societies studied which can then be tested in a more rigorous fashion. Thus it may well be the case that the brilliant investigator can use a projective test to useful effect whereas the Grub Street tester can produce nothing. An outstanding example of this sensitive use of tests and procedures which are far from scientific is to be found in Carstairs' (1957) study of the Rajputs in central India. Sampling was not random in that Carstairs set himself up in a village and sought volunteers. The data themselves were biographies, interviews and Rorschach responses, yet so deft is the handling of this material that there can be few readers who do not feel that they have reached a good understanding of the personalities of these subjects. Nevertheless this does not mean that these data gathering techniques are suited for scientific investigation. The value of scientific tests lies in their objectivity — their ability to give the same result regardless of tester.

However, we do not propose to abandon the use of projective techniques in the cross-cultural study of personality. What we propose for the research use of projective tests in alien cultures is the procedure used by Holley, in numerous investigations and fully described in Holley (1973) with the Rorschach test. In this Holley scored the Rorschach dichotomously for the presence or absence of various schizophrenic signs, whose scoring was highly reliable. The protocols from depressives, schizophrenics and normals, were then subjected to G correlational analysis (Holley and Guilford, 1964) in which correlations between people were computed, followed by Q factor analysis and a Varimax rotation. These investigations revealed that depressives could be separated from normals with a validity of 1 (i.e. perfectly), a result which Holley (1973) attributed to error-free statistical analysis. There seems little doubt that the most significant feature of these results from the viewpoint of the scientific utility of projective tests lies in the reliable scoring procedure although the G index is a useful correlational index in the study of groups. That the method is useful with other projective tests is revealed by on-going studies of criminal psychiatric subjects by Hampson and Kline (1977) where these were clearly separated from controls and fell into meaningful groups using this form of statistical anslysis with the TAT, House Tree Person Test and Family Relations Indicator. Of course to interpret the nature of the discriminating test factor needs considerable further study which is why, at present, the method is suggested as for research use only. Certainly it would be highly interesting to administer a battery of projective tests to samples from a wide variety of different societies and attempt to see empirically by the use of G methodology how they might be discriminated. Thus, to take a concrete example, if we thought that two societies offered particularly good chances for different Freudian defences to develop, this method with the right projective tests, free enough to allow such mechanisms to be observed, could put the theory to a rigorous test. The same procedure could be adopted with typically anal and oral cultures.

This review of the problems involved with different methods of psychological assessment in cross-cultural studies indicates clearly that there is no technique in which we can have any great confidence. In fact most investigations have to be examined individually since even a normally dubious test can, if subjected to special scoring procedures which have demonstrated reliability and validity, yield useful data. Generally, however, as we have indicated the results of most cross-cultural investigations fall far short of the scientific rigour desirable to test Freudian theory.

The remainder of this chapter will now be taken up with a consideration of the results obtained from the various kinds of cross-cultural research.

IV. RESULTS OF HOLOGEISTIC STUDIES

Since the hologeistic approach, despite its problems (see p. 58), still seemed the best suited to the study of Freudian theory we shall look at these results first.

Whiting and Child (1953) in their classic study utilized the ethnographic data from 75 societies to examine the effects of child training on personality. They concentrated on the psychoanalytic concept of fixation modified (but not so greatly that it renders the work inappropriate to the study of Freudian theory) thus: positive fixation was hypothesized to result from a high degree of indulgence of a particular form of behaviour, while negative fixation was held to result from a high degree of frustration of a particular form of behaviour. Although psychoanalytic psychosexual theory has concerned itself most with fixation at the oral and anal phase of development (Freud, 1905) Whiting and Child (1953) looked at the effects of fixation not only on putative oral and anal characteristics but on dependence, aggression and the origins of guilt. Although it is difficult to summarize the results of so large a study both briefly and accurately, it is probably fair to argue that they found that the effects of negative fixation were as hypothesized in psychoanalytic theory whereas the role of positive fixation was not supported. In the case of positive fixation progressive satisfaction was related to indices of positive fixation, more so than was initial satisfaction at an early stage of childhood. However, with negative fixation there was evidence for its relation to later behaviour, especially in the case of oral, dependence and aggressive systems of behaviour where early socialization anxiety was clearly implicated. The evidence for the effects of negative fixation on the anal and sexual systems was much less although not entirely absent. Whiting and Child (1953), however, feel that it would be going far beyond the evidence of these results to argue that Freudian theory exaggerated the importance of the anal and sexual systems of behaviour and failed to recognize the importance of dependency and aggression systems partly because, as they realize, there are defects in the methodology of this hologeistic method.

Before discussing the value of this study to the elucidation of Freudian theory we must mention also the results of the same authors' study of the origins of guilt, which in the psychoanalytic mould they hypothesized would arise from identification with the parents. Here there was some support for this claim although, as Whiting and Child (1953) admit it was not so strong as was the case with negative fixation. Despite all the problems associated with the hologeistic method it seems to us that this research does offer some support for psychoanalytic theory, and is a most valuable investigation for the following reasons. In the first place in as much as some of the hypotheses were supported it demonstrates that Freudian theories can be extended, as has always been claimed in the theory, to societies very different from early twentieth-century Vienna. Indeed the huge range of societies suggests that the concepts might even be universals, although obviously better samples need to be used. Furthermore in view of the dubious quality of some of the ethnographic reports the fact of significant correlations at all is remarkable in as much as error tends to reduce correlations and eliminate significance. Hence it could be the case that the true correlations are in fact larger than those apparent in this study. Finally the results suggest that the method is a viable means of examining those psychoanalytic hypotheses which are concerned with the effect of cultural practices on personality. Thus this pioneering study seems to suggest (rather than convincingly demonstrate) that the Freudian concept of negative fixation was sound and an important variable in personality development in a wide range of societies. It more powerfully demonstrates the utility of this method in the study of Freudian theory.

Whiting *et al.* (1958) utilized similar methods in a study of the Oedipus complex in 56 societies which sampled 45 of the 60 culture areas of Murdock (1957), the basic data being the ethnographic literature relevant to these societies. In "Totem and Taboo" it was argued by Freud, largely on the basis of the anthropological work of Fraser and Robertson Smith, that totemism and initiation rites could be used as an index of Oedipal conflict in a culture. Whiting *et al.* (1958) assumed that an ideal environment for the Oedipus complex was a long post-partum sexual taboo. Hence they tested the hypothesis that societies with a long post-partum sexual taboo will be more likely to have initiation rites than will societies with a short taboo, since in almost all societies the infant sleeps with its mother until usurped by the returning father. The results of this investigation supported the psychoanalytic theory in that significantly more cultures (80%) with long taboos had initiation ceremonies. It is by no means easy to formulate an alternative explanation for this relation between long post-partum sexual taboo and male initiation rites and the results again support the utility of the method for investigating Freudian theory and confirm the applicability of psychoanalytic ideas to societies very different from Vienna at the turn of the century.

Stephens (1961, 1962) also used the hologeistic method in a study of the

Oedipus and castration complexes in 72 societies. An indirect approach was used in that the actual hypothesis under investigation concerned menstrual taboo. He argued that the extent of menstrual taboo in a society reflects the intensity of castration anxiety felt by the men of that society. The psychoanalytic reasoning behind the hypothesis is that the sight of or contact with blood from female genitals would arouse castration anxiety. Since it was difficult to obtain a measure of castration anxiety Stephens measured its antecedents, the child-rearing procedures connected with Oedipal conflict and linked these to the length of menstrual taboo. Ten such techniques were investigated: diffusion of nurturance, the post-partum sex taboo, severity of masturbation punishment, severity of sex training, severity of aggression training, pressure for obedience, severity of punishment for disobedience, strictness of father, whether father is main disciplinarian, importance of physical punishment as discipline and a total score based on these ten variables. The relation of each of these variables to the menstrual taboo scale was examined. All were related in the expected direction, four of them at the 0·05 level or better. The total score was related to the menstrual taboo scale at the 0·000001 level. From this Stephens concluded that the castration complex was a widespread phenomenon (rather than a Viennese one) and that it originated in the Oedipal situation. That these child-rearing techniques were related to menstrual taboo does seem impressive evidence for the concept of castration anxiety and for this aspect of Freudian theory. There does not seem to be a convincing alternative explanation of these results. Again when we bear in mind the possible errors in the ethnographic reports these results are even more striking. It seems to us that these studies alone support the value of the hologeistic method in the study of Freudian theory.

These three hologeistic investigations not only demonstrate the utility of the method but show also that there is some objective support for the concepts of the Oedipus and castration complexes and negative fixation. Harrington and Whiting (1972) are well aware of the defects in methodology such as we have discussed earlier in this chapter and point out that some attempts have been made to overcome them. Thus Whiting (1963) in her study of six cultures actually organized data collection, thereby ensuring the relevance and comparability of data in the different cultures. However, this means that the correlational technique over a wide number of societies has to be abandoned — which was a particularly useful feature for testing Freudian theory. Furthermore the methods of data collection are inevitably below the standard desirable for scientific investigation (e.g. the problem of cross-cultural measuring instruments) problems which are more important in a small sample of cultures than in the original method. Since the expense of mounting large-scale cross-cultural studies of the six cultures type is considerable some workers have concentrated on one small problem in one culture and then replicated it in another. Studies of the couvade by Munroe and Munroe (e.g. 1971) are relevant to psychoanalytic theory and will be discussed below. To finish our discussion of the hologeistic cross-cultural studies, therefore, we will examine some of the further findings of the traditional approach and those investigations where the data have been deliberately collected to be relevant to psychoanalytic theory.

One set of investigations has concentrated upon the view of gods held by a society. The interest of this for Freudian theory lies in the fact that we should predict from it that views of gods reflected images of parents. Thus in societies where infants were harshly treated the gods should be regarded as malevolent, malignant, harsh; whereas in societies where infants were indulged the opposite view should obtain. Spiro and D'Andrade (1958) working with 11 societies, Lambert et al. (1959) using 62 and Whiting (1959) all found this hypothesis supported. The data and scores were similar to those in the original investigation of Whiting and Child (1953). Spiro and D'Andrade found that societies where infants were indulged also felt that the gods could be controlled. This was seen by them as further evidence that relationships to gods reflected the early familial situation since indulged infants in fact control their parents by crying or otherwise attracting attention when in need. Whiting (1959) found that in societies where children were indulged ghosts were not feared at funerals. This again supports Freudian theory in that ghosts would be held to be projections of parental images. From this it is clear that these investigations give general support to the psychoanalytic view of god and religion as well as supporting the notion of projection. The evident importance of the infant's relationship with his caretakers is also confirmatory of psychoanalytic theory.

We have mentioned above how Harrington and Whiting (1972) have advocated the combination of the concepts of Whiting and Child's (1953) work and original field-work so that the data impinge directly on the hypotheses under investigation. Price-Williams (1965) carried out just such a study among the Tiv of Northern Nigeria, an investigation related to those in the previous paragraph. Price-Williams (1965) accepted the argument of Spiro (1961) that the existence of malevolent supernatural beings is a projection or displacement of repressed impulses and put it to the test by observing the severity of independence training and indulgence of aggression in child rearing. In addition folk tales and stories were also studied for the importance in them of various behaviour systems especially succorance, nurturance and aggression. The Tiv are particularly useful for the investigation of this hypothesis because they attribute severe or protracted illness either to the offence of *akombo*, a supernatural agency, or to the attack of *mbatsav*, generally malevolent supernatural beings. As postulated by psychoanalytic theory and by Spiro (1961), aggression was a common theme in the folk tales of the Tiv and aggression was suppressed as far as possible in the child-rearing procedures although the ratings of these (carried out by students) were not as reliable as desired. Nevertheless this one-culture study does support the previous cross-cultural results and hence Freudian theory.

Munroe and colleagues have carried out a series of experiments into cross-sex identity. The research concerned the phenomenon of male pregnancy symptoms and its relation to cross-sex identification — positive in Freudian theory. Munroe and Munroe (1971) compared males with symptoms and controls in three societies — Boston in the United States, the Black Caribs of British Honduras and the Logoli of Kenya. The hypothesis was that males with symptoms would show, on measures of sex identity, female or exaggeratedly male responses. It was also considered likely that the symptom group would have had less contact with males (as models) during childhood. The hypotheses were supported in the Boston group (26 with symptoms and 30 controls) where measures of sexual identity were: Franck drawing completion test, Gough brief scale of femininity, semantic differential descriptions of family roles, concealed figures test and a questionnaire on interest, activities and early background. On overt measures the experimental group was exaggeratedly masculine but feminine on the covert measures.

In the Black Carib different experimental procedures had to be adopted. In this group couvade is common, a custom which would apparently reflect strong cross-sex identity in itself. Certainly, as confirmation of the hypothesis, pregnancy symptoms among males are more common among the Caribs (90%). Since the Franck test was not suitable for this sample and since so high a proportion of the sample showed symptoms, rho's were computed between intensity of symptoms and couvade practices, baby care, family role description, sex-role preferences, early experience and exaggerated masculinity as measured in ratings for bravery, drinking and wife-beating. In fact the symptoms were associated with indices of exaggerated masculinity — cursing, wife-beating, drinking and gambling. Practising the couvade was also related. Similar findings were obtained in the third society, the Logoli where 13 of the 20 males examined showed symptoms. This linking in three societies of male pregnancy symptoms, couvade (where appropriate) and male pregnancy symptoms is good support for Freudian theory.

Finally before we leave the hologeistic method we shall briefly discuss some investigations, which are relevant to Freudian theory although in a less obvious way than those we have previously examined, and one which attacks a more general psychoanalytic proposition. Bacon *et al.* (1963) carried out a cross-cultural survey in the original style (Whiting and Child, 1953) using 48 mainly non-literate societies. The relation of theft and personal crime to early child-rearing procedures was the focus of the research. Personal crime, defined as assault, rape or malignant sorcery, for example, and theft in societies where it was forbidden, would both be related to defective superego development in Freudian theory. Thus it is highly interesting and confirmatory of the theory that both these classes of offence were related to lack of opportunity for the child to identify with the father, a finding similar to that in the West with criminal populations (e.g. Bowlby, 1944). Theft alone was associated with socialization anxiety and status differences among adults and personal crime was associated with suspicion and distrust. This study by Bacon et al. (1963) supports, in the most general terms, the Freudian theory of the implication of the superego in crime.

Bacon et al. (1965) carried out a series of studies on adult drinking habits using a similar methodology. Although these investigations are not of primary concern to the student of Freudian theory one finding was relevant. In the 139 societies the indulgence or severity of child-rearing practices was positively related to presence and extent of ceremonial drinking (e.g. communion wine), the general consumption of the society and the frequency of drunkenness. The correlations indicated that the indulgence of dependency need both in childhood and adulthood was related to a low incidence of drinking and insobriety. Since dependency is an oral characteristic in Freudian psychosexual theory (Glover, 1924) it would follow that orally fixated persons whose dependency was not indulged would resort to other oral gratifications and this would account for the correlations noted.

Allen (1967) investigated in 58 societies which had been previously rated by Whiting and Child in respect of their child-rearing practices the broad psychoanalytic proposition that adult ego strength would have a curvilinear relationship to severity of child training. Either indulgence or deprivation would result in low ego strength. A seven point rating scale for ego strength was developed which was satisfactorily reliable (0·74). At one extreme were societies characterized by passive acceptance of problems and rigid methods of solution, while at the other pole were societies noted for flexibility of problem solving and a tolerance to frustration. The curvilinear hypothesis was not supported by this investigation in that satisfaction was positively related to ego strength and anxiety was negatively related, so that satisfaction would not appear to be as bad for ego strength as Freudian theory claims. Allen (1967) however tries to avoid rejecting the theory by arguing that cross-cultural studies (by using averages for societies) do not contain the extremes of deprivation and indulgence that may be found in any one society. This is because societies as a whole are not as extreme as the abnormal individuals with whom psychoanalysis has had to deal. This does not seem to us a convincing argument, indeed it seems that the opposite could as easily be maintained (see p. 58). Nevertheless, despite this, the fact that child-rearing procedures were related to measures of ego strength is some general support for psychoanalytic theory.

Enough now has been said to illustrate the value of the hologeistic method both in its original form and the more modern extension of it, as used by Whiting (1963). What is now needed it seems to us is for the method to be taken up with the specific intention of studying Freudian hypotheses.

The investigation of societies by the British anthropological school (Kuper, 1973), as we have seen, has eschewed psychological explanations and is thus usually of little relevance to our purpose. However anthropological studies by psychoanalysts, e.g. Roheim (1934) or Kardiner (1945), are likely to be more useful as is the work of the culture and personality group, provided that the findings are not vitiated by the methodological imperfections we have previously discussed (see p. 62). Free associations are not better among the Alor than among the Viennese as scientific data! Thus to review all these anthropological and cultural findings would be absurd. We shall restrict ourselves to those that can bear on the validity of Freudian theory.

One of the first fruits of the anthropological investigation of Freudian concepts has become so famous that we shall not here discuss the research in any detail. We refer to the work of Malinowski in the Trobriand islands, summarized in "The Sexual Life of Savages". However this work deserves mention because it highlights all the features, advantageous and otherwise, of this cross-cultural approach. As is well known, Malinowski demonstrated that among the Trobriand islanders the Oedipus complex was not as Freud had found it in Vienna. Here the triangular relationship was not between son, mother and father but between brother, sister and sister's son. The Oedipus complex was therefore not universal but was, as described by Freud, merely one of a series of possible nuclear complexes. Which complex actually develops depends upon the family unit within the culture. Jones (1924) rebutted Malinowski's claims arguing that the non-recognition of the biological relationship between father and son which Malinowski had stressed in his description of the Trobriands was in fact a denial of Oedipal conflicts. Indeed the matrilineal social organization was itself an institutionalized defence against such Oedipal conflicts. Furthermore the hostility between son and uncle, which was for Malinowski the Trobriand equivalent of the Viennese father–son hostility, Jones saw as a displacement. In other words Malinowski's data were not refutatory to the traditional concept of the Oedipus complex.

As Parsons (1969) has pointed out, to continue this debate is no longer useful. In fact most psychoanalysts have now modified their views of the Oedipus complex to regard it as a cultural phenomenon depending upon the family environment (e.g. Fenichel, 1945), not a universal inherited instinct. Indeed object relations theory (Fairbairn, 1952) which has tended to replace the older instinct theory of psychoanalysis (see Bowlby, 1969) suggests that there is no necessity for any particular family member to be incorporated into a complex, so that Malinowski's findings do not present any longer even a theoretical problem. Indeed Parsons' (1969) own work in Naples where she appears to have found yet another variant of the Oedipus complex (the "Madonna complex") adds empirical support to the argument. In one sense, therefore, Malinowski's work might be thought of as having contributed towards achieving one of the aims of cross-cultural research into Freudian theory — changing it. Thus even if Malinowski's findings did not directly change the psychoanalytic view, they were influential in its modification. However from the viewpoint of the scientific standing of Freudian theory it is doubtful whether these anthropological observations are sufficiently rigorous to modify it.

Muensterberger (1969) contains many excellent papers reporting research relevant to Freudian theory. The majority of these however, as was the case with the work of Parsons (1969), constitute further psychoanalytic evidence rather than the scientific, objective evidence for which we are searching in this chapter. Thus Muensterberger (1969) himself tries to link orality and dependence in the Southern Chinese. This paper is highly convincing in the sense of persuasive. Only when we apply the critical apparatus of the psychological scientific method and discount the attractive literary style are its failings clear. The data were obtained from interviews in English with fifteen men and six women in the Chinese quarters of New York and San Francisco. The sample was chosen on the grounds of availability rather than social class, background or education. These sampling procedures are sufficient to rob the study of scientific validity. From these interviews Muensterberger (1969) was satisfied that boys were orally indulged (more than girls) up to the age of one year and that this accounted for the typical oral characteristics of the Chinese: their preoccupation with food, rest, gambling (asking fate — mother — for protection), opium, reliance on others for help and the use of the go-between in Chinese society. The evidence for these assertions is in effect little more than anecdotal and since it conflicts with the Chinese stereotype of long and hard work Muensterberger is forced to refer to this as pseudo-activity in which the Chinese hide themselves from dangers. Again we can have little confidence in results such as these although they are useful as a basis for hypothesis.

We have now made it clear that these studies are valuable as sources of hypotheses for putting to a more rigorous test but are insufficient to be regarded as the scientific evidence for which we are looking. Some anthropological findings, however, despite these difficulties deserve notice.

Devereux (e.g. 1947) has carried out extensive psychoanalytic anthropological studies of the Mohave Indians. Although his reports of Mohave sexuality linked to child-training practices are fascinating the validity of the original data is for reasons we have discussed dubious. However his reports of beliefs in the society are less likely to be distorted than personality and behavioural assessments so that we can pay more attention to these. Mohave mothers do not nurse orphan children because they feel that their own baby will be angry and die to spite them. Similarly if sucklings have to be weaned early (because pregnancy has dried the milk) they tend not to thrive, even to die. These "spite suicides" are equated with the spite deaths above and are held to be caused by impotent rage. The jealous infant wishes to deprive another of the right to live (the foetus) which is contrary to the Mohave ethic of complete generosity. Hence the sequence is in terms of psychoanalytic theory, oral frustration (no milk), rage and aggression to foetus, self aggression and suicide. This theory of rage, self aggression and suicide is held by Mohave shamans who are called in to attempt treatments for these ills. What is interesting in addition to the theory, is that the characteristic quality of a shaman is that he can remember what his infantile thoughts were (whence the theory) and indeed can even draw upon interuterine memories. The resemblance to the theories of Melanie Klein could hardly be closer. Whether Devereux was influenced by her theories in his interpretations of the Mohave information cannot of course be determined. Nevertheless it is worthy of note that a culture which claims that its shamans have special knowledge of infantile life should have elaborated theories so close to the one analytic theory which has concentrated on this age group.

Horton (1961) in his study of the Kalabari Ijaw of Nigeria found another interesting parallel with orthodox psychoanalytic theory. They believe that conscious feelings, desires and thoughts originate in the *biomgbo* but that in turn everything in the *biomgbo* is brought about by the *teme* which is the driving force of the personality although largely unconscious. In some individuals the *teme* is in conflict with the conscious, and here a diviner is called in who has to find the underlying wishes of the *teme* and get his patient to reject them, usually by some dramatic rite. This is so like classical psychoanalysis that one would like to know whether sessions are strictly timed and paid for. These findings have been quoted more for interest than for any strong belief that they support psychoanalytic theory.

Gorer (1943) and La Barre (1945) among the Japanese and Berkley-Hill (1921) among the Hindus have argued that anality is the key to understanding their national characteristics. However, as Kerlinger (1953) pointed out, many of the "facts" about child-rearing in these cultures that were assumed to be true by these writers are simply false. Thus even if their assessment of personality were correct (and we have no reason to think that it is) the results could still not be taken at their face value. Certainly these impressionistic literary studies can have no place in the validation or extension of Freudian theory. Of course as Axelrad (1969) has pointed out in his comments on the effectiveness of anthropology to illuminate Freudian theory, the whole notion of a national character related to some form of child-training procedure implies almost impossible sampling and measurement problems, which we have previously discussed.

These strictures on methodology preclude using the results even of such influential investigators as Kardiner and Roheim as other than suggestive of hypotheses. Again we do not argue that their work is worthless. On the contrary we feel that it is equivalent to the best psychoanalytic clinical work — insightful and fascinating but insufficiently tied to reputable data to form a basis for a scientific theory.

Mention of Roheim brings us to one source of cross-cultural evidence that might be usable in the study of Freudian theory — dreams. Roheim (1947) contains an excellent discussion of the use of dream material in anthropology and many of the points are relevant to the use of such material in the investigation of the scientific validity of Freudian theory. Thus Seligman (1924) in discussing dreams argued that the essential psychological mechanisms that were seen in Western man could also be observed in the primitive tribes that were then the subject of anthropological investigation. However, as Roheim points out, Seligman discussed no individual dreams and thus there were no associations. Lincoln (1935) collected together a number of dreams from the Navaho and the Solomon Islands but there were few associations. As Roheim emphasizes, dream interpretation is impossible without associations. Roheim himself in his field-work aimed to find the unconscious meaning of an institution or belief by dream analysis of the dream in which it had occurred. Roheim then proceeds to exemplify his method and results.

However, the description of this work shows clearly that it is unsuitable for the purposes of validating Freudian theory. Thus in the validity studies we are seeking for direct evidence that dreams contain unfulfilled wishes, that there is a latent content underlying the actual (manifest) content. Certainly the collection of typical dreams from other cultures can achieve none of these aims. Thus even if it turns out that dreams are common to many different cultures (e.g. a falling dream or a pursuit dream) this tells us nothing about the psychological mechanisms, if any, underlying them. Furthermore Roheim's methods are identical to those of psychoanalysis.

Thus all that Roheim could demonstrate is that similar results are obtained using free associations to dreams with tribe X as are found with European samples. What is needed is some treatment of dream material, similar to that of Hall (1966) perhaps, which does not do violence to the Freudian theory of dreams but which does not simply mimic Freudian methods. Actually the work of Lee (1958) (see below) illustrates how such investigations can be carried out. All this discussion makes it clear that we cannot use anthropological work, however suggestive, as scientific support for Freudian theory.

V. CROSS-CULTURAL PSYCHOLOGICAL STUDIES

We now come to our fourth group of cross-cultural studies, those conducted by workers who are psychologists and who use first and foremost psychological methods. As we saw there are enormous problems with psychological tests when they are used in non-Western cultures. Suffice it to repeat here that the favourite method (projective tests) of cross-cultural psychologists can carry little weight as evidence and we can find in the literature no attempt to use objective procedures to test Freudian theory, as we suggested might be possible in cross-cultural investigations. Furthermore as our survey (Kline, 1973) of tests available for testing Freudian theories showed, there are relatively few such tests available and the only one that has been used cross-culturally is the present author's. However, as mentioned earlier, two investigations, in Ghana (Kline, 1969) and in India (Kline and Mohan, 1974), were not successful in elucidating Freudian theory, although it appears to be the case that in some cultures, at least Ai3Q could be used. Indeed we are forced to conclude that at present cross-cultural study of Freudian theory by current tests should not be attempted, although it would be relatively easy to develop the necessary tests given time. Since tests are not useful we must turn therefore to the study of variables which do not require psychological tests.

One of the most striking cross-cultural studies of Freudian theory was that of Lee (1958) who studied the dreams of 600 Zulu subjects (120 in great detail). Since this was a large-scale study of the hysterical crying to which the Zulu women in this area are prone all we can do here is summarize rather baldly the results of the detailed study of the dreams of these 120 women. First of all it was found that dream content was limited almost exclusively to areas of social experience permitted by the culture in the indigenous system of sanctions of some 50 to 100 years ago. For example women in these dreams never handled cattle (as was then tabooed) although now in fact women are used as herders. Lee argues that this supports the Freudian notion that the superego is formed from the early introjection of the parents. Since these parents in their turn had formed their superegos early on in life we should expect dream content to show a considerable cultural lag and this indeed seems to be the case with Lee's Zulu.

These findings, on their own, of course, could not support the Freudian hypothesis of superego introjection because too much inference is required in interpreting the data. However, one finding among these Zulu, where the most important thing for a woman was to have children and as many as possible as a protection against old age, was unequivocal. The dreams of women who had a poor obstetric history (who were barren or who had recently lost children) were compared with the dreams of the rest. Those who dreamed of "a baby" had much the worst record of married infertility. Those who had borne children had lost more than half of them and these were the youngest group — an important qualification, since had they been the eldest group such deaths would not have been so surprising. Since, as Lee (1958) shows, in this society there is a powerful psychological need for a baby such dreams must indicate wish-fulfilment — as Freud claimed. It is to be noted that the wish is directly expressed in the manifest content of the dream, a phenomenon in Freudian theory typical of children (Freud, 1935). Further support that these dreams represented wishes comes from the findings that nine of the 21 subjects who had "baby" dreams said a baby was their main wish and four said children were their main desire. Of the 97 other subjects only 18 gave a baby or children as their main wish — a difference that is significant at the 1% level. Again sufferers from pseudocyesis (false pregnancy), a common complaint in the area, tended to have more baby dreams than the others. Finally Lee presents further data linking dreams of still water and flooding to conflicting desires for more children (the cultural norm) among those who already have sufficient of their own. This of course enters the world of symbolism which the research is intended to test rather than use so that we shall not here discuss it further. However, one clear example of symbolism occurred (Lee, personal communication) namely that there was only one dream of a dead snake and this belonged to a woman who was married to the sole impotent man in the community.

There can be little room for doubt that this study by Lee (1958) is good evidence that among these Zulu dreams do express wishes and that one dream symbol at least — the snake — is as Freudian theory describes. This study is an impressive illustration of the power of cross-cultural studies based on careful observation of specified samples and the quantitative analysis of the resulting data without relying on psychological tests, which as we have seen are liable in cross-cultural studies to produce data which are invalid but (even worse) appear valid. Very important in a study of this kind is the fact that it cannot be argued that the dreams were contaminated by subjects' knowledge of what they were expected to dream about, a jibe frequently aimed at analysts of the relevant persuasion. These Zulu were undoubtedly ignorant of psychoanalytic theory. In conclusion it seems to us that this study by Lee could well be taken as a model of how to investigate Freudian theory cross-culturally. The rich knowledge of the culture typified in the best anthropology was combined with proper sampling, data collection and statistical analysis.

Two studies of language deserve mention. Mosak (1955) examined the gender of words for Freudian symbols in French, Spanish and German. Now as we have argued elsewhere (Kline, 1972) this investigation contains within itself an inherent contradiction. It assumes that, if Freudian theory were correct, the gender of symbolic words in languages would accord with their symbolism. If this were true we ought to look at the gender of such words in the basic root languages. However, if only unconscious factors affected the gender of these words we should also expect the gender of such words when derived from the same root language to be the same. Thus since Spanish and French are both derived from Latin the gender of symbolic words in each language should be the same. If it is not then this is evidence that some external factors are affecting gender. If this is the case then the study of Freudian theory by looking at the gender of symbolic words is a poor strategy. Thus the failure of Mosak to find the theory confirmed (in that the gender of symbolic words was not in accordance with the theory) cannot be held to disconfirm the theory. Mullen (1968) also examined the gender of symbolic words in French, German and Spanish. However, the same faults vitiated this work, which failed to confirm Jungian and Freudian theory. What is really needed with this approach is to study basic root languages which are preferably unconnected.

Minturn (1965) carried out such a study, accepting that the gender of words is unlikely to be determined entirely by their symbolic referents. She therefore sought to test Freudian theory by examining the direction of gender classification of symbolic words in several languages rather than the magnitude of the direction in one language. She used 54 male and 60 female symbols, judged as unequivocally masculine or feminine. To avoid contamination of findings the fact that certain languages have a common origin, languages with distinct etymological roots were selected: six Indo-European languages (French, German, Russian, Greek, Irish and Maharata) and four non-Indo-European Languages (Arabic, Tunica, Nama and Hausa) were studied. Not only were the symbolic words classified for gender but equally important a random selection of nouns in each language was also investigated — a procedure which ought to allow for the other external influences on gender which we have previously discussed.

First expected frequencies based upon the random samples for each language were compared with the gender frequencies for the symbolic words and in most cases the Freudian hypotheses were supported. Then a chi-square analysis was computed to test the association between symbolic classification and actual gender. This was significant in the expected direction in eight out of ten cases. Since it has been admitted that other variables than their symbolic significance affect the gender of words constancy of results across languages is a crucial test. For female symbols the difference between observed and expected frequencies is correct only five out of eight times but for male symbols it is correct seven out of eight times (sig. 3% level). From this it can be concluded that male symbols do tend to be classified as male in a wide variety of languages not only of Indo-European derivation, although there is less consistency concerning female symbols — some support for Freudian theory.

VI. CONCLUSIONS

The conclusions from our discussion of cross-cultural studies of Freudian theory are clear. We have shown how cross-cultural investigations fall into a number of categories the main ones being anthropological, hologeistic and psychological. We have illustrated the strengths and weaknesses of each method from the viewpoint of the scientific validation of Freudian theory which we have taken to be the purpose of our examination of this work. We demonstrated that social anthropology has characteristically ignored the psychological aspects of its data so that much of it although intrinsically relevant to Freudian theory cannot be used for our purposes. In addition we have called into question the sampling procedures and the sources of information commonly used in anthropology which appear to fall short of the scientific rigour necessary for theory verification. We also found that the work of anthropologists who were avowedly psychoanalytic in their outlook could not be used to validate Freudian theory because usually their data were of the same kind that formed the basis of the original theory and which produce little confidence in its veracity.

The hologeistic method and its modern derivation where the concepts are studied in single cultures with data specially collected for the purpose, despite the disadvantages of having to use ethnographic reports of dubious validity and the problems of sampling, were useful in the study of Freudian theory and investigations were discussed where substantive findings were made. It was concluded that hologeistic studies specifically designed to test relevant Freudian hypotheses could still provide a sound source of evidence for the validity of Freudian theory.

Psychological studies were reviewed and here the main problem was found to be the use of psychological tests in non-Western non-literate cultures. Certainly the normal use of projective techniques followed by subjective interpretation cannot be recommended but a method was suggested which might prove valuable. There seems to be no *a priori* reason why tests suitable for use in a wide variety of cultures ("trans-cultural" variables in the terminology of Price-Williams (1965)) should not be developed although the effort would be considerable and would involve cooperation between psychologists in many different countries. Finally other psychological studies were examined where the variables were not based upon tests and in one case at least (that of Lee, 1958) a very promising methodology was exhibited. In this investigation we found the combination of quantified observational data from a specific sample subjected to a proper statistical analysis and of sound background knowledge of the sample involved including familiarity with the language. Such a study as this is not all that different from the modern extensions of the hologeistic method to which we have already referred.

Thus it would seem to us that cross-cultural studies of Freudian theory can be highly useful in the scientific study of Freudian theory if they combine the best features of anthropology, the profound knowledge of the background of the society under investigation, and the best features of psychology, the emphasis on quantification and sampling and rigorous methodology. Essential to this must be the development of special psychological tests. This specification makes it clear why this chapter has been forced to concentrate on the difficulties and problems of procedures rather than expound a corpus of results. When we couple to all these demands the necessity for a sound knowledge of the languages of the cultures and a knowledge of psycho-analytic theory we can see that investigations of the kind we have prescribed are necessarily rare. For to be successful cross-cultural studies demand rare combinations of skills and knowledge; yet if successful they can put Freudian theory to the scientific test in a way that is unique and powerful. This is the prize that awaits the cross-cultural investigator of Freudian theory.

REFERENCES

Allen, M. G. (1967). *J. soc. Psychol.* **71**, 53–68.
Axelrad, S. (1969). *In* "Man and his culture" (Ed. W. Muensterberger), 273–274. Rapp and Whiting, London.

Bacon, M. K., Child, I. L. and Barry, H. (1963). *J. abnorm. soc. Psychol.* **66**, 291–300.

Bacon, M. K., Child, I. L. and Barry, H. (1965). *Q. J. Study Alcohol Suppl.* **3**, 29–48.

Bakan, D. (1958). "Sigmund Freud and the Jewish Mystical Tradition." Van Nostrand, Princeton.

Berkley-Hill, O. (1921). *Int. J. Psycho-Analysis* **2**, 306–321.

Boas, F. (1938). "Race, Language and Culture." Heath, Boston.

Bowlby, J. (1944). *Int. J. Psycho-Analysis* **25**, 1–57.

Bowlby, J. (1969). "Attachment", Vol. 1: "Attachment and Loss." Hogarth Press and Institute of Psychoanalysis, London.

Campbell, D. T. and Naroll, R. (1972). *In* "Psychological anthropology" (Ed. F. L. K. Hsu), 435–463. Schenkman, Cambridge, Mass.

Carstairs, G. M. (1957). "The Twice-Born." Hogarth Press, London.

Cattell, R. B. (1957). "Personality and Motivation Structure and Measurement." New York Book Co., Yonkers.

Cattell, R. B. (1973). "Personality and Mood by Questionnaire." Jossey Bass, San Francisco.

Cattell, R. B. and Kline, P. (1976). "The Scientific Study of Personality." Academic Press, London and New York.

Cattell, R. B. and Warburton, F. W. (1967). "Objective Personality and Motivation Tests." University of Illinois Press, Urbana.

Conant, J. B. (1947). "On Understanding Science." Yale University Press, New Haven.

Cronbach, L. J. (1970). "Essentials of Psychological Testing." Harper-Row, Chicago.

Deregowski, J. B. (1966). "Difficulties in Pictorial Perception in Africa." Institute for Social Research, University of Zambia.

Devereux, G. (1947). *Psychoanal. Q.* **16**, 519–546.

Du Bois, C. (1944). "The People of Alor." University of Minnesota Press, Minneapolis.

Eysenck, H. J. (1953). "Uses and Abuses of Psychology." Penguin Books, Harmondsworth, Middlesex.

Eysenck, H. J. (1959). "Personality Tests and Reviews." (Ed. O. Buros), 897–899. Gryphon Press, New Jersey.

Eysenck, H. J. (1960). "The Structure of Human Personality", 2nd Edition. Methuen, London.

Eysenck, H. J. and Wilson, G. D. (1973). "The Experimental Study of Freudian Theories." Methuen, London.

Fairbairn, W. R. D. (1952). "Psychoanalytic Studies of the Personality." Tavistock, London.

Farrell, B. A. (1964). *Inquiry* **7**, 104–122.

Fenichel, O. (1945). "The Psychoanalytic Theory of Neurosis." Norton, New York.

Freud, S. (1905). "Three essays on Sexuality", Standard Edition of the Complete Psychological Works of Sigmund Freud, Vol. 7, 235–243. Hogarth Press and Institute of Psychoanalysis, London.

Freud, S. (1913). "Totem and Taboo", Standard Edition of the Complete Psychological World of Sigmund Freud, Vol. 13. Hogarth Press and Institute of Psychoanalysis, London.

Freud, S. (1935). "An autobiographical study," Standard Edition of the Complete
Psychological Works of Sigmund Freud, Vol. 20, 7–74. Hogarth Press and
Institute of Psychoanalysis, London.
Glover, E. (1924). "On the Early Development of Mind." (1956). Mayo Pub. Co.,
London.
Gluckman, M. (1962). "Essays on the Ritual of Social Relations." Manchester
University Press, Manchester.
Gorer, G. (1943). Trans. N.Y. Acad. Sci. 2, 106–124.
Grygier, T. G. (1961). "The Dynamic Personality Inventory." N.F.E.R., Windsor.
Hall, C. S. (1966). "The Meaning of Dreams." University of Chicago Press,
Chicago.
Hampson, S. and Kline, P. (1977). Brit. J. Criminol. In press.
Harrington, C. and Whiting, J. W. M. (1972). In "Psychological Anthropology."
(Ed. F. L. K. Hsu), 469–507. Schenkman, Cambridge, Mass.
Holley, J. W. (1973). In "New Approaches in Psychological Measurement." (Ed. P.
Kline), 119–155. Wiley, London.
Holley, J. W. and Guilford, J. P. (1964). Educ. psychol. Meas. 24, 749–753.
Horton, R. (1961). Africa. 31, 110–116.
Hudson, W. (1960). J. soc. Psychol. 52, 183–208.
Hudson, W. (1967). Int. J. Psychol. 2, 89–107.
Jones, E. (1924). "Essays in Applied Psychoanalysis" (1964). International
University Press, New York.
Jones, E. (1957). "The Life and Work of Sigmund Freud." Basic Books, New York.
Kardiner, A. (1945). "The Psychological Frontiers of Society." Columbia University
Press, New York.
Kerlinger, F. N. (1953). Soc. Forces 31, 250–258.
Kilbride, P. L. and Robbins, M. C. (1969). Am. Anthrop. 71, 293–301.
Kline, P. (1969). Br. J. Soc. Clin. Psychol. 8, 201–210.
Kline, P. (1971). "Ai3Q." N.F.E.R., Windsor.
Kline, P. (1972). "Fact and Fantasy in Freudian Theory." Methuen, London.
Kline, P. (1973). In "New Approaches in Psychological Measurement" (Ed. P.
Kline), 179–209. Wiley, Chichester.
Kline, P. (1975). Psych. Stud. 20, 1–6.
Kline, P. and Mohan, J. (1974). J. soc. Psychol., 94, 137–138.
Kuper, A. (1973). "Anthropologists and Anthropology." Allen Lane, London.
La Barre, W. (1945). Psychiatry 8, 314–342.
Lambert, W. W., Triandis, L. and Wolf, M. (1959). J. abnorm. soc. Psychol. 58,
162–169.
Lee, S. G. (1953). "TAT for African Subjects." University of Natal Press,
Pietermaritzburg.
Lee, S. G. (1958). J. soc. Psychol. 47, 265–283.
Lincoln, T. S. (1935). "The Dream in Primitive Cultures." Cresset Press, London.
Lindzey, G. (1961). "Projective Techniques and Cross-Cultural Research."
Appleton-Century-Crofts, New York.
Malinowski, B. (1929). "The Sexual Life of Savages." Routledge and Kegan Paul,
London.
Martin, M. (1964). Inquiry 7, 80–98.
Menninger, W. C. (1943). Psychoanal. Q. 12, 161–193.
Minturn, L. (1955). Ethnology 4, 336–342.

Mosak, H. R. (1965). *J. consult. Psychol.* **14**, 108.
Muensterberger, W., ed. (1969). "Man and his Culture." Rapp and Whiting, London.
Mullen, F. G. (1968). *Percept. Mot. Skills* **26**, 1041–1042.
Munroe, R. L. and Munroe, R. H. (1971). *J. soc. Psychol.* **84**, 11–25.
Murdock, G. P. (1957). *Am. Anthrop.* **59**, 664–687.
Naroll, R. and Cohen, R., eds. (1970). "A handbook of method in cultural anthropology." Natural History Press, Garden City.
Newson, E. and Newson, J. (1963). "Infant care in an urban community." Allen and Unwin, London.
Parin, P. and Morgenthaler, F. (1969). *In* "Man and Culture" (Ed. W. Muensterberger), 187–210. Rapp and Whiting, London.
Parsons, A. (1969). *In* "Man and Culture" (Ed. W. Muensterberger), 331–384. Rapp and Whiting, London.
Phillips, H. P. (1965). "Thai Peasant Personality." University of California Press, Berkeley.
Popper, K. (1959). "The Logic of Scientific Discovery." Basic Books, New York.
Price-Williams, D. R. (1965). *J. soc. Psychol.* **65**, 1–15.
Radcliffe-Brown, A. R. (1952). "Structure and Function in Primitive Society." Free Press, New York.
Rapaport, D. and Gill, M. M. (1959). *Int. J. Psycho-Analysis* **40**, 153–162.
Roheim, G. (1934). *In* "Essays presented to C. G. Seligman" (Eds E. E. Evans-Pritchard *et al.*). Routledge and Kegan Paul, London.
Roheim, G., ed. (1947). "Psychoanalysis and the Social Sciences." Hogarth Press, London.
Seligman, C. G. (1924). *Jl R. anthrop. Inst.* **14**, 46.
Semeonoff, B. (1973). *In* "New Approaches in Psychological Measurement" (Ed. P. Kline), 89–118. Wiley, Chichester.
Shouksmith, G. (1968). "Assessment through Interviewing." Pergamon Press, Oxford.
Spain, D. H. (1972). *In* "Psychological Anthropology" (Ed. F. L. K. Hsu), 267–308. Schenkman, Cambridge, Mass.
Spiro, M. E. (1961). *In* "Studying Personality Cross-Culturally (Ed. B. Kaplan), 93–128. Row, Peterson, Evanston.
Spiro, M. E. (1968). "International Encyclopedia of the Social Sciences" (Ed. D. L. Sills), 558–663. Macmillan and Free Press, New York.
Spiro, M. E. (1972). *In* "Psychological Anthropology" (Ed. F. L. K. Hsu), 573–607. Schenkman, Cambridge, Mass.
Spiro, M. E. and D'Andrade, R. G. (1958). *Am. Anthrop.* **60**, 456–466.
Stephens, W. N. (1961). *Genet. Psychol. Monogrs* **64**, 385–416.
Stephens, W. N. (1962). "The Oedipus Complex Hypothesis: Cross-Cultural Evidence." Free Press, New York.
Vernon, P. E. (1964). "Personality Assessment." Methuen, London.
Vernon, P. E. (1969). "Intelligence and cultural environment." Methuen, London.
Vernon, P. E. and Parry, J. B. (1949). ."Personal selection in the British Forces." University of London Press, London.
Whiting, B. (1963). "Six Cultures." Wiley, New York.
Whiting, J. W. M. (1959). *In* "Nebraska Symposium on Motivation", 174–195. University of Nebraska Press, Lincoln.

Whiting, J. W. M. (1968). *In* "Handbook of Social Psychology" (Eds G. Lindzey and E. Aronson), Vol. 2. Addison Wesley, Cambridge, Mass.

Whiting, J. W. M. and Child, I. L. (1953). "Child Training and Personality." Yale University Press, New Haven.

Whiting, J. W. M., Kluckhohn, H. and Anthony, A. (1958). *In* "Readings in Social Psychology" (Eds E. E. Maccoby, T. M. Newcomb and E. L. Hartley), 359–370. Holt, New York.

Wober, M. (1967). *Br. J. Psychol.* **58**, 29–38.

3 | Malnutrition and Mental Development in Rural Guatemala

ROBERT E. KLEIN, MARC IRWIN, PATRICIA L. ENGLE AND CHARLES YARBROUGH

Though the problem of malnutrition is a very old one, an accurate understanding of its effects has only recently begun. Stimulated by international attention to the losing race between population growth and world food production, the last decade has witnessed a proliferation of studies of the effects of malnutrition on human development. Many such studies have focussed on the relationship between malnutrition and mental development. In agreement with folk wisdom, an association between malnutrition and deficient mental development has not been difficult to establish. Yet, unequivocal evidence as to a causal relationship has eluded investigators. At least some of the reasons why are not difficult to understand. Problems of definition and measurement of nutritional status are considerable. Such problems are equally great for mental development, and these are complicated by the fact that the effects of malnutrition are generally studied in developing countries, by social scientists employing instruments and concepts foreign to the research setting. Thus, the problem of cross-cultural understanding and measurement is usually present in research on the effects of malnutrition and mental development. Finally, the usual research strategies are difficult to apply to the study of the effects of malnutrition; one can neither cause malnutrition in order to observe its effects, nor erase the poverty, illness and social deprivation which almost invariably exist simultaneously with malnutrition, and which constitute plausible alternative explanations of deficient mental development.

This paper will briefly describe previous research on the effects of malnutrition on mental development (for more extensive reviews, see those of Birch, 1972; Klein *et al.*, 1971; Latham, 1974; Read, 1975; Warren, 1973)

and then describe in some detail the design and findings to date of one such research project, the Institute of Nutrition of Central America and Panama's (INCAP) on-going longitudinal prospective study of the effects of malnutrition on mental development in rural Guatemala.

I. A SELECTIVE REVIEW OF THE LITERATURE

In this brief review of the published literature, we will focus on several areas of research conception and design which have been troublesome in previous studies. These include adequate definition of nutritional status, consideration of the effects of the timing of malnutrition, appropriate operationalization of mental development, effects of the age of measurement of mental development, and attribution of causality.

A. Definitions of Malnutrition

Malnutrition is a difficult concept to operationalize because, while it refers in part to input, or the food a person eats, the only measures usually available are output measures (i.e. growth or health status). Thus the criteria for classification (summarized in Jelliffe, 1966) are all inferential, with past malnutrition inferred from present physical state. In particular, protein–calorie malnutrition (PCM) has been variously defined using indicators of physical growth, various clinical signs, and biochemical indicators. It is generally agreed that PCM is a continuum, with clinically identified kwashiorkor (caused primarily by protein deficiency) and marasmus (primarily a calorie deficit) at one end, and "good" nutritional status (maximal growth, appropriate weight for height) at the other. The primary indicator is low weight for age or low weight for height and the extreme category is defined as having less than 70% of expected weight for age. In this range kwashiorkor is indicated by the presence of oedema, skin rash, changes of colour of hair, and apathy, while marasmus is indicated by wasting, little subcutaneous fat, and irritability. The moderately malnourished child is usually thought to be identified only by growth retardation, say, of less than 90% of the normal weight for age. It may be accompanied by biochemical indications and/or evidence of reduced food intake, but almost never by clinical signs. Finally, designation of malnutrition is complicated by the fact that children with deficient diets may also exhibit signs of various vitamin and mineral deficiencies in addition to the signs of protein–calorie malnutrition described here.

The majority of studies of human malnutrition and mental development have dealt exclusively with the effects of severe malnutrition (Birch *et al.*, 1971; Botha-Antoun *et al.*, 1968; Brockman and Ricciuti, 1971; Cabak and Najdanvic, 1965; Champakam *et al.*, 1968; Chase and Martin, 1970; Cravioto *et al.*, 1966; Cravioto and DeLicardie, 1970; Cravioto and Robles, 1965; DeLicardie and Cravioto, 1974; Edwards and Craddock, 1973; Evans *et al.*, 1971; Hertzig *et al.*, 1972; Liang *et al.*, 1967; Mönckeberg, 1968; Montelli *et al.*, 1974; Pollit and Granoff, 1967; Stein *et al.*, 1972a, b; Stoch and Smythe, 1963, 1967). Typically, subjects have been children hospitalized for one of two forms of acute malnutrition, marasmus or kwashiorkor (Birch *et al.*, 1971; Brockman and Ricciuti, 1971; Cabak and Najdanvic, 1965; Champakam *et al.*, 1968; Chase and Martin, 1970; Cravioto and Robles, 1965; DeLicardie and Cravioto, 1974; Evans *et al.*, 1971; Hertzig *et al.*, 1972; Mönckeberg, 1968; Montelli *et al.*, 1974; Pollit and Granoff, 1967). These studies of severe malnutrition typically find an association between early PCM and poor cognitive performance. However, one could easily suspect that the trauma associated with having a serious illness and being hospitalized has in itself negative effects on mental development. Also, there is a problem of selection: though usually unlikely, the possibility does exist that some children become malnourished because they are in some ways more difficult children, perhaps with more feeding problems. These problems, as well as a variety of others to be discussed shortly, have made it difficult to make unambiguous causal statements about the effects of malnutrition on mental development.

Fewer investigations have focussed on less severe forms of malnutrition, although the number of children affected is far greater. Though severe malnutrition is a relatively rare condition except during times of natural disaster, it has been estimated that 75% of all children growing up in developing countries are malnourished to some degree (Béhar, 1968). The effects of mild-to-moderate PCM have been studied by Boutourline-Young *et al.* (1973), Chávez *et al.* (1974), McKay *et al.* (1969), Montelli *et al.* (1974), Mora *et al.* (1974), and Patel (1974). Like the studies of severe PCM cited, these studied have typically reported an association between malnutrition and poor cognitive performance. However, these investigators have not been able to make strong causal statements because possible alternative explanations for their findings exist.

B. Timing of Malnutrition

In all but a few studies (e.g. Cravioto *et al.*, 1966; Cravioto and DeLicardie, 1970; Edwards and Craddock, 1973; McKay *et al.*, 1969; Mönckeberg *et al.*,

1972), diagnosis of malnutrition has been made during the first few years of life. Since most studies have consisted of follow-ups of previously hospitalized children, nutritional-status data are reported for only one or at most two points in time. While these are important data, we would be in a stronger position to specify effects of malnutrition if we had nutritional-status measures collected during the child's entire early life, including the prenatal period. This kind of data has various advantages: it allows precise estimation of the effects of malnutrition on mental development at the time of the malnutrition and its long-term effects on later mental development. Such information also permits inferences to be more readily made concerning the mechanisms involved in these effects; a consistent association of prenatal malnutrition with retarded mental development, for example, would suggest the possibility of a neuroanatomic mechanism, because of the rapid growth and vulnerability of the nervous system during gestation, while greater effects of later appearing malnutrition might suggest that the mechanism involved was insufficient energy levels available for environmental exploration and stimulation. Data collected over a long period of time also allow the investigator to define nutritional status directly, in terms of nutrient ingestion, rather than indirectly, as physical growth. Only long-term longitudinal investigations allow the collection of such data. Longitudinal investigations other than the INCAP study are those of Stoch and Smythe (1963 and 1967) in South Africa; Botha-Antoun et al. (1968) in Lebanon; McKay et al. (1969) and Mora et al. (1974) in Colombia; Boutourline-Young et al. (1973) in Tunisia; and those of Chávez et al. (1974) and DeLicardie and Cravioto (1974) in Mexico. To date none of these studies excepting those of Stoch and Smythe and Botha-Antoun et al. have published final results.

C. Definitions and Measurement of Mental Development

No consensus exists among scientists concerning an appropriate definition of mental development. The term subsumes an almost infinite number of human characteristics that could be evaluated, and in fact, there exist hundreds of tests designed to measure mental ability, which is simply level of mental development at a given point in time. However, in spite of this profusion of tests, the majority of investigators have chosen to employ IQ (or in the case of infants, DQ) scores as their operationalization of the construct (Birch et al., 1971; Botha-Antoun et al., 1968; Boutourline-Young et al., 1973; Cabak and Najdanvic, 1965; Chase and Martin, 1970; Chávez et al., 1974; Cravioto and Robles, 1965; DeLicardie and Cravioto, 1974;

Edwards and Craddock, 1973; Evans *et al.*, 1971; Hertzig *et al.*, 1972; Liang *et al.*, 1967; Mönckeberg, 1968; Mönckeberg *et al.*, 1972; Montelli *et al.*, 1974; Mora *et al.*, 1974; Patel, 1974; Pollit and Granoff, 1967; Stoch and Smythe, 1963, 1967).

While the use of IQ scores can be defended on some pragmatic grounds (i.e. the tests are well known, well standardized in some settings, and predict school success), their use does not focus attention on possible mechanisms which might link malnutrition to mental development, or on possible differential effects of malnutrition on various mental capacities. A few attempts to study such specific effects have been made; some studies have reported several subscale scores for infant psychomotor scales (Chase and Martin, 1970; Chávez *et al.*, 1974; Cravioto and Robles, 1965; Mönckeberg, 1968; Mönckeberg *et al.*, 1972; Montelli *et al.*, 1974), describing deficits in malnourished infants on each subscale. Others have addressed themselves to specific types of cognitive performance such as intersensory integration (Champakam *et al.*, 1968; Cravioto *et al.*, 1966; Cravioto and DeLicardie, 1970; Klein *et al.*, 1969; McKay *et al.*, 1969; Witkop *et al.*, 1970). Such studies have been informed by the hypothesis that malnutrition causes neurointegrative deficits. Results of these studies have to date been equivocal, with Cravioto *et al.* (1966), Cravioto and DeLicardie (1968), Champakam *et al.* (1968), and Witkop *et al.* (1970), reporting an association of deficient intersensory integration and malnutrition, but Klein *et al.* (1969) and McKay *et al.* (1969), reporting none. Champakam *et al.* (1968) assessed performance in four general areas: memory, perceptual ability, abstract thinking and verbal ability. They found deficits associated with malnutrition in all four areas. These deficits were greatest in abstract thinking and perceptual ability. As we shall show in the latter part of this paper, the INCAP study has attempted to go considerably beyond previous investigations in the range of its infant and preschool mental test batteries. Such inclusiveness should permit testing of hypotheses concerning specific and differential effects of malnutrition. Furthermore, with this information it may be possible to choose among hypothetical mechanisms linking malnutrition and mental development.

A further problem related to the definition of mental development concerns the cultural validity of the operational definition of mental development employed. Intellectually competent behaviour and the mental development which makes such behaviour possible takes place in, and is inextricably tied to, a particular environmental context. Thus, as Berry (1969), Irwin *et al.* (1974), and Scribner and Cole (1973) have argued, measurement instruments employed in any cultural setting must be appropriate to that setting. They must also be interpretable to scientists. In general, investigators in the area of malnutrition and mental development have concerned themselves with the latter requirement and paid little attention to the question of local, or emic validity (Berry, 1969). This problem would appear to be insignificant in testing children during the first one or two years of life. However, for preschool and older children, the question of emic validity in cognitive test performance is a serious one. In a few cases the problem has been ignored, with unadapted Western tests employed (Edwards and Craddock, 1973; Hertzig et al., 1972). Even where cultural adaptation of Western tests has been attempted (e.g. Cabak and Najdanvic, 1965; Champakam et al., 1968; Evans et al., 1971; Liang et al., 1967; Stoch and Smythe, 1963, 1967) such attempts do not assure emic validity of measurement. This would require that the tests actually measure traits (in this case, facets of intellectual competence) which have meaning in the context of the local culture, and that their operationalizations, the test items and tests employed, measure these traits accurately. Even where Western psychometric instruments have been successfully adapted to employ indigenous materials and concepts (and it is generally very difficult to determine on the basis of published research reports to what extent this has been achieved), nothing can be known about the relationship of test performance to local definitions of competence and the ability to function as an effective member of the community, without the collection of independent measures of such competence and ability. Where IQ tests are adapted to measure a population fairly, they may, as Biesheuvel (1949) has suggested, simply measure Western educability. Such information is of value as one index of the effect of nutritional status. It is, however, at best a culture-bound and limited index of the effects of malnutrition on mental development and intellectual competence, and one which may be unlikely to reveal how early malnutrition will affect the adult lives of its victims. For a more extensive discussion of the methodological problems of establishing both emic and non-emic validity of measurements in cross-cultural field studies, the reader is referred to Irwin et al. (1975). To address the problems of both emic, or local, validity, and non-emic, or Western, validity, the INCAP project has employed a variety of non-psychometric measures which are described in the second half of this paper.

D. Age of Measurement of Mental Development

Mental development is, of course, a process which unfolds over time. Measurements of cognitive performance are snapshots of the status of development at particular points in time. As such, these measurements have meaning first in relation to the age or developmental period in which they are made, and much less to other periods, such as adulthood. However, mental test performances measured in later childhood (from age seven onwards) are more similar to and predictive of adult performances than are performances measured in earlier childhood (c.f. Bayley, 1968). Since malnutrition and mental development researchers are ultimately most interested in the effects of malnutrition on adult functioning and competence, studies which report the mental test performance of older children are of more intrinsic interest than those which report the performances only of very young children, such as those of Cravioto and Robles (1965), Pollit and Granoff (1967), Brockman and Ricciuti (1971), and Montelli et al. (1974). The optimal design to measure mental development at various ages is, again, the long-term longitudinal prospective study, which enables description of the relationship of malnutrition to cognitive ability and to the ability to cope with the various tasks of childhood as development proceeds.

E. Attribution of Causality

The classical scientific paradigm for generating inferences of a causal effect of one variable on another is experimental manipulation of the first variable accompanied by control or randomization of other variables representing alternative causal explanations. The experimental manipulation possible in malnutrition research is limited by ethical considerations; investigators do not malnourish children in order to observe the effect of malnutrition on mental development. One form of experimental manipulation is possible, however. Where malnutrition exists, nutrition can be improved through supplementation of inadequate diets, and the effect of this intervention can be observed. The effects of deprivation are measured indirectly by observing the extent of *improvement* with adequate nutrition. The present investigation has employed such a design. So have the longitudinal investigations of McKay et al. (1969), Boutourline-Young et al. (1973), Chávez et al. (1974), and Mora et al. (1974).

Other studies have employed observational, rather than experimental designs; naturally occurring severe or moderate malnutrition has been identified, and correlated mental development has been measured. With the single exception of Stein et al.'s (1972a, b) follow-up study of children of the Second World War pregnant famine victims (who were malnourished for a relatively brief period, with average birth-weight never dropping to levels common in the third world today), every one of these observational studies has found associations between early severe or moderate malnutrition and deficient mental development. The near unanimity of these findings is impressive. However, alternative causal explanations do exist. One is that poverty and accompanying social deprivation almost invariably co-exist with malnutrition. In those studies where social variables have been measured (Chase and Martin, 1970; Chávez et al., 1974; Cravioto and Robles, 1965; Evans et al., 1971; Mönckeberg et al., 1972; Mora et al., 1974; Patel, 1974; Schlenker et al., 1968; Stein et al., 1972a, b; Stoch and Smythe, 1963, 1967), this association has been confirmed. Since social deprivation may well play a causal role in deficient mental development (e.g. Hess et al., 1968, 1969; Whiteman and Deutsch, 1968), the effects of nutritional and social variables on mental development are confounded. Klein et al. (1972) have attempted to estimate both the independent and the combined contributions of social deprivation and malnutrition to mental development. Their conclusion is that both malnutrition and social factors contribute importantly to psychological test performance. Analyses of the kind performed by these investigators require either the collection within a longitudinal prospective study of quantitative social status and social deprivation data of the kind that will permit statistical control of social factors, or a design that separates nutritional status and conditions of social deprivation, or preferably both.

II. THE INCAP STUDY

The preceding literature review indicated a number of characteristics of the design and choice of variables in major studies linking malnutrition and mental development that have prevented firm conclusions about the effects of mild-to-moderate PCM on intellectual functioning. The following section describes the design of the INCAP study; the final section summarizes the major results to date of that study.

A. Design

The INCAP investigation is a longitudinal quasi-experimental intervention study. Four villages from an Eastern, Spanish-speaking section of Guatemala, where malnutrition is endemic, were matched on a number of demographic, social, and economic characteristics. The experimental intervention was differential supplemental feeding of two matched groups; two villages were selected at random as "experimental" villages, in which a high protein–calorie drink similar to a popular corn-base gruel (atole) was made available twice daily at a central dispensary for all residents; and two were selected as "control" villages in which a drink was also made available to all who wished to partake. This drink (*fresco*), similar to Kool-Aid, contained about one-third of the calories contained in the *atole*. Both drinks contain enough iron, vitamins and minerals so that none of these substances should be limiting. In both experimental and control villages, free outpatient medical care has also been provided since the inception of the study.

The design is longitudinal; all children in the villages from birth to 7 years of age have been measured on both independent and dependent variables since 1969. Our primary concern here is with the children for whom we have information on supplemental food ingested by mother or child since the child's conception. The design is prospective in that data about a child's health and feeding are collected in advance of mental testing.

This design also permits us to examine change over time, from one testing to another, and thus to ask whether supplemental feeding during a certain period is related to increases in test performance during that same period, or at what stage of mental development the largest effects of the supplemental feeding are likely to appear, and whether there are critical periods in development during which malnutrition has an effect on mental development. Finally, the longitudinal design allows one to ask whether effects seen at one age persist to later ages, or are erased by intervening circumstances. However, these analyses require that the measures of mental development be highly reliable over short periods of time. A large amount of effort has therefore been directed at accurately assessing test–retest reliability at all ages.

B. Definition of the Independent Variable

The desired measure of nutritional status in this study is total nutrient ingestion by the mother during pregnancy and lactation and by the child up to the point of mental testing. This measure would be a sum of supplemental feeding and level of home diet of the mother and child during these periods. Home diet information that is individually reliable is extremely difficult to obtain because of vagaries of individual reporting, variability in what a child eats from day to day, and real changes in the biochemical and nutrient composition of various foods from year to year. In fact, estimates of the total home diet, based on dietary surveys, are less precise than supplemental food ingested, which can be measured very accurately. Thus, home diet serves as a family background variable that permits us to be sure that our villages do not differ in this respect.

C. Definition of the Dependent Variable

The dependent variable, mental development, has been measured with a series of tests that represent various theories and constructs about the processes of mental development. The approach has been purposely eclectic. In the light of the paucity of evidence on specific cognitive effects of malnutrition (e.g. evidence that there are effects on one type of processing and not on another) it was felt that this approach would provide the greatest chance of identifying which specific kinds of functioning are affected by malnutrition.

As previously noted, testing has been longitudinal; testing is begun with the newborn and repeated at 6, 15, and 24 months, then annually from 36 months to 84 months. At each age emerging abilities are measured, and the Test Battery becomes increasingly larger and more varied.

Neonates are tested within 10 days of birth with the Brazelton Neonatal Scale, and then at 6, 15, and 24 months with an infant scale composed of items compiled from the Bayley, Cattell, Gesell, and Merrill–Palmer Infant Scales. From 36 months to 7 years, children are tested annually on a battery of 24 tests chosen to tap memory, language, perceptual reasoning, learning, and abstract reasoning ability.

The Brazelton Scale was designed by T. Berry Brazelton and his colleagues, and is currently being employed by a number of investigators (e.g. Freedman and Freedman, 1969; Horowitz, 1973; Scarr-Salapatek and Williams, 1973). The scale assesses behavioural state (varying from deep sleep to crying), reaction to distal stimulation, and incipient social responses, in addition to neonatal reflexes. Inter-observer reliability among INCAP's testers has ranged from $r = 0.93$ to $r = 0.97$. Test–retest reliabilities for the summary variable employed in our analyses is $r = 0.67$ for a sample of 20 infants.

At 6, 15, and 24 months of age, infants in our study are tested with an infant battery called the Composite Infant Scale (CIS). Items are scored as mental or motor, according to traditional infant batteries. Test–retest and inter-observer reliabilities for the CIS are presented in Table 1. With the exception of the 24-month motor sub-scale ($r = 0.44$), these reliabilities are high, ranging from 0.82 to 0.99. The 24-month motor sub-scale appears to be approaching a ceiling at this age.

From 3 to 7 years of age, all children in the study are tested on an extensive battery of tests, known as the Preschool Battery. The tests in the Preschool Battery derive from a number of psychological theories. Some have their origins in learning theory (Digit and Sentence Memory, Memory for Designs and for Objects, Incidental Learning, and Reversal Discrimination Learning). The Embedded Figures Test (EFT), Matching Familiar Figures

Table 1
Test–retest and inter-observer reliability of psychological test measures

VARIABLE	Test–retest	N	Inter-observer	N
Brazelton Neonatal Assessment				
BG 1	0·67	20	0·97	20
Composite Infant Scale				
6 months mental	0·88	20	0·82	15
6 months motor	0·92	20	0·82	15
15 months mental	0·88	20	0·87	15
15 months motor	0·87	20	0·87	15
24 months mental	0·86	20	0·85	15
24 months motor	0·44	20	0·85	15
Preschool Battery (36 months)				
Cognitive Composite	0·87	40	—[a]	—
Embedded Figures Test Sum	0·81	20	0·99	140
Embedded Figures Test Time	0·63	20	0·99	140
Embedded Figures Test Adaptability	0·63	20	—[a]	—
Digit Span	0·65	20	0·99	140
Sentence Span	0·60	20	0·99	140
Reversal Discrimination Learning Sum	0·60	40	—[a]	—
Reversal Discrimination Learning Time	0·40	20	N.A.	—
Naming	0·86	20	1·00	140
Recognition	0·91	20	0·99	140
Verbal Inferences	0·62	20	N.A.	—
Line Velocity	0·65	20	0·99	140
Persistence on an Impossible Puzzle	0·45	20	0·97	140

[a] Not appropriate; score is constructed, not observed.

Test (MFF) and Haptic Visual Matching Test (HVM) are tests of perceptual analysis. Another sub-set are problem-solving tasks similar to those found in well-known intelligence tests (Picture Vocabulary, Incomplete Figures, Verbal Analogies (inferences), Block Design, a concept matching task, a coding task, and the Knox Cubes test, itself an early IQ test). Three tests are Piagetian (conservation of area, of continuous quantity and of matter (Piaget and Inhelder, 1969)), and one other is designed to measure neurological changes occurring between 5 and 7 (perception of the midline). Finally, two tests measure the non-cognitive capacities of inhibition and control (Draw-a-Line-Slowly) and persistence (measured by persistence in attempting to solve an impossible puzzle). This complete battery is administered to 5- to 7-year-olds, with 3- and 4-year-olds receiving only ten of the tests. Of those ten, two were not initiated until the Spring of 1971, and the data for these tests are still too sparse for profitable analysis. The remaining eight come primarily from the learning area (Digit and Sentence Memory and Discrimination Learning) and the problem-solving tasks

(Picture Vocabulary and Verbal Inference). The EFT is also administered, as well as two non-cognitive tests (Line Velocity on the Draw-a-Line-Slowly task, and Persistence on an Impossible Puzzle).

For a few tests, response time is measured (EFT and, Reversal Discrimination Learning) and an additional variable, "adaptability", has been generated for the EFT. This variable assesses how well the child adjusts his response time to the difficulty of each item. The Vocabulary test has two scores: number of pictures named and number recognized, which presumably measure somewhat different capabilities. In all, the Preschool Battery administered at 3 and 4 years yields 12 measures.

In addition to these variables, a composite variable, known as the Cognitive Composite, has also been constructed and is reported in the present paper. It consists of an equally weighted, standardized combination of five tests chosen to tap cognitive rather than motor or response time characteristics, and to give approximately equal representation to verbal and perceptual skills. Although the basis of selection was theoretical, the choice of variables and equality of weighting is congruent with a factor analysis of the test battery. The tests composing the Cognitive Composite at 3 and 4 years are Digit Memory, Vocabulary Recognition, Verbal Inferences, Embedded Figures, and Reversal Discrimination Learning.

Tests in the Preschool Battery were adapted to the research setting by a team consisting of American and Guatemalan psychologists, a Guatemalan cultural anthropologist, and Guatemalan testers and cultural informants (Klein et al., 1969). Two years of pre-testing, during which some tests went through as many as ten revisions, were devoted to developing test materials and instructions which both the intuitions of testers, as well as the performances of local (pilot sample) children of various ages suggested were appropriate and meaningful.

Both emic or local validity as well as Western validity of these measures has been assessed (Irwin et al., in press). Emic validity was assessed, first by employing adult's ratings of children's smartness (Klein et al., 1973), which is translated as "listura", in Spanish, and is associated with the concepts of alertness, independence, verbal facility, and good memory. Also employed in emic validity studies have been parental judgments of children's intellectual ability, as revealed by their assignments of chores to their child at early ages, and by their decisions concerning sending their child to school (and thus losing an important labour source), or not sending him (Irwin et al., in press). Non-local, or Western, validity has also been evaluated, through free behavioural observations of children's ability to engage in self-managed sequences (Nerlove et al., 1974; and Irwin et al., in press), and by school performance measures (Irwin et al., 1976; and Irwin et al., in press).

The result of these validity studies has been a considerable amount of converging evidence of both emic and Western validity; *listura* ratings, parental judgment measures, self-managed sequences and school performance have all been found to correlate significantly with various tests in the Preschool Battery. Each of these measures correlates with a different pattern of tests, suggesting that intellectual competence is a multi-dimensional concept in our rural Guatemalan research setting, and one which is somewhat different from the Western concept. Furthermore, the local concept of intellectual competence appears from our data to be defined quite differently for girls than for boys (Irwin *et al.*, in press).

D. Intervening Variables

The eventual aim of investigation in this area is a causal statement about nutritional effects on mental development. For instance, one would like to be able to assert convincingly that supplemental feeding has or has not contributed to or caused an improvement in mental functioning at a particular age. If we were manipulating only the independent variable, then the only considerations in making causal statements would be the statistical ones of significance and power. However, our treatment (the supplement) is voluntarily consumed, so it becomes important to be sure that observed relationships are not due to a third factor related to both. For instance, the association between family socio-economic level and mental test performance of these children is well documented (Klein *et al.*, 1972), and if the present study had found a positive association between amount of supplement ingested and socio-economic level (e.g. if richer families were more likely to make use of the supplemental feeding) then a positive association between mental test performance and supplement ingested could be attributed to the relationship each has with family SES rather than to a real relationship between nutritional status and mental development. However, our experimental design allows us to control for differences in SES; since the feeding is freely available to all those who wish it, lower SES children who attend frequently may be as well fed as children from higher SES levels who do not attend the supplementation centre, but have adequate home diets.

E. Results to Date

This section must be introduced with a caveat characteristic of longitudinal studies in progress: the data which will be presented in this paper are necessarily incomplete. Though the project was conceived as a study, from birth to 7 years, of cognitive development and its antecedents, data have thus far been collected in sufficient quantity to examine effects only to 48 months of age. Furthermore, as previously noted, data have not yet been analysed for all tests employed in the study, as many are not given before age five. Finally, only a portion of the planned analyses of the data now available has been completed. Even though our analyses are preliminary, those results which are available are both interpretable and provocative.

Two types of analyses have been performed to examine the effects of nutritional status on mental development. The first consists of analyses of variance employing a categorical measure of supplementation history. For these analyses, each child is assigned to one of three categories on the basis of the number of quarters (3-month intervals) during which he (or his mother during pregnancy and lactation) was well supplemented. To be labelled well-supplemented, a child had to receive adequate supplementation in at least 75% of the time intervals (3-month intervals) he has passed through. The required quantity of supplement, measured in calories, varies by age of the child. During pregnancy (3 intervals), the mother must have consumed at least 20,000 calories. When the child was between 0 and 6 months, the mother had to ingest 10,000 calories per quarter; from 6 to 24 months, either mother or child had to consume 10,000 calories per quarter, depending on whether the child was being breast fed; and from 24 to 84 months of age, the child had to ingest 10,000 calories per quarter. Children who had received (either directly or through the mother) less than 5,000 calories per quarter in at least 75% of their time intervals (10,000 during pregnancy) were labelled "poorly supplemented"; all other children were considered intermediate.

The second type of analysis performed employs a continuous measure; the total amount of supplement ingested by the child or by his pregnant or lactating mother. As will be noted, similar results were obtained with each type of analysis.

1. The Effects of Nutritional Supplementation on Psychological Test Performance

Table 2 presents a comparison of mean psychological test performance by level of supplementation and results of analyses of variance. Neonatal psychomotor development is indexed in Table 2 by Brazelton variable BG1, which includes the positive signs of vigour, visual following, social interest in the examiner, and motor maturity. No significant effects of nutritional status were obtained for this variable. Other analyses have revealed a strong effect

Table 2

Means and standard deviations of psychological test scores by supplementation ingestion category, and analyses of variance

Test	Nutritional status category: 0 $\bar{X}$	1 $\bar{X}$	2 $\bar{X}$	F	S.D. (pooled)	Sig. level
Brazelton Neonatal Assessment						
BG 1	38·83 (42)	36·00 (32)	39·05 (83)	0·66	13·12	NS
Composite Infant Scale						
6 months mental	74·17 (161)	76·45 (223)	77·81 (101)	2·54	13·44	<0·100
6 months motor	70·11 (161)	70·96 (223)	72·72 (101)	1·06	14·14	NS
15 months mental	61·77 (177)	66·30 (255)	72·31 (77)	16·40	14·14	<0·005
15 months motor	73·62 (177)	77·35 (255)	82·60 (77)	7·36	17·61	<0·005
24 months mental	59·44 (245)	65·39 (220)	67·85 (80)	17·46	13·76	<0·005
24 months motor	67·33 (237)	74·61 (218)	79·07 (80)	13·56	20·28	<0·005
Preschool Battery						
36 months						
EFT Sum	9·43 (270)	10·03 (232)	9·70 (50)	1·91	3·44	NS
EFT Time	3·15 (270)	3·01 (232)	2·89 (50)	1·58	11·45	NS
EFT Adaptability	0·009 (270)	0·013 (232)	0·072 (50)	1·48	0·240	NS
Digit Span	10·11 (224)	10·87 (197)	12·92 (44)	2·22	8·33	NS
Sentence Span	12·06 (228)	14·22 (210)	14·60 (48)	1·85	12·85	NS
RDL Sum	23·18 (232)	23·83 (220)	20·93 (45)	0·38	20·52	NS
RDL Time	2·34 (232)	2·07 (220)	1·83 (45)	5·13	11·49	<0·010
Vocabulary Naming	6·44 (262)	7·44 (227)	8·06 (50)	5·07	4·31	<0·010
Vocabulary Recognition	19·40 (262)	20·62 (227)	20·70 (50)	2·83	5·67	<0·050
Verbal Inferences	1·25 (120)	1·52 (106)	2·08 (12)	3·28	1·22	<0·050
Draw-A-Line Slowly (cm/sec)	10·59 (250)	9·34 (220)	9·44 (50)	4·84	4·55	<0·010

(*contd.*)

Table 2—(*contd.*)
Means and standard deviations of psychological test scores by supplementation
ingestion category, and analyses of variance

Test	Nutritional status category: 0 $\bar{X}$	1 $\bar{X}$	2 $\bar{X}$	F	S.D. (pooled)	Sig. level
Persistence on an Impossible Puzzle	5·98 (203)	5·86 (223)	6·46 (50)	0·25	5·40	NS
Cognitive Composite	−5·28 (278)	48·97 (237)	54·20 (50)	2·75	280·39	<0·100
48 months						
EFT Sum	4·63 (205)	4·83 (236)	5·55 (31)	1·74	2·60	NS
EFT Time	2·90 (205)	2·69 (236)	2·85 (31)	1·54	1·24	NS
EFT Adaptability	0·022 (205)	0·054 (236)	0·024 (31)	2·02	0·175	NS
Digit Span	21·05 (200)	21·43 (233)	19·24 (29)	0·409	12·37	NS
Sentence Span	30·07 (204)	34·10 (231)	36·07 (28)	2·62	20·37	<0·100
RDL Sum	33·48 (209)	37·93 (240)	40·97 (31)	3·69	20·15	<0·050
RDL Time	1·69 (209)	1·55 (240)	1·58 (31)	2·66	0·64	<0·100
Vocabulary Naming	11·70 (212)	13·89 (238)	14·10 (30)	11·18	5·19	<0·005
Vocabulary Recognition	25·59 (212)	27·30 (238)	26·63 (30)	5·83	5·35	<0·005
Verbal Inferences	2·76 (155)	3·05 (191)	3·00 (23)	1·50	1·54	NS
Draw-A-Line Slowly (cm/sec)	7·30 (203)	5·97 (229)	4·44 (31)	9·65	4·18	NS
Persistence on an Impossible Puzzle	9·01 (184)	9·06 (236)	8·00 (31)	0·359	6·62	NS
Cognitive Composite	−17·53 (215)	56·52 (241)	67·87 (31)	4·08	291·50	<0·025

of gestational supplementation on birth-weight, and a relationship between birth-weight and various measures from the Brazelton scale (Lasky *et al.*, 1975; Lechtig *et al.*, 1975). However, the relation of maternal supplementation to the Brazelton variable is almost zero. Presently, both Brazelton himself and we at INCAP are experimenting with construction of new summary variables, and the possibility of an effect of nutritional status on neonatal behaviour cannot yet be ruled out.

Also presented in Table 2 are the results of analyses of data for the Composite Infant Scale. Data for two summary variables are presented at each age at which the test is administered: mental score and motor score. Again, little effect is seen at 6 months of age. However, significant effects of supplementation ingestion emerge by 15 months, and these are particularly strong at 24 months. Individual items in the Composite Infant Scale at 15 and 24 months have also been examined separately. In general, these analyses indicate that the impact of supplement ingestion is more closely related to motoric and manipulative items within both the mental and motor scales than to more linguistic or cognitive items.

Table 2 presents, in addition, means and F ratios by nutritional status category for psychological test performance at 36 and 48 months of age. At 36 months, significant effects of supplementation category were found for response time on Reversal Discrimination Learning and on Vocabulary Naming, Vocabulary Recognition, Verbal Inferences and Draw-a-Line-Slowly. Cognitive Composite showed a marginally significant ($p < 0.10$) effect.

At 48 months as well, several tests showed significant effects associated with categories of supplementation ingestion: Vocabulary Naming, Vocabulary Recognition, Reversal Discrimination Learning Sum Correct, Draw-a-Line-Slowly, and Cognitive Composite score all showed significant effects at least at the 0·05 level, and Sentence Memory and Reversal Discrimination Learning response time were significantly different at the 0·10 level. Again, as at 36 months, well supplemented children responded faster on Reversal Discrimination Learning.

All analyses described thus far have combined data for boys and girls. We have also examined the possible existence of sex differences within our data by performing two-way ANOVAS of the supplementation ingestion categories by sex on the Composite Infant Scale at each age it is administered and on 36-month Preschool Battery scores. Small sample sizes prevented a similar analysis at 48 months. The only main effects for sex were on the Cognitive Composite ($F = 4.75$, $p < 0.05$) and Digit Memory tests ($F = 2.86$, $p < 0.10$) at 36 months, both favouring girls. A differential effect of supplement ingestion by sex was found for Draw-a-Line-Slowly. Well supplemented females succeeded in drawing a line significantly more slowly than poorly supplemented females ($F = 4.65$, $p < 0.05$) while the analogous comparison was not significant for males. In summary, neither strong mean sex differences nor differential responses to nutritional supplementation of the sexes are apparent in our data.

We have also examined the possibility that non-nutritional variables may be confounded with and responsible for the apparent effects of supplementation on mental development observed in our data. Among such variables considered have been testing effects, morbidity of subjects, parental cooperation with the project, village differences and attendance to supplementation centres. Following statistical analyses, all of these variables have been ruled out as possible alternative explanations of our observed effects.

Effects of repeated testing, for example, are not in evidence up to 48 months of age. Correlations between morbidity and psychology scores are near zero, as are those between field staff ratings of family cooperation with the project and psychology scores. Village differences were not present at the time the project began, according to baseline evaluations done at that time. Furthermore, we have recently compared the least well-supplemented (and presumably least affected by our project) children from our two types of villages (*fresco* and *atole*) to determine whether these two groups of children differ significantly in psychological test performance on any test. They do not.

In addition to examining the possibility of confounding effects of testing, morbidity, family cooperation and village differences, we have also examined the effect of attendance to the supplementation centres on Preschool Battery test performance. Children who come to the centres could conceivably be intellectually stimulated by attending *per se*. However, within-child regression analyses have revealed that for every 100 days of attendance, an increment of 0·007 standard deviation units on cognitive composite score was produced. Thus, attendance *per se* does not appear to be a significant confounding variable.

2. Timing of Nutritional Supplementation and Psychological Test Performance

Having found evidence of an effect of nutritional supplementation on psychological test performance, we wished to learn whether this effect is a cumulative one or whether a crucial period exists when supplementation is particularly likely to exert an effect on test performance. On an *a priori* basis, logical arguments could be advanced for each of these alternatives; if cognitive development is conceived of as a process of active and continual interchange with the environment (as Piaget, for example, has frequently argued) one might expect the effects of good or bad nutrition, mediated by energy levels, to cumulate throughout childhood. On the other hand, since central nervous system development is extremely rapid during pre- and immediately post-natal life, one might expect the effects of poor nutrition to be strongest during gestation or very early in life.

Our results to date are consistent with the latter hypothesis. Table 3 presents correlations and partial correlations of CIS Mental Scores at 6, 15

Table 3

The association of psychological test performance with supplement ingestion

Test	I — With supplement ingested during pregnancy		II — With total supplement ingested to time of testing		III — With total supplement ingested to time of testing (II), controlling for supplement ingested during pregnancy (I)		IV — With supplement ingested during pregnancy (I), controlling for post-natal supplement ingested to time of testing (II)	
	Boys	Girls	Boys	Girls	Boys	Girls	Boys	Girls
Composite Infant Scale — 6 months mental scale	0·11	0·13[a]	0·04	0·01	-·07	-·18[b]	0·13[a]	0·15[a]
Composite Infant Scale — 15 months mental scale	0·09	0·24[b]	0·14[a]	0·12[a]	0·11	-·07	0·01	0·22[a]
Composite Infant Scale — 24 months mental scale	0·20[b]	0·15[a]	0·19[b]	0·13[a]	0·11	0·04	0·12[a]	0·09
36 months Cognitive Composite	0·09	0·11	0·04	0·10	0·00	0·04	0·12[a]	0·05
36 months Verbal Inferences	0·36[b]	0·25[b]	0·20[b]	0·12[a]	0·04	-·03	0·33[b]	0·23[b]

N = approx. 250 for all tests except Verbal Inferences.
N = approx. 120 for Verbal Inferences.
[a] p <0·05.
[b] p <0·01.

and 24 months, and Cognitive Composite and Verbal Inferences scores at 36 months with supplement ingestion. Column I shows the correlation between supplement ingested during pregnancy by the mother and the child's later test performance; Column II shows the correlation between cumulative supplement ingested by the child and mother up to the time of psychological testing and the child's test performance; Column III shows the partial correlation of cumulative supplementation with test performance when maternal gestational supplementation is controlled by partialling; and Column IV shows the correlation of supplement ingested during pregnancy with child's test performance controlling for post-natal supplement ingestion. It will be noted that once gestational supplementation is partialled out of the correlations between total cumulative supplementation and test scores, virtually no relationship remains between later cumulative supplementation and test performance. On the other hand, the association of prenatal supplementation and subsequent test performance is unaffected by controlling for later supplementation. Thus, pregnancy appears to be the crucial period for supplementation as far as psychological test performance up to 36 months is concerned. The effect of supplementation during pregnancy on test performance after 36 months will be examined as more data become available for children followed since conception.

An additional analysis examining the importance of the timing of food supplementation on psychological test performance involves the comparison of siblings whose mothers ingested different amounts of the supplement across two successive pregnancies. These analyses have the advantage of controlling for potentially confounding variables which are constant within families. The slopes of gestational supplementation regressed on 6, 15 and 24 month total Composite Infant Scale performance are significant and much larger than those of cumulative supplement ingested at any later point up to the time of testing, replicating the results of our partial correlation analyses.

3. Family Socio-economic Status and Psychological Test Performance

Family socio-economic status has been measured regularly since the study began. We use a scale which combines ratings of each family's house (number of rooms and type of construction), parents' use of more modern clothing, and amount of direct teaching of children by parents and older siblings. This Composite SES score is standardized within village to control for inter-village differences in house style, etc., and then averaged across three surveys spanning five years.

The relationship of family SES to both home diet and supplement ingestion have been examined at 36 months. Home diet protein and calorie ingestion show modest correlations with family SES (for males: r prot. $= 0{\cdot}11$, p<$0{\cdot}05$; r cal. $= 0{\cdot}20$, p<$0{\cdot}01$; for females: r prot. $=0{\cdot}09$, n.s.; r cal. $= 0{\cdot}15$, p<$0{\cdot}01$). In contrast, a non-significant tendency was observed for children with lower family SES scores to ingest more food supplement.

We have also examined the relationship between family socio-economic status and psychological test performance. No relationship between SES and performance is evident for the Brazelton Neonatal Scale or for the Composite Infant Scale at 6, 15 or 24 months. We are in the midst of analyses of SES effects on 36- and 48-month variables but it appears that SES by 48 months becomes an important determinant of mental test performance.

We have also begun to examine the interactive effects of supplementation and family SES on cognitive test performance. The question motivating our examination of such an interaction is whether the effects of nutritional status or supplementation are greater among children from low as opposed to high SES families in our study villages. Two kinds of analyses have been performed to explore this question. The first has consisted of comparing test scores of least and best supplemented children (nutritional status categories 0 vs 2) in low and in high family SES groups. Such analyses have to date been performed for the Composite Infant Scale and for the preschool battery at 36 months. For the Composite Infant Scale, there is no evidence that effects of supplementation are greater among low SES children. However, at 36 months, several tests show a significant effect of supplementation only in the low SES group. These tests differ by sex, with an effect confined to low SES boys for Embedded Figures Sum Correct and Adaptability, Reversal Discrimination Learning Time and Vocabulary Recognition. Significant supplementation effects were confined to girls from low SES families for Embedded Figures Adaptability and Reversal Discrimination Learning Time.

Another type of analysis investigating the associations between nutritional status and psychological test performance within high and low SES groups has also been performed. This has consisted of constructing contingency tables examining a child's relative risk of being in the lowest (or highest) pentile (20%) of test performance as a function of being in each nutritional supplementation category.

These tables were first constructed for the entire population of children available, regardless of SES level. These, as well as tables broken down by SES, are shown in Table 4. Since before 15 months of age no association exists between supplementation category and relative risk of extreme test performance, tables for the Brazelton and 6-month Composite Infant Scale are omitted. For the Composite Infant Scale at 15 and 24 months and for the

Table 4
Relative risk of falling into extreme 20% according to supplementation ingestion and
socio-economic status

Sample size (N's)	Percentages	Chi-square
	Psychological test performance group	

VARIABLE: COMPOSITE INFANT SCALE 15-MONTH MENTAL SCORE

Total sample

		Low^a	Med.^{b}	High^c	Tot.	Low	Med.	High	Tot.	X^b	d.f.	p
Supplementation category:	0	52	101	24	177	29	57	14	100	27·1	4	<0·01
	1	44	157	54	255	17	62	21	100			
	2	5	46	26	77	6	60	34	100			
	T	101	304	104	509	20	60	20	100			

Low SES

	Low	Med.	High	Tot.	Low	Med.	High	Tot.	X^b	d.f.	p
0	23	50	6	79	29	63	8	100	18·4	4	<0·01
1	22	79	29	130	17	61	22	100			
2	2	28	13	43	5	65	30	100			
T	47	157	48	252	19	62	19	100			

High SES

	Low	Med.	High	Tot.	Low	Med.	High	Tot.	X^b	d.f.	p
0	27	45	18	90	30	50	20	100	11·7	4	<0·05
1	22	75	25	122	18	61	20	100			
2	3	18	13	34	9	53	38	100			
T	52	138	56	246	21	56	23	100			

VARIABLE: COMPOSITE INFANT SCALE 15-MONTH MOTOR SCORE

Total sample

		Low^a	Med.^{b}	High^c	Tot.	Low	Med.	High	Tot.	X^b	d.f.	p
Supplementation category:	0	43	114	20	177	24	64	11	100	16·2	4	<0·01
	1	45	159	51	255	18	62	20	100			
	2	5	54	18	77	6	70	23	100			
	T	93	327	89	509	18	64	17	100			

Low SES

	Low	Med.	High	Tot.	Low	Med.	High	Tot.	X^b	d.f.	p
0	17	55	7	79	22	70	9	100	9·1	4	NS
1	20	85	25	130	15	65	19	100			
2	3	29	11	43	7	67	26	100			
T	40	169	43	252	16	67	17	100			

High SES

	Low	Med.	High	Tot.	Low	Med.	High	Tot.	X^b	d.f.	p
0	23	55	12	90	26	61	13	100	7·6	4	NS
1	24	72	26	122	20	59	21	100			
2	2	25	7	34	6	74	21	100			
T	49	152	45	246	20	62	18	100			

Table 4—(*contd.*)

Sample size (N's)				Percentages				Chi-square		
				Psychological test performance group						

VARIABLE: COMPOSITE INFANT SCALE 24-MONTH MENTAL SCORE

Total sample

	Low[a]	Med.[b]	High[c]	Tot.	Low	Med.	High	Tot.	X^b	d.f.	p
0	70	140	35	245	29	57	14	100	35·5	4	<0·01
1	30	137	53	220	14	62	24	100			
2	3	53	24	80	4	66	30	100			
T	103	330	112	545	19	61	21	100			

Low SES

0	41	59	14	114	36	52	12	100	25·9	4	<0·01
1	18	69	27	114	16	61	24	100			
2	2	24	14	40	5	60	35	100			
T	61	152	55	268	23	57	21	100			

High SES

0	28	78	21	127	22	61	17	100	11·7	4	<0·05
1	12	68	25	105	11	65	24	100			
2	1	29	10	40	3	73	25	100			
T	41	175	56		15	64	21	100			

VARIABLE: COMPOSITE INFANT SCALE 24-MONTH MOTOR SCORE

Total sample

	Low[a]	Med.[b]	High[c]	Tot.	Low	Med.	High	Tot.	X^b	d.f.	p
0	65	127	45	237	27	54	19	100	20·4	4	<0·01
1	34	131	53	218	16	60	24	100			
2	6	49	25	80	8	61	31	100			
T	105	307	123	535	20	57	23	100			

Low SES

0	34	55	20	109	31	50	18	100	11·3	4	<0·05
1	18	63	32	113	16	56	28	100			
2	5	26	9	40	13	65	23	100			
T	57	144	61	262	22	55	23	100			

High SES

0	30	71	24	125	24	57	19	100	15·7	4	<0·01
1	16	68	20	104	15	65	19	100			
2	1	23	16	40	3	58	40	100			
T	47	162	60	269	17	60	22	100			

Table 4—(*contd.*)

	Sample size (N's)				Percentages				Chi-square		

VARIABLE: COGNITIVE COMPOSITE SCORE AT 36 MONTHS

Total sample

Supplementation category:	Low[a]	Med.[b]	High[c]	Tot.	Low	Med.	High	Tot.	X^b	d.f.	p
0	67	162	49	278	24	58	18	100	5·9	4	NS
1	39	145	53	237	16	61	22	100			
2	8	31	11	50	16	62	22	100			
T	114	338	113	565	22	60	20	100			

Low SES

	Low	Med.	High	Tot.	Low	Med.	High	Tot.	X^b	d.f.	p
0	39	71	13	123	32	58	11	100	10·1	4	<0·05
1	22	72	26	120	18	60	22	100			
2	4	16	5	25	16	64	20	100			
T	65	159	44	268	24	59	16	100			

High SES

	Low	Med.	High	Tot.	Low	Med.	High	Tot.	X^b	d.f.	p
0	26	88	36	150	17	59	24	100	0·5	4	NS
1	17	73	26	116	15	63	22	100			
2	4	15	6	25	16	60	24	100			
T	67	176	68	291	16	60	23	100			

[a] Lowest pentile.
[b] Middle 60% of scores.
[c] Highest pentile.

Cognitive Composite Score at 36 months, poorly supplemented children were much more likely to be in the lowest than the highest pentile of test scores. Well supplemented children were much more likely to be in the highest than the lowest pentile of test scores. Chi-square tests performed on the entire contingency tables (including the middle 60%) are significant at 15 and 24 months.

To examine the effect of SES on the relationship between nutritional status category and risk of falling in the lowest or highest pentile, contingency tables were constructed within low and high SES groups. As was the case for contingency tables constructed with the entire sample, no significant associations in either high or low SES groups were seen before 15 months.

At 15 and 24 months, the relative risk of falling into the lowest pentile of test performance as a function of nutritional status category was accentuated in the low SES group. For 15-month mental scores, for example, poorly supplemented (category 0) children in the low SES group were nearly four times as likely to be in the lowest pentile as in the highest pentile (29% vs 8%), whereas in the high SES group, the poorly supplemented child's probabilities of falling into lowest and highest pentiles were more similar (30% vs 20%). Similar accentuation of nutritional status category effects in the low SES group were observed for 15-month motor scores, 24-month mental scores, and also 24-month motor scores, though the accentuating effect of SES was less for this last score. The greater similarity between percentages of poorly supplemented children falling into highest and lowest pentiles observed among high SES children suggests that these children can be high scorers even without nutritional supplement, but that the low SES children's chances of being high scorers are more related to their nutrition. In both high and low SES groups, well supplemented children were more likely to be high than low scorers.

These patterns were repeated at 36 months; in the high SES group, a poorly supplemented child was about equally likely to fall into low or high pentile (17% vs 24%) but in the low SES group, a poorly supplemented child was about three times as likely to be in the lowest rather than the highest pentile (32% vs 11%). Also, in both high and low SES groups, well supplemented children were more likely to be high than low performers. In the low treatment group, SES and mental test performance were associated (p<0·01), but not in high (or middle) treatment groups.

Chi-square analyses performed on tables which include a performance category containing the middle 60% of children were more often significant for the low SES group than the high SES group. This was the case for the Composite Infant Scale mental and motor scores at 15 months, the mental score at 24 months, and the Cognitive Composite score at 36 months.

III. DISCUSSION

In this paper, we have presented some preliminary results from an on-going longitudinal study of the effects of nutritional and other environmental factors on mental development. Employing voluntarily consumed dietary supplementation, we have to date accumulated considerable evidence of an effect of nutritional status on mental development up to 48 months of age. These effects do not become apparent before 15 months, but are evident in performances on mental and motor infant scales at 15 and 24 months, and on a variety of cognitive tasks administered at 36 and 48 months of age. Our data suggest that the locus of these effects is in maternal nutrition during pregnancy.

While the INCAP study is not the first to find evidence of a relationship between malnutrition and mental development, these findings are especially important for several reasons. Unlike most previous studies, the present investigation has employed a prospective and precisely monitored intake measure of nutritional status, rather than approximate measures such as growth or retrospective reports and clinical records of episodes of malnutrition. Furthermore, by supplementing a population suffering from endemic mild-to-moderate malnutrition as opposed to studying severely malnourished clinic cases, we have been able to focus on the effects of levels of malnutrition which afflict enormous numbers of children growing up today.

In addition to differing in its definition of nutritional status and in level of malnutrition studied, the present study has employed a wide variety of culturally appropriate measures of mental development, as compared with the single global IQ-type measures frequently used in previous studies. At present it is difficult to discern patterns of effects on specific cognitive skills, since data for only a subset of tests and ages are yet available in sufficient quantity for analysis. However, the beginnings of such a description can be made. Our data indicate that general verbal reasoning processes are most consistently affected at 36 and 48 months. Variables showing an effect at these ages include Verbal Inferences, Vocabulary Naming, Vocabulary Recognition, and Response Tempo measures. Other tests showing an effect, and, of potentially equal importance, tests showing no effect, are heterogeneous and difficult to characterize, though relatively little effect was seen for Perceptual Analysis, Verbal Memory, and Persistence measures. Further specification of the nature of nutritional effects on mental development, and a subsequent attempt to identify mechanisms involved in such effects, must await collection of more data. So, of course, must resolution of the crucial question of whether the effects of malnutrition on mental development persist into later childhood and beyond.

As we have noted, previous studies of the relationship between malnutrition and mental development have not been able to go beyond the description of an association between the two to a convincing statement that malnutrition plays a causal role in deficient mental development. We have in the present paper reported a variety of analyses investigating and ultimately eliminating non-nutritional explanations of our findings. Poverty and accompanying social deprivation consistently accompany malnutrition and constitute plausible alternative explanations for the poor cognitive performances of malnourished children. Thus, the within-family regression analyses we have described, which indicate effects of nutritional status on cognitive performance while controlling for family SES level, constitute the strongest evidence ever gathered for a direct and causal link between malnutrition and deficient mental development.

Out data permit us to dismiss the possibility that family socio-economic level alone can explain the lower test performances of less well nourished sample children. However, our findings also indicate an important role of socio-economic level in mental development. SES was seen to interact with nutrition such that children from poorer families were more strongly affected by nutritional supplementation than children from less poor families. Furthermore, the pervasive power of poverty to depress intellectual development was attested to by the presence, within a population among whom the range of wealth and opportunity is severely restricted, of significant cognitive test score differences between children from poorer as compared to less poor families.

ACKNOWLEDGEMENTS

We would like to acknowledge support by Contract N01-HD-5-0640 from the National Institute of Child Health and Human Development, Bethesda, Maryland.

Portions of this paper were presented at the Fourteenth Meeting of the PAHO Advisory Committee on Medical Research, Washington, DC, USA, July 7-10, 1975, and at a Conference on Ecological Factors in Human Development, The University of Surrey, Guildford, England, July 13-17, 1975.

REFERENCES

Bayley, N. (1968). *Am. Psychol.* **23**, 1–17.
Béhar, M. (1968). *In* "Malnutrition, Learning and Behavior" (Eds N. S. Scrimshaw and J. E. Gordon), p. 30. MIT Press, Cambridge, Mass.
Berry, J. W. (1969). *Int. J. Psychol.* **4**, 119–128.
Biesheuvel, S. (1949). *In* "The Yearbook of Education" (Ed. G. B. Jeffrey), p. 90. Evans, New York.
Birch, H. G. (1972). *Am. J. publ. Hlth.* **62**, 773–784.
Birch, H. G., Piñeiro, C., Alcalde, E., Toca, T. and Cravioto, J. (1971). *Pediat. Res.* **5**, 579–585.
Botha-Antoun, E., Babayan, S. and Harfouche, J. K. (1968). *J. trop. Pediat.* **14**, 112–115.
Boutourline-Young, H., Manza, B., Louyot, P., El Amouri, T., Redjeb, H., Boutourline, E. and Tesi, G. (1973). "Social and environmental factors accompanying nutrition." Biannual Meeting of the International Association of Behavioural Sciences. Symposium on the Effects of Nutrition and Development, Ann Arbor, Mich., August 21–24.

Brockman, L. M. and Ricciuti, H. N. (1971). *Devel. Psychol.* 4, 312–319.
Cabak, V. and Najdanvic, R. (1965). *Archs Dis. Childh.* 40, 532–534.
Champakam, S., Srikantia, S. G. and Gopalan, C. (1968). *Am. J. clin. Nutr.* 21, 844–852.
Chase, H. P. and Martin, H. P. (1970). *New Eng. J. Med.* 282, 933–939.
Chávez, A., Martínez, C. and Yoschine, T. (1974). *In* "Early Malnutrition and Mental Development" (Eds J. Cravioto, L. Hambreus and B. Vahlquist), p. 211. Almquist and Wiksell, Uppsala.
Cravioto, J. and DeLicardie, E. R. (1968). *In* "Malnutrition, Learning and Behavior" (Eds N. S. Scrimshaw and J. E. Gordon), p. 252. MIT Press, Cambridge, Mass.
Cravioto, J. and DeLicardie, E. R. (1970). *Am. J. Dis. Child.* 120, 404–410.
Cravioto, J. and Robles, B. (1965). *Am. J. Orthopsychiat.* 35, 449–464.
Cravioto, J., DeLicardie, E. R. and Birch, H. G. (1966). *Pediatrics* 38, 319–372.
DeLicardie, E. R. and Cravioto, J. (1974). *In* "Early Malnutrition and Mental Development" (Eds J. Cravioto, L. Hambreus and B. Vahlquist), p. 134. Almquist and Wiksell, Uppsala.
Edwards, L. D. and Craddock, L. J. (1973). *Med. J. Aust.* 1, 880–884.
Evans, D. E., Moodie, A. D. and Hansen, J. D. L. (1971). *S. Afr. Med. J.* 45, 1413–1426.
Freedman, D. G. and Freedman, N. C. (1969). *Nature* 224, 1227.
Hertzig, M. E., Birch, H. G., Richardson, S. A. and Tizard, J. (1972). *Pediatrics* 49, 814–824.
Hess, R. D., Shipman, V. C., Brophy, J. E. and Bear, R. M. (1968). "Report to the Graduate School of Education." University of Chicago, Chicago.
Hess, R. D., Shipman, V. C., Brophy, J. E. and Bear, R. M. (1969). "Report to the Graduate School of Education." University of Chicago, Chicago.
Horowitz, F. D. (1973). Personal communication.
Irwin, M., Schafer, G. and Feiden, C. (1974). *J. Cross-cult. Psychol.* 5, 407–423.
Irwin, M., Engle, P. L., Klein, R. E. and Yarbrough, C. (1976). DDH-INCAP. In preparation.
Irwin, M., Klein, R. E., Engle, P. L., Yarbrough, C. and Nerlove, S. (In press). *Ann. N.Y. Acad. Sci.*
Jelliffe, D. G. (1966). "The Assessment of Nutritional Status of the Community." World Health Organization, Geneva.
Klein, R. E. (1971). *In* "Amino Acid Fortification of Protein Foods" (Eds N. S. Scrimshaw and M. Altschul), p. 339. MIT Press, Cambridge, Mass.
Klein, R. E. (1976). DDH-INCAP. In preparation.
Klein, R. E., Gilbert, O., Canosa, C. A. and De León, R. (1969). "Performance of malnourished in comparison with adequately nourished children on selected cognitive tasks (Guatemala)." Annual Meeting of the Association for the Advancement of Science. Boston, Mass., December.
Klein, R. E., Habicht, J-P. and Yarbrough, C. (1971). *Adv. Pediat.* 18, 75–91.
Klein, R. E., Freeman, H. E., Kagan, J., Yarbrough, C. and Habicht, J-P. (1972). *J. Health Soc. Behav.* 13, 219–225.
Klein, R. E., Freeman, H. E. and Millett, R. (1973). *J. Psychol.* 84, 219–222.
Lasky, R. E., Lechtig, A., Delgado, H., Klein, R. E., Engle, P., Yarbrough, C. and Martorell, R. (1975). *Am. J. Dis. Child.* 129, 566–570.
Latham, M. C. (1974). *Physiol. Rev.* 54, 541–565.

Lechtig, A., Delgado, H., Lasky, R. E., Klein, R. E., Engle, P. L., Yarbrough, C. and Habicht, J-P. (1975). *Am. J. Dis. Child.* **129**, 434–437.
Liang, P. H., Hie, T. T., Jan, O. H. and Giok, L. T. (1967). *Am. J. clin. Nutr.* **20**, 1290–1294.
McKay, H. E., McKay, A. C. and Sinisterra, L. (1969). "Behavioral effects of nutritional recuperation and programmed stimulation of moderately malnourished preschool age children." Meeting of the American Association for the Advancement of Science Symposium. Boston, Mass.
Mönckeberg, F. (1968). *In* "Malnutrition, Learning and Behavior" (Eds N. S. Scrimshaw and J. E. Gordon), p. 269. MIT Press, Cambridge, Mass.
Mönckeberg, F., Tisler, S., Toro, S., Gattás, V. and Vega, L. (1972). *Am. J. clin. Nutr.* **25**, 766–772.
Montelli, T. B., Ribeiro, M., Ribeiro, M. and Ribeiro, M. A. C. (1974). *J. trop. Pediat.* **20**, 201–204.
Mora, J. O., Amézquita, A., Castro, L., Christiansen, J., Clement-Murphy, J., Cobos, L. F., Cremer, H. D., Dragastin, S., Elias, M. F., Frankling, D., Herrera, M. G., Ortiz, N., Pardo, F., Paredes, B. de, Ramos, C., Riley, R., Rodríguez, H., Vuori-Christiansen, L., Wagner, M. and Stare, F. J. (1974). *Wld Rev. Nutr. Diet.* **19**, 205–236.
Nerlove, S. B., Roberts, J. M., Klein, R. E., Yarbrough, C. and Habicht, J-P. (1974). *Ethos.* **2**, 265–295.
Patel, B. D. (1974). *In* "Early Malnutrition and Mental Development" (Eds J. Cravioto, L. Hambreus and B. Vahlquist), p. 155. Almquist and Wiksell, Uppsala.
Piaget, J. and Inhelder, B. (1969). "The Psychology of the Child." Basic Books, New York.
Pollit, E. and Granoff, D. (1967). *Rev. Interam. Psicol.* **1**, 93–102.
Read, M. S. (1975). IBRO Satellite Symposium on the Growth and Development of the Brain. New Delhi, India, October. Raven Press, New York. In press.
Scarr-Salapatek, S. and Williams, M. L. (1973). *Child Dev.* **44**, 94–101.
Scribner, S. and Cole, M. (1973). *Science* **182**, 553–559.
Schlenker, J. D., Bossio, V. and Romero, E. R. (1968). *Arch. Latino-amer. Nutr.* **18**, 173–184.
Stein, Z., Susser, M., Saenger, G. and Marolla, F. (1972a). *Science* **178**, 708–713.
Stein, Z., Susser, M., Saenger, G. and Marolla, F. (1972b). *T. Soc. Geneesk.* **50**, 766–774.
Stoch, M. B. and Smythe, P. M. (1963). *Archs Dis. Childh.* **38**, 546–552.
Stoch, M. B. and Smythe, P. M. (1967). *S. Afr. Med. J.* **41**, 1027–1030.
Warren, N. (1973). *Psychol. Bull.* **80**, 324–328.
Whiteman, M. and Deutsch, M. (1968). *In* "Social Class, Race, and Psychological Development" (Eds M. Deutsch, I. Katz and A. R. Jensen), p. 86. Holt, Rinehart and Winston, Inc., New York.
Witkop, C. J., Baldizón, G. C., Castro, O. R. P. and Umaña, R. (1970). *In* "Second Symposium on Oral Sensation and Perception" (Ed. J. S. Bosma). Thomas, Springfield, Illinois.

4 | Coping with Unfamiliar Cultures

RONALD TAFT

I. INTRODUCTION

Life requires a continual series of adaptations to new environments since no situation is ever quite identical with the one that has gone before. This chapter deals with a special case of human adaptation: namely that required to cope with a new and unfamiliar culture. Usually this is associated with a change from one society, or subsection of a society, to another, although even minor changes in social environment can create the need for short-term cultural adaptation. This paper, however, is concerned with the major cultural gaps that occur either as a result of the person's locomotion from one society to another, or owing to revolutionary changes in his social environment.

The process of coping with a new culture requires the learning of new responses and skills, and the acquisition of new information. This chapter will be largely devoted to an analysis of the process of culture learning in its various manifestations. The analysis will use concepts derived from psychology, sociology and anthropology and an attempt will be made to place the process of coping with new cultures within the context of the literature on such basic social processes as socialization (and resocialization), the social psychology of the relationship between an individual and social groups, the concept of competence and a general theory of behaviour involving such basic processes as cognition and skilled motor behaviour.

This approach implies that adaptation to unfamiliar cultures should be viewed as a special case of responding to a new environmental event, where that event is complex, enduring and social in nature and where it has a cultural context that is unfamiliar to the actor. The approach also implies that a wide variety of situations can be treated as examples of adaptation to unfamiliar cultures. It is to this latter point that we now turn.

II. THE VARIETIES OF CULTURE COPING SITUATIONS

This section will illustrate a variety of situations that involve the need to cope with unfamiliar cultures, some due to locomotion to a new locality and some not. Many of these situations have been subjected to theoretical analysis and research investigation, but there has, on the whole, been considerable compartmentalization between the studies with little attempt to integrate them.

An extensive list of examples of situations that involve cultural adaptation is presented in Table 1 under five main headings: Sojourning, Settling, Sub-cultural Mobility, Segregation, Changes in Society. The first two imply geographical locomotion, while the latter three do not. Examples of non-locomotive changes that require coping with new cultures have been dealt with by writers on "adult socialization" and "resocialization" (e.g. Brim and Wheeler, 1966; Riley *et al.*, 1969; Coulter and Taft, 1973) referring to such situations as the treatment of social deviants, adjustment to retirement, and induction into a profession. Studies of such processes as adjustment to marriage, transition from school to work, and induction into university are also relevant, as are those on the acceptance of cultural innovations (e.g. Rogers, 1962) and "modernization" (e.g. Inkeles and Smith, 1974). Then there are the situations in which a person is incorporated into a new, encompassing society such as armed services (e.g. Dornbusch, 1955; Rootman, 1972), religious orders (Wick, 1971), residential university (Newcomb, 1943), prison (Garabedian, 1963), concentration camp (Bettelheim, 1943), prison camp (Schein, 1956), rehabilitation centre (Curle, 1947), and mental hospital (Goffman, 1961).

There is another set of studies that deal with situations that arise from locomotion to new locations; these include studies of foreign students (e.g. Bennett *et al.*, 1958; Bochner and Wicks, 1972), Peace Corps trainees (Guthrie, 1975), foreign business men, missionaries, diplomats, technical advisors and administrators (Foa and Chemers, 1967). These studies, strangely enough, seldom refer to the related problems of anthropologists doing field-work (treated specifically in Kimball and Watson, 1972) nor to the coping problems met by sight-seeing tourists (De Sola Pool, 1958; MacCannell, 1973).

Finally, there are studies of the adjustment of settlers who have immigrated from one community to another with the intention of participating as a *member* of the new society (e.g. Taft, 1966). Since my own work on cultural contacts has mainly been concerned with this latter situation, much of my treatment will be oriented towards it. Immigration represents a classical situation where a newcomer is required to cope with an unfamiliar culture, although it has some characteristics that are not universal

Table 1

A categorization of situations requiring coping with an unfamiliar culture

Geographical locomotion		Non-locomotion		
Sojourning	Settling	Sub-cultural mobility	Segregation	Changes in society
Explorers, anthropologists and other social scientists	Voluntary immigrants	Social-class mobility	Prisoners	Colonized or occupied nation
Journalists	Internal migrants from rural to urban areas	Entry into a profession	Segregated minorities	Natural disaster or imbalance
Business representatives	Refugees	Transition from school to work	Army and Navy recruits	Social disorganization
Colonial officials and diplomatic representatives	Participators in group immigration e.g. members of a migrant's family, employees of a "migrating" business	Retirement	Religious order members	Cultural destruction
Espionage agents		Inter-communal contacts within a pluralistic society	Boarding school and college residents	Innovation and modernization
Army personnel		Marriage	Old age home residents	Fashion swings
Technical consultants and aid workers	Captives and slaves		Hospital patients	
Limited contract workers (Gastarbeiter)			Mentally ill patients	
Tourists				
Students				

to cultural coping. For example, an immigrant needs to be concerned with his relationship to the new society while a temporary sojourner or traveller does not necessarily have to be so.

It seems unfortunate that so little attempt has been made to analyse the communalities and differences between situations that require coping with unfamiliar cultures. Brein and David's excellent review (1971) for example, deliberately deals only with the adjustment of sojourners and no mention is made at all of the literature on immigrants, let alone that on segregatees entering a total institution. Similarly, Alfred Schutz's treatment of the "stranger" (1964) specifically excludes transient contacts. All of these studies could help to inform each other, since all of the situations involve the necessity for participating in social contacts with new protagonists, learning to perceive new social cues and communicating information to others using unaccustomed signs, symbols and media.

A. Variations in the Difficulty of the Coping Task

The magnitude of the coping task imposed by a change in one's cultural environment varies considerably according to the size of the gap, the abruptness of the discontinuity, the salience of the changes to the person's behavioural functioning, and the degree to which the new environment encompasses that functioning. Sometimes the gap is an easy one to bridge and sometimes it is difficult. Sister Dignam (1966) has aptly described the "seemingly interminable gap" that occurs in the transition of a young woman from secular life to life within a religious order, where she relinquishes her grasp of the familiar past structure but has not yet taken a firm grasp of the new. Dignam uses Erik Erikson's analogy of a trapeze artist in mid-air to describe the situation: the greater the distance between the trapeze bars, the more difficult the transition.

The most extreme case of persons in contact across cultures are those described by Gajdusek (1970) in his treatment of the behaviour of isolated natives in their first confrontation with Western explorers, missionaries or officials. They had no relevant knowledge at all of how to interact with the strangers, but attempted to cope by engaging in echopraxia and echolalia, so that, for instance, when the stranger stroked his chin or smiled they stroked their chins or smiled, respectively.

B. Factors determining the difficulty of culture coping

The greater the disparity between the familiar and the unfamiliar culture, the more difficult it is to bridge the gap. Such factors as the language used and known by the members of the new society, its economic structure and level of technology, the size and complexity of the formal society and its political structure, its specific ceremonies and rituals, and the style of primary social relationships are all highly relevant to the size of that gap. The greater the differences in these respects, the more difficult the task of coping, other things being equal.

One of the relevant variables that may not be "equal" is the abruptness of the change; this can be modified either by the existence of a transitional stage or by the lack of pressure to change. The transitional period may be a contrived training course preparatory to making the change such as, for example, the America Peace Corps training schools, or courses aimed at the integration of recent arrivals into a new society, such as the Ulpanim courses in Hebrew for new immigrants in Israel.

In the case of immigrants, the abruptness of the cultural change is partly a function of the circumstances of immigration; thus, a refugee who has left his country under conditions of crisis has to undergo a more abrupt change than a voluntary emigrant who has had time to contemplate and prepare for his transition. Gradualness in change may arise in other ways also; familiogenic changes between generations are less abrupt than the idiogenic changes that occur in one person's lifetime, despite all that has been said (by Stonequist and others) about the cultural stresses in second generation immigrants. Idiogenic changes in a newcomer to a culture are less abrupt when he is able to fall back into a familiar and accepting group within the new society for his primary social relationships, his recreation and catharsis for his frustrations and balm for his psychic wounds.

The effect of the abruptness of the change on the style of coping is not a simple one. No relationship was found, for instance, between the degree of identification with Australia and the presence of a large community of recent immigrants from the same country (Taft, 1966, p. 67). Nor were there any consistent differences in this respect between refugees and voluntary immigrants: for example, Polish refugees (mostly former peasants) were better integrated to life in Australia in almost every respect than were voluntary immigrants from Italy.

Whether or not an abrupt change from one culture to another is debilitating to a person's functioning will depend partly on the degree to which the change is salient to his behaviour. The definition of *salience* is not easy, but it involves the concept that some areas of activity are more central to the ego than are others; i.e., they are more closely associated with the person's self-esteem. For example, a stranger who has high need for autonomy would find it more difficult to adapt to a culture which denies him much space of free movement; if the need for autonomy is central to his self concept, he may even despise himself for accepting this lack of indepen-dence without a struggle. Apart from its relationship to the ego, the salience of cultural differences to the functioning of a newcomer may also be related to such factors as his degree of emotional responsiveness to the particular aspect of living (e.g. what and how to eat), the age at which he was enculturated in this aspect, and the complexity of its association with other aspects of his life. Further, the relevance of the cultural difference to the difficulty of coping is affected by the person's attitude towards change itself: if his original culture is one that accepts the need for, and even the value of, cultural change, this will make it easier for him to cope with a new one than if he has been taught that continuity of tradition is a virtue.

Finally, it is suggested that the difficulty in coping is a function of the degree to which the new culture is all-encompassing. Persons who move into new societies often do not wish to adapt any more than they need to, and it is possible to minimize this requirement by such devices as avoiding contact as much as possible, or by immersing oneself in a group in the new society that embodies the old culture. For example a foreign student can reduce his adaptation to the bare minimum required in order to fulfil his role as a student, and otherwise he may confine his social life to his fellow countrymen.

Very often the reason for a sojourn in a new country is a pragmatic one — perhaps to learn a vocation, obtain a degree or even merely to enhance one's prestige in the eyes of the folks back home — and this may require little adaptation. It could be just another Western misconception to project into the mind of a student from a developing country an intrinsic desire to learn about the language and culture of the Western society to which he has come for study, beyond the minimal level required for coping with everyday life. A peripheral contact with the new culture is typical of many culture contact situations; for example, Ruth Hartley (1960) found in her study of the effect of entry into college that some of the students could minimize their involvement with the institution by still using their neighbourhood group as their primary reference group. It would have been different if the students had been "totally immersed" in college by being in residence on an isolated campus, as in the studies at Bennington (Newcomb, 1943) and Vassar (Sanford, 1956).

The best representation of a fully encompassing society is Goffman's description of a total institution which he defines as "a place of residence and work where a large number of like-situated individuals, cast off from the society for an appreciable period of time, together lead an enclosed, formally administered round of life" (1961, p. 11). The examples given by Goffman are mental hospitals and prisons in which the inmates are involuntary and in which they are differentiated almost completely from the staff who enforce certain standards of behaviour from them. He points out that even such encompassing institutions as these often do not totally control the behaviour of their inmates who can engage in "secondary adjustment" behaviour; that is, unauthorized, but acceptable, ways of pursuing individual gratification. The existence of such opportunities varies with the totalness of the institution. The same applies to the situation in which a settler or sojourner who enters an authoritarian society may find himself. If the new society is totalitarian or one that follows some ideological orthodoxy, the newcomer may need to conform rapidly to assigned roles which cover all aspects of his life, much like the inmate of a total institution, and there may even be a class of guardians of the orthodoxy (police, priests' assistants, vigilantes) corresponding to the staff of these institutions. A similar position pertains in a partial way even to non-totalitarian societies if the newcomer is an indentured labourer who has immigrated under a restrictive contract as, for example, was the case with refugees in Australia in the years 1948-52, and in other labour-hungry countries in the seventies (the Gastarbeiter), as well as for Africans in the South African mining areas.

III. LEARNING TO BECOME A MEMBER OF A SOCIETY

The process of adapting to a new society corresponds in some respects to that involved in becoming a member of society in the first place, although there is the important difference that resocialization and reculturation involve a transformation of an existing state of affairs. In order to investigate the nature of these transformation processes we shall first examine briefly the nature of socialization and enculturation.

A. Socialization and Resocialization

"Socialization refers to all the factors and processes which make one human being fit to live in the company of others" (Kelvin, 1970, p. 270). This includes training in basic human social processes, for example dialogue, bargaining, status awareness, emotional control and sense of obligation, without which an individual could not cope with any society, whether it be his indigenous one or an alien one. The form in which this training is given is relevant to the particular culture and is embodied in the enculturation process.

Berger and Luckmann (1967) point out that in primary socialization the cultural forms for expressing basic social behaviour are internalized from the teaching of early "significant others" and become "*the* world, the only existent and conceivable world" (p. 134), with a strong emotional and protective overtone. The products of primary socialization provide the child with an "understanding" of his world and with "institutionalized programs for everyday life". These are responded to quasi-automatically as the real world and they form part of the child's concept of his own identity. The "familiar" culture then is the "home world", the one that is associated closely with the family, or quasi-family. In obverse, an "unfamiliar" culture is one that is at variance with the primary socialization, and is out of harmony with the person's basic values and concept of self.

The products of secondary socialization which are derived from "the sub-worlds of institutions" have a lower level of reality for the person than those based on the primary and are more readily adapted to a changed situation. They have a lower level of "subjective inevitability" and require regular validation by the external society in the course of social interaction. Typically, the new environment can be coped with by making use of past learning adapted slightly to fit the situation in the same way as in secondary socialization to the original culture.

The distinction between primary and secondary socialization, however, is one of degree rather than of kind and Berger and Luckmann seem to exaggerate the sharpness of the boundaries. Some of the features of secondary socialization can be associated with dynamic aspects of personality that are as important to an individual as some of the features of his primary socialization; for example the professional identity of an actor may be so important to his status or his self-expression needs that the lack of work in his profession may lead to mental breakdown (see Taft, 1961, for examples of this in the case histories of actors).

The fact that extreme cultural discontinuities require resocialization of the concept of self raises the question whether some kind of desocialization is also necessary before resocialization can occur. Eisenstadt (1954) has argued that immigration automatically implies desocialization, that is, a shrinkage of social roles and a transformation of the self-image and values. This is supported by Bar-Yosef (1968) who refers to a "disturbance of the immigrant's role system" and the undoing of his socialized "adjustment patterns". Clearly, as resocialization takes place in the course of coping with new cultures, some old social learning is shed, at least in the sense that new responses are adopted in situations that would previously have evoked different ones. But it takes a more profound and all-encompassing situation to require the desocialization of the concept of self and values to which Eisenstadt refers. Brim (Brim and Wheeler, 1966, pp. 27–28) argues that it is virtually impossible to resocialize the basic values of adults and suggests that the only changes that can be hoped for would be in overt role behaviour; a person can be pressed to conform to role requirements but not to agree with the values underlying it. Goffman (1961), also doubts whether true resocialization often occurs in practice — even in a "total institution" — and he describes the more typical process rather as one of "disculturation" (Sommer's term) in which old, presumably undesirable, role performances and attitudes are "untrained". As he puts it "total institutions do not really look for cultural victory" (1961, p. 23), and in this sense the situation of the inmate is closer to that of a sojourner than a settler.

Sometimes, however, even in the case of a sojourner, the new culture does have "a victory" and the newcomer becomes fully resocialized as a result of group support, institutional legitimation of the new identity, and the presence of new "significant others" to replace those of the person's childhood. Even then, as Berger and Luckmann point out, total transformation is accomplished only in stages during which the resocializing individual passes through a series of supportive group memberships, commencing as probationers and novitiates and only slowly advancing to their new identity. During this transition period they are segregated from their old social groups to protect them from conflicting validations of their identity.

Other writers have described situations in which primary resocialization has actually occurred, usually under conditions involving extreme stress (e.g. concentration camp inmates, Bettelheim, 1943; prisoners of war, Schein, 1956; and returned prisoners of war, Curle, 1947). In each one of these cases the common features associated with the change were the shock effects involving heightened emotions associated with suffering, and the importance of social relationships — either between peers or between authorities and inmates. Curle deliberately set up transitional communities in order to provide a new reference group to help the former prisoners accept "the cultural validity of new roles" in civilian society, apparently with considerable success (Curle and Trist, 1947).

A dramatic and moving (and possibly fictional) account of desocialization under quite different circumstances is presented in the writings of Carlos Castaneda who describes his period of 10 years "apprenticeship" with the Yaqui Indian sorcerer, Don Juan. He learnt to divest himself of his "personal history", or to "stop the world". In Don Juan's words: "What stopped inside you yesterday was what people have been telling you the world is like. You see, people tell us from the time we are born that the world is such and such and so and so, and naturally we have no choice but to see the world the way people have been telling us it is," (1974, p. 268). In other words Castaneda has (or, rather, claims that he has) divested himself of his primary socialization, but, unlike the other resocialization situations described, the philosophy which Castaneda has now accepted is that one should have "no personal history", no person or group to "pin you down with their thoughts" (p. 29), i.e., no society and no norms, neither the original one nor a replacement for it.

All of the examples given of resocialization involve prior desocialization which might seem to suggest that this is necessary. They also represent extreme situations applying to "segregatees" where there is a total environmental control; the need for desocialization may not apply to the other comparable situations described in Table 1. There is evidence, both experimental (e.g. Bem, 1967) and naturalistic (Taft, 1966) that changes in behaviour can lead to changes in expressed attitudes without any obvious desocialization occurring. However, such changes are effected only gradually and under certain circumstances and it is not known how deeply they go in altering the concept of self and basic attitudes towards life. A further consideration of this question will be raised in connection with the relationship between acculturation and changes in identification.

B. Enculturation and Reculturation as Psychological Processes

In the course of becoming a member of a society a child is enculturated to the particular ways and general style of life that constitute its culture, and as a consequence becomes culturally competent. For this purpose we shall follow Inkeles' definition of a culture as "the knowledge, skills, attitudes, values, needs and motivation, cognitive affective and conative patterns which shape [an individual's] adaptation to the physical and projective cultural setting in which they live" (1969, pp. 615–16).

This section will be devoted to an analysis of the main psychological processes involved in becoming competent in a particular culture. These processes will be treated with respect to three broad discriminable but interrelated aspects: the cognitive, the dynamic, and the performance.

1. Cognitive Aspects of Enculturation

The cognitive training imparted by a society in the course of enculturation includes the belief systems about the nature of the world — cosmic, physical and social — and the knowledge that is necessary for functioning effectively. The culture partly shapes the individual's way of dealing with his perceptual world and provides such cognitive structures as schemata, concepts, categories, stereotypes, expectations, attributions, subjective probabilities, associations and images. At a more molar level the culture provides rules, systems of logic, collective memories, beliefs, ideologies, connotation networks for understanding social roles, and verbal and non-verbal language systems. (There is space here for dealing with only a few of these aspects. A broader coverage is to be found in Triandis *et al.* (1971).) By definition, an unfamiliar culture is one with respect to which such knowledge is lacking and a central issue in cross-cultural psychology is the question of how we get to know other cultures.

The process of enculturation to a society can be treated as the acquisition of the means by which an individual's behaviour may be rendered meaningful to the other members of his society, and vice versa. This is achieved by the dissemination of the necessary knowledge and skills so that both intentional and unintentional communications can be understood and responded to appropriately. Thus, the major dissonance generated by the advent of a newcomer to an unfamiliar culture lies in the sphere of communication. This is recognized, for example, in Brein and David's treatment of the adjustment of sojourners (1971) which is oriented towards the problems of intercultural communication.

Since we are interested specifically in the adaptation to a culture of persons who are unfamiliar with it, a further cognitive aspect of enculturation that handicaps the social functioning of an adult newcomer should be mentioned. I refer to the common memories, myths, and historical traditions that help to facilitate communication between the members of a society and also to heighten a feeling of common identity. The newcomer who does not know the culture may be handicapped as much by his ignorance of the information that is more or less common to the members of the society as by his ignorance of, say, the conventions of colloquial language usage. One of the problems in the rehabilitation of former prisoners, for example, is their feeling of incompetence arising from their ignorance of recent events and social developments that are well known to their primary groups and to the public at large.

The orderliness of cultures. Kelvin (1970) has suggested a psychological approach to the role of the culture of a society in enabling its members to understand and respond effectively to each other. He argues that behaviour depends upon prediction of events; one cannot cope with one's environment unless one has expectations with respect to it and unless those expectations correspond with reality to a reasonable extent. It is comparatively easy for an individual to hold realistic expectations about the physical world because of its orderliness, and the fulfilment of the expectations enables him to act upon the physical environment in a manner that is effective for the achievement of his intentions. Commerce with the social environment is more problematic because it is less inherently orderly than the physical, but an individual acts towards others as if the latter's likely behaviour is almost as predictable as that of objects. The fact that it is not causes errors and makes social relations harder to cope with than everyday relations with objects. Obviously the less a person knows about the likely response of others to his behaviour the more difficult he will find it to cope with the interaction. Society makes the behaviour of its members more predictable to each other by enculturating them to certain role requirements, a knowledge of which is required in order for a member of the society to be able to grasp the meaning of the behaviour of other persons with whom he interacts, and to behave in a meaningful way himself.

The social behaviour of an individual is effective to the extent that he holds realistic implicit beliefs about orderliness of the social environment. These beliefs depend on the availability of relevant cognitive structures for imposing on that environment, and on the possession of valid models of the rules followed by the actors. This leads us to a consideration of cognitive categories and social rules.

Cognitive categories. An ability to categorize events in a social world in a consensually validated fashion is dependent partly on the way the culture is represented to the individual and by him; for example, the representation of objects through the use of words, or the representation of roles through social position names. Without a considerable degree of consensus about the use of the categories, communication between individuals, and ultimately all social interaction, becomes very difficult. Donald Campbell (1964) examines the implications for cross-cultural communication, and for the practice of anthropology, of the fact that different people classify objects differently. He points out that communication across cultures and languages sometimes becomes possible only by the perceiver inferring how the other person is constructing the world from his reactions to commonly perceived events. Campbell suggests an analogy with the way a colour-blind person learns to discriminate colours whose hues in fact all look the same to him but which have secondary characteristics that are perceived in a similar fashion by the colour sighted and the colour-blind. It is only by extending the areas of common perception by inference that a person can begin to comprehend the categorizing system of another.

Differences in the way that experience is categorized constitutes one of the main differences between cultures, although the task of investigating these differences has, so far, been relatively neglected by cross-cultural scholars, excepting for some linguistic analysts. Davidson (1974) has pointed out that Australian aborigines of the Murngin tribe categorize common objects, such as plants, animals and colours, according to which of two tribal moieties they fit, and this in turn, determines their perceived cosmic relations with each other. Davidson reports that Murngin adolescents explained environmental phenomena spontaneously in terms of moiety classifications. A similar, albeit less cosmic, categorization of objects exists in those languages that classify nouns into gender, a procedure that causes difficulty for Engligh-speaking learners of such languages, especially when the gender contradicts the sex of the object.

The place of rules in enculturation. The orderliness of societies is based on the existence of generally accepted social rules. These are acquired by a child initially through identification with parents and subsequently with more general social models from outside the home. The rules associated with social role behaviour are seldom explicitly verbalized and a person who has been brought up in a particular culture usually finds it impossible to formulate them.

The technique used by Triandis and Malpass for analysing subjective culture (see Malpass, in press) represents a method for developing sets of rules that are specific to given types of actors in given situations. This is an important contribution to the possible description of explicit cultural rules because of the specificity of the application of the rules, but it raises questions about the degree to which anyone using them is able to generalize to other situations.

The limited place of explicit rules in a culture, and the difficulties posed by trying to learn the culture by acquiring them is brought out in the learning of second languages. Most language rules have exceptions, and, although attempts may be made to formulate rules about the exceptions, eventually certain specific instances must be learnt by rote. Anyone who tries to speak, or write, a new language strictly according to sets of rules is likely to produce incorrect, or at least quaint language, that may be understandable but markedly "foreign".

Because the rules of a culture are usually not clear or completely known even to well enculturated persons, it is necessary for people to operate with premises of mini-hypotheses which they treat as if they were rules. These are employed because, in the light of the present state of the person's knowledge about the culture and his perception of the world, they appear to have the highest probability of being valid and relevant; but when the person is not familiar with the culture he has to work with hypotheses of low probability. (See Sarbin *et al.*, 1960, especially Chapter 5 on the "Operative probability of modules".) Whether an actor will take a risk by acting on a hypothesis of low probability as if it were a rule also depends on the utility of successful coping and the disutility of failure. In real life much of our behaviour does not risk much, one way or the other, i.e. the utilities and disutilities are not high, and we tend to treat our hypotheses as if they were rules even when they have been disconfirmed. Where, however, the stakes are high, for example when to operate on an invalid rule can cause severe punishment to a foreigner, his action will tend to be paralysed through lack of any hypothesis that he would dare to use.

This treatment of utilities and disutilities leads on to a consideration of the dynamic aspects of culturally derived behaviour and the cultural performance.

2. Dynamic Aspects of Enculturation

These refer to the goals, social attitudes and values that are embodied in culturally defined behaviour; the habits, traits, and defensive and expressive styles that characterize the behaviour of the members of the society; the role expectations and feelings of obligation and propriety concerning that behaviour; and the related feelings of social identity.

To deal with the way in which a particular culture shapes the "raw" biological being into a uniquely functioning personality which is nevertheless culturally defined would take us into a long excursion into the fields of personality development and the general relationship between culture and personality functioning. For the present purposes it is sufficient to stress that there are certain universal human needs and modes of functioning that must be satisfied in all cultures. In broad terms these needs refer to the maintenance of life processes, the need to maintain a structural society to enhance as well as regulate social relationships, and to provide for the self-expressive needs of individuals. While these needs are universal, each culture prescribes different modes for satisfying them.

Strangers who enter a new society can attempt to satisfy their needs either by participating in the culturally approved means of doing so or by belonging to sub-societies within the larger one in which they can pursue their needs in the familiar manner of their original culture. Most newcomers employ a mixture of the two methods, although this will vary in accordance with the degree to which the new society permits cultural pluralism. Considerations of the difficulties that are met by newcomers to a culture frequently focus on the culturally defined means of satisfying social relationship needs; for example, the mores relevant to dominance and compliance; or etiquette practices related to the presentation of self and the protection of face. These types of need are important to the persons concerned and they represent "bear-traps" into which the unwary newcomer is continually in danger of falling.

Less attention is usually given to the satisfaction of the self-expressive needs of newcomers. These refer to the needs for artistic, spiritual and intellectual expression and stimulation and also to the development and practice of various competencies for their own sake. Needs of this sort are often difficult to gratify within an alien cultural environment, and, if they are to be satisfied at all, the newcomer may have to make a partial withdrawal from the new culture until he has learnt to make the necessary cognitive changes, and has acquired the skills that are necessary for him to gain satisfaction for his self-expression needs in commerce with the culture.

3. The Relationship between the Dynamic and Cognitive Aspects

The differentiation between the cognitive and dynamic aspects of enculturation is not a firm one, but it is highlighted by the useful distinction made by Ruesch *et al.* (1948) in their concepts of "internal" and "external" symbols. The former involve the ego and are associated with feelings of shame, guilt and anxiety when violated; i.e., these symbols are associated with primary socialization. Full acculturation requires the attachment of these affective reactions to the external symbols in the right amount and on the right occasions, and this involves a much more fundamental change in the learner than just learning to handle the external symbols. When the external and internal aspects of the acculturation are in harmony, the person *knows* the new culture. This implies that a person's knowledge of the cultural rules and possession of the language skills are integrated with appropriate postural, emotional and motoric responses; for example, his non-verbal behaviour is consonant with his verbal; his goal directed behaviour is matched by emotions that aid the achievement of the goal; his behaviour is consistent with his self concept.

Unless an integration is achieved between the cognitive and dynamic aspects of the culture as they coexist within a person, enculturation has not occurred, i.e., the person is not able to perform the necessary social skills with competence. This is what is meant when we say that an alien culture is "meaningful" to us; we don't mean just that we know how members of that culture behave; we mean that we can physically empathize with that behaviour, that we can put ourselves into their set. As a Japanese-Canadian put it when commenting on his feeling of alienation during a visit to Japan "You don't know when to laugh, you don't understand why others laugh." The importance of empathy in overcoming a cultural gulf is demonstrated in Guiora *et al.*'s (1975) report that students who were independently demonstrated to possess high empathic qualities were relatively good at imitating the pronunciation of foreign phrases.

Empathizing with the attitudinal set of other persons involves not only a knowledge of what to expect in their overt behaviour — the role behaviour that they are carrying out, the language that they are using, and even such subtleties of expressive behaviour as gestures and tempo — but also it involves the capacity to simulate the covert affective aspects of the behaviour including muscle tonus and readiness for action and states of excitement or depression. When this occurs the new culture is no longer unfamiliar or alien to us, but instead "we have a feeling for it", implying that we participate fully in it and it is "familiar" to us. This integration of the cognitive and the dynamic is difficult to achieve for anyone who has to learn to cope with an unfamiliar culture in adulthood, but it forms a significant part of the socialization process in which children develop the social skills needed for perceiving and performing social roles.

4. Performance Aspects of Enculturation

The ultimate test of enculturation is not whether the person has acquired the appropriate cognitive knowledge, or whether he feels the appropriate affect, but whether he carries out the appropriate role performances. This is dependent, of course, on the cognitive and dynamic enculturation but it also calls for the possession of the appropriate skills. These skills are of two types: technical and social.

Technical skills are required as instruments for the performance of roles; for example, the language, hunting skills, crafts, academic skills. These are more specific than the skills that are required in order to perform roles in social interaction, and they are often incorporated in training programmes for the children of the society. A newcomer who comes into contact with the culture after the normal age for training the children of that society in these technical skills may have special difficulty in coping because there are probably few facilities for providing the necessary instruction and training to adults. In industrialized societies this is the usual position with regard to training in literacy and in skilled crafts, and it means that adult immigrants suffer a handicap in comparison with the native born group whose socialization includes such cultural knowledge.

The acquisition of the social skills of a culture provides us with the competence to perform required roles without undue resort to rule dominated behaviour. As Miller *et al.* put it, "Both skills and instincts are on-going patterns of action, directed toward the environmental conditions that activate and guide them and organized hierarchically into action units with more than one level of complexity" (1960, p. 93). As these authors point out, the learner may start from a "communicable plan" (read "formulated rules") but, through practice and repetition, redundancies are eliminated and integrated sequences developed that can be executed in a relatively inflexible and automatic form. A person who is familiar with a culture can perform the required roles most of the time without having to formulate a plan of action in accordance with postulated rules and hypotheses. Formulated rules are only a "learner's crutch", and when a culture learner has established sufficiently high levels of probability in the confirmation of his expectations, he can afford to lay down his crutch. (But he shouldn't throw it away beyond his reach — he may need it again if things go wrong.) This action is sometimes accompanied by definite feelings of self-confidence and trust in the world ("Look Dad; no hands!").

When the performance of social roles — and, of course, the use of a language — have become automatic, an environmental or internal cue brings into action a mental set which trips off the skilled sequence of behaviour without intervention of internal mini-hypotheses. These "mental sets" are equivalent to the engagement of a system of unformulated postulates and premises, which then operate in a learned sequence, appropriate to the intentions of the person, his own cognitive and motor aptitudes, and the demands of the environment. In so far as these automatic actions are successfully executed and bring the desired secondary results, they may elicit the positive emotions or even the exhilaration associated with recognition of mastery.

The conception of role behaviour as a skilled performance is a useful one for consideration both of enculturation and reculturation processes. In the course of enculturation, a person develops: (1) perceptual readiness to select certain events for attention — culturally based "stances" towards the world: (2) readiness to respond in set ways to those events when the context is appropriate — dynamic "sets", and (3) repertoires of learned behavioural sequences for coping with the situation — the actual "role performances". These performances represent smooth flowing sequences of actions directed towards the attainment of an end state, i.e. coping. This concept of social behaviour as a skill owes much to Argyle, 1967 and Kelvin, 1970.

Most skills, and certainly all social skills, require more than the possession of repertoires of complex sequences; they also imply that the actor engages in interaction with the environment by correctly perceiving the context and responding appropriately to feedback cues from it. These responses to the actual situation pertaining at the time that the behaviour takes place enable the actor to elaborate more subtly on the general rules of behaviour and guide him on when to depart from them to advantage. The actual execution of a skilled performance is not a blind process; the performer continually monitors his own behaviour and its effect on the environment so that he can adapt his actions to changes in the signals and can note unexpected feedback occurrences, i.e. discrepancies between his expectations and his observations. Although the performance of skilled behaviour may be virtually automatic, it ceases to be so when there is a breakdown in the confirmation of expectancies, and operating rules may then be brought into play deliberately as an attempt to cope with the situation. (See the treatment of rules, above.)

A stranger who is attempting to learn to act in accordance with the role prescriptions of a new culture suffers from all of the disadvantages of an unskilled performance. First, his stance is inappropriate, i.e., he is not primed to respond to stimuli that are relevant to the role; then, his set to respond is not appropriate, and, finally, his actual performance is awkward. The correct sequences of behaviour do not flow freely, smoothly and automatically, the stranger fails to notice feedback, or when he does notice it, he doesn't know how to use it. The major components of his lack of skill derives from his inability to develop the correct expectations of the behaviour of others, and to impart congruent expectations to others about his own behaviour. Thus, the behaviour and the feedback are out of harmony with each other.

Learning cultural skills. In order to improve the efficiency of his cultural performance, the newcomer may fall back on a number of possible strategies. As a result of trial and error he may eventually learn to accommodate better to feedback, and, with practice, his performance will improve. He may also improve by observing and imitating the behaviour of others — if only he can work out the rules that will guide him in deciding who to imitate. He will also deduce general rules and operating and stop rules for their application from his observation and experience. In rare cases, if he is fortunate, he may have an individual human guide who will advise him on his behaviour, demonstrate the correct behaviour, point out his errors, instruct him, and deliberately supervise his cultural performance. This personalized instruction and supervised practice involving immediate feedback is probably the most efficient way in which a newcomer can learn an unfamiliar culture, depending, however, upon the qualities of the learner and the guide and the relationship between the two.

The analysis of cultural competence as a skill throws light on methods of training persons for another culture, but lack of space prevents a detailed treatment here. Suffice to say that the strategies used for teaching motor, artistic and professional skills to novices — for example, playing tennis, painting, and school teaching — have application also to teaching cultural skills to persons who are about to enter an unfamiliar culture, or who have recently done so. Typically, instructors in skills use such techniques as: expounding general and specific performance rules; modelling correct performances; practising sub-routines and full sequences with the learner in non-competitive situations (i.e. providing role-playing practice), correcting incorrect performances, and reinforcing good ones. All of these methods may be employed in teaching new skills — or perfecting old ones for that matter — and they play a part in varying proportions in culture training schemes.

Nevertheless, skills can only be imparted by a teacher up to a point: in the main *it is the learner who learns rather than the teacher who teaches* and this applies to a person learning a new culture as much as to a learner of other skills. On the whole a stranger is on his own, and even when he is furnished with a guide to act as translator, instructor and model, he will still learn mainly by trial and error, and practice and observation, often incidentally rather than deliberately.

As skill acquisition proceeds, irrespective of whether it is a motor or a cultural skill, the performance begins to become part of the actor's self concept. He moves from being a person who knows how to converse in Cantonese to being a Cantonese speaker, and perhaps to being a Cantonese. This process of "ego-incorporation" or "self-projection" (depending on one's point of view) is a most important aspect of culture learning and is relevant to the transition from mere cognitive learning to acculturation and identification with the new culture. In other words, the culture becomes familiar. We now see that familiarity is the result of an integration of the cognitive, dynamic and performance aspects of participating in a culture, a process which, even under the most ideal conditions, takes some time.

IV. CULTURE SHOCK

When an individual finds himself in an unfamiliar cultural environment, where his previous learning is inadequate for coping, he may suffer some degree of emotional disturbance, a condition often referred to as culture shock. The degree of disturbance may range from virtually nil to complete debilitation depending on the personality of the individual, on the extent of the unfamiliarity of the culture, and on the size of the personal stakes involved. Where only minor needs are at stake, the person may simply not bother to make the effort to solve the problem. Where the difficulty of finding a solution is slight only, he may easily summon up the necessary energy to meet the challenge, and the amount of adjustment required would be no more than that often called for in the normal course of life within his original culture. Under these conditions, no particular stress is engendered by having to cope with an unfamiliar culture, and in fact, the experience may stimulate well integrated action. Where, however, the coping task is a difficult one, the dissonance between a person's enculturation and the present cultural demands may cause him debilitating stress, or "shock".

Oberg (1960) appears to have been the first to use the term "culture shock", in connection with the experience of anthropologists who have to learn to handle the violation of social reality implicit in unfamiliar social norms, values and mores. This represents a challenge to their primary value socialization since the accustomed validation of the basic values and role concepts virtually ceases. But well before Oberg's work, Margaret Wood (1934) had referred to the "well of loneliness" of the cultural stranger who feels the absence of people with sufficiently similar experiences to understand how he feels.

Alfred Schutz (1964) also referred to the stress that derives from the stranger not knowing the implicit structure of the society or the rules of role behaviour. He is lost in a "labyrinth in which he has lost all sense of his bearings" (p. 37) and he does not possess the relevant "matter of course recipes for action".

The referents for "culture shock" are different in these three cases, and these do not exhaust the possibilities. Here is a listing of at least six different senses in which the term has been used. (In a later work (in Kimball and Watson, 1972) Oberg himself lists a wide variety of aspects of shock which encompasses many of the meanings listed here.)

1. Strain due to the effort required to make the necessary adaptations. Guthrie (1975) calls this "culture fatigue" rather than shock, and describes the symptoms in Peace Corps volunteers as irritability, dissatisfaction, insomnia and psychosomatic disorders. As we have seen, trying to operate in a social environment where the cues and rules of behaviour are not clear requires the stranger to work with conscious rules and to maintain vigilance. He, therefore, cannot resort to automatic performance and consequently suffers from cognitive overload. Those who have travelled will know the strain involved in adapting to new people, new ways and new environments, and of having to encode and decode an unfamiliar language. This strain is also reminiscent of the physical tiredness and stiffness that besets a person learning a skill such as skiing or car driving at the initial learning stage when he has to think consciously about his performance. The strain of having to adapt may explain the findings of Wardwell et al. (1964) that there is a high rate of coronary heart disease in persons who moved from farm to cities in the USA and in upwardly mobile children of immigrants. Seymour Levine and his co-workers (1972) have also produced evidence of physiological malfunctioning related to the need to adapt to unfamiliar environments. These researchers have shown that when expectancies have been built up through habituation, a failure of the environment to provide the expected feedback causes a rise in pituitary-adrenal activity which at best alerts the person for action and at worst causes agitation.

2. Sense of loss arising from being uprooted from one's original surroundings and a feeling of deprivation in the new one with respect to such aspects of life as companions, profession, "edible" food, recreation, cultural stimulation and social status. Losses of this type are obviously present in the case of forced refugees or segregatees but they also apply to voluntary

settlers and sojourners who may be filled with longing for their old environment. Perhaps the loss in the latter cases is mainly of the familiar and comfortable sensory and perceptual experiences of "home" (sights, smells, noises and tastes), or of old friends. Cultural shock, in this sense characterizes the anthropologist in the field who "has an imperative need for social contact and a certain measure of approval" (Kimball and Watson, 1972, p. 21). Richardson (1974, pp. 32ff) describes the depression pattern that commonly overtakes the initial elation of recent British immigrants in Australia as a result of sensory shock at the environment, nostalgia for their old country and for familiar people and the realization of hardships that lie ahead for them. Thus the shock associated with loss may consist both of realistic feelings of deprivation and of sentimental feelings of nostalgia.

3. Rejection by the newcomer of the host population, or the opposite process — a feeling by the newcomer that he is rejected by the new society. This latter feeling may well be realistic and it is likely to colour the whole attitude of the person towards the new society to the extent of making him anxious and self-deprecating and unwilling to try to become integrated in any way. The most disturbing situation of all occurs when the newcomer feels rejected and yet is under pressure to engage in close interaction with the local group; for example, a member of a threatened group, such as Chinese traders in parts of South East Asia, who nevertheless has to interact in apparent "goodwill" with the local population in order to make a living; or to take an opposite example, an administrator in an occupied colonized land, who has to work with a hostile local population. Brein and David (1971), describe cases of culture shock among both foreign students and Peace Corps workers in which the sojourner either felt inferior to the local population or he felt vastly superior. In both of these cases, the feelings of status discrepancy sometimes led to maladjusted states associated with anxiety, depression and alienation in the sojourner.

4. Confusion in one's role and role expectations and in one's values and feelings of self-identity. This may extend from mere ambivalence or uncertainty in behaviour to emotional paralysis. This type of cultural confusion may become a focus for neurotic mechanisms leading to phobias, psychosomatic symptoms, depression, etc., all of which have frequently been observed in recently arrived immigrants and others who have been subjected to cultural change (see, for example, the review by Coelho, 1972 and the treatment by Brody, 1970). However, the evidence is by no means clear that these groups have particularly high rates of mental breakdown; the figures suggest that some groups do and others do not (see, for example, the review by Murphy, 1974). In any case, there are many possible causes of mental breakdown and the studies do not demonstrate that cultural confusion is the cause rather than merely a symptom of the breakdown. The

case for culture conflict as a source of stress has been overstated by some writers, for example de Vos and Hippler, (1968), (see Taft, 1974 for an analysis of the differing senses in which the term has been used, and for some data which suggest that persons in bi-cultural situations only rarely suffer severe stress as a result of it). Some degree of culture conflict is more likely to be present when the circumstances force a bi-cultural person to choose between two sets of role performances, values, or competing national identities in cases where strong negative emotions such as shame, guilt, or fear, apply to one set rather than the other. Problems of this type occur mostly when one of the cultures is associated with an identity from which the bi-cultural person would like to escape.

5. A realization of the differences between the cultures, accompanied by feelings of surprise, discomfort, anxiety, indignation or disgust — in other words "shock" in the everyday sense of being scandalized (Spiro, 1961, p. 121, calls it "moral anxiety"). Even volunteers to the US Peace Corps are not exempt from such moral indignation at what they regard as the violation of their values (Brein and David, 1971) nor are tourists (de Sola Pool, 1958). Merely being a witness to, let alone a participant in, the violation of deeply held values can cause profound feelings of guilt, or at least shame (see Oberg, 1960). The shock accompanying these violations of propriety may cause a state of social spasticity that may render any effective adaptation impossible.

6. The most common meaning of culture shock is the feeling of impotence on the part of the stranger who cannot deal competently with his environment owing to unfamiliarity with the cognitive aspects of the culture and inability to perform the necessary role playing skills. This incompetence may well exacerbate shock in some of the senses described earlier; for example, it may lead to culture fatigue, to a sense of loss, and to actual rejection by the host society with consequent damage to self-esteem. The loss of mastery is equivalent to infantile regression; that is, the newcomer is reduced to a state of ignorance and weakness in which seemingly everyday matters have to be explained to him so that he becomes dependent on the goodwill of persons who act as cultural bridges by guiding, translating and modelling. The shock aspect of this can be clearly seen in the common example of the immigrant mother who has to employ her young child as a go-between in dealings with the school principal and even with her gynaecologist. In addition to the effect that the newcomer's incompetence may have on his self-esteem there are other possible consequences of the type that often follow frustration; for example, apathy, aggression and even panic.

In view of all of the possible manifestations of culture shock mentioned in the six types, one may be justified in asking how a person could ever sufficiently overcome the emotional barriers in order to cope eventually with an unfamiliar culture. The answer is that the required adaptation is usually not so severe as to cause irreversible shock. As literature on the behaviour of people under extreme conditions (e.g. war, concentration camps, extreme isolation) will testify, the adaptability of the human animal is greater than is usually believed. The writings of Victor Frankl about adjustment to the Auschwitz death camp (e.g. 1959) bring this out clearly. The human being can take many shocks to his system and still retain his resilience; in addition, society often provides protective, custodial or restorative institutions to enable, or perhaps force, persons suffering from culture shock to learn to adjust. If these are not provided by the society at large, they are often incorporated into sub-systems set up by the newcomers themselves, e.g. foreign student associations. There are, however, some groups of con-quered, or otherwise pressurized people, who are not provided with any support to help them recover from profound culture shock, and whose continued social existence is, as a consequence, at extreme risk; for example, detribalized but rejected Aborigines in the Australia of but yesterday, and perhaps of today. (This type of extreme disturbance is treated as "acculturative stress" by Berry and Annis, 1974.)

V. MULTI-CULTURALISM

We shall now consider the situation of a person who has acquired more than one culture either as part of his original enculturation, or as the result of a successful acculturation to one or more new cultures, without the loss of the old ones. By definition, such persons are able to function in more than one culture with no more than minimal adaptation required from one to the other. It is impressive that a bi-lingual person is able to keep apart the two language systems with a minimum of interference between them, almost as if at any one time the speaker is "switched in" mentally to a plug which allows only one language to operate. Like the bi-lingual, a true bi-cultural has the skills to perform competently the roles required by each cultural context and he is able to avoid gaffes that could result from inappropriate switching between cultures. One of the characteristics of a well developed and integrated skill is that it resists interference from associated but irrelevant experiences; consequently each set of cultural skills, because of the way in which the components are integrated, stands on its own with little deterioration resulting from the coexistence of the other.

The relationships of the cultures that coexist within the one individual will be different if the language and role playing skills associated with them are not highly competent. In such cases it could be expected that the compartmentalization would not work perfectly and there would tend to be interference between the cultures — as can be seen in the case of a school child in the early years of learning a foreign language. It can also be seen when one culture is learnt before the other — thus the adult learner of a new language has trouble with pronunciation, syntax, vocabulary and phrase usage in the second one owing to interference from the first. This, of course, is the subject matter towards which this whole chapter is directed — the problems of coping with an unfamiliar culture when competence in a familiar one has already been acquired. A question that is worth asking at this point is what happens to the original cultural skills when new ones are acquired. Not only does the latter not eliminate the former, but there also need not necessarily be a preference for one over the other. Where a person's competence in one of the cultures is greater than in the other, he is likely to prefer it wherever possible and to avoid situations requiring the skills associated with the other. But given equal proficiency in the two cultures, the cultural choice — for example the language chosen — may be made on purely pragmatic grounds in relation to the particular context that evokes it. There also may be a general preference for engaging one set of skills rather than the other because of its greater compatibility with the person's values, and because it represents his preferred national identification. Lambert (1967) has shown, for example, that there is a relationship between national identification and language proficiency in bi-linguals. Competence in the English language in immigrants in Australia is influenced by their interest in becoming integrated with Australia, and is a consequence more than a cause of their degree of social acceptance by Australians (Taft, 1966).

When a bi-cultural person moves into the exclusive ambience of just one of the cultures, it might seem that he would easily be able to cope with this situation because he already possesses the necessary competence. This view, however, overlooks the deprivation that may occur as a result of the lost use of the other competencies. He may not be satisfied just to be able to cope with the existing environment and he may feel less than fulfilled without being able to employ his other skills. I cannot quote any scientific studies on the needs of multi-culturals to exercise all of their cultural competencies from time to time, but ethnic novels often refer to nostalgic jags on the part of the characters who are ostensibly fully integrated members of the majority society. Perhaps this also explains the often puzzling experience when an apparently well acculturated native suddenly "goes bush", i.e., temporarily abandons his Westernized style of life in order to engage in some ritual activity with his tribal people; for example, the University student who drops out of his course in order to participate in a ritual revenge war. While such behaviour may give the multi-cultural person a reputation for flightiness it does call for a greater understanding by society of the advantages of providing social conditions that cater to the divergent needs of multi-cultural individuals.

Given appropriate social conditions, the advantages of multi-culturalism should out-weigh the disadvantages for both society and for the individual. In the case of the latter there is some evidence that being bi-lingual has more positive than negative features for him, and the same could apply to bi-culturalism in general although evidence on this is lacking at present.

There is some evidence that the possession of more than one language is an advantage in linguistic competence, when other variables such as socio-economic class are controlled (e.g. Peal and Lambert, 1962; Carringer, 1974). This advantage probably derives from the increase in the number of verbal strategies available and an extension of the connotations of words in the two languages together compared with just the one (Carringer). In the general realm of culture, beyond mere language, multi-culturalism can lead to enrichment of resources for coping with situations and an increase in the possibilities of communicating and communing with a diverse group.

Adler (1974) has presented a useful treatment of multi-culturalism but has stressed much more than I would the strain that arises from the conflict that is imposed on the multi-cultural person. According to him, a multi-cultural man is vulnerable to all kinds of pressures and conflicting messages and is likely to take refuge from his lack of a clear-cut identity by becoming alienated from society, if not by becoming completely nihilistic. This alleged negative effect of multi-culturalism on personality functioning tends to dominate much of the thinking on the subject, despite the evidence presented by Adler himself of some cases of successful multi-cultural functioning in persons who had to undergo a painful process of resocialization to acquire cultures additional to their original one.

As was pointed out above in connection with culture shock, the reports on the debilitating effect of multi-culturalism on an individual are largely specific to situations where one of his identities is held in low esteem by the dominant society. Excepting in these cases, most multi-cultural persons are able to move relatively freely between their individual cultures and to employ the normal methods of coping with the multiple identity that lies within everyone (one can go back at least to William James' "multiple selves" for a psychological treatment of the subject).

After reviewing empirical studies on the need for consistency of identity, Gergen (1968) has concluded that this applies mainly where the pressures of the environment force it, and that, under normal circumstances people tolerate inconsistency within themselves (despite claims to the contrary by

Prescott Lecky, Carl Rogers and Leon Festinger). This is not to deny that a given multi-cultural individual can suffer from a neurotically debilitating cultural conflict, especially when he is under external pressure to declare himself in one way or the other in his actions. But, in most instances, it is relatively easy for a bi-cultural person to solve his cultural conflicts in a number of possible ways: by simply ignoring the existence of the conflict; by suppressing one set of culturally defined prescriptions and following the other one completely; or by applying each set in its appropriate situation, for example, by speaking one language at home and another at school. It may also be possible for an unusually mature bi-cultural individual to rise above both cultures by following superordinate social prescriptions that serve to integrate more specific, but contradictory ones, e.g. "be just", "be thoughtful of others' needs".

VI. A MULTI-FACET FRAMEWORK FOR ANALYSING LONG-TERM ADAPTATION TO NEW CULTURES AND SOCIETIES

This final section will propose a framework derived from the study of immigrants that may prove useful for the analysis of a wide variety of cultural adaptation situations. The process of coping with an unfamiliar cultural situation is treated here in relation to four major aspects of the adaptation process:

(1) *Cultural adjustment:* The functioning of the personality in the changed cultural environment.
(2) *Identification:* Changes in the person's reference groups and personal models, and in his social identity.
(3) *Cultural competence:* Acquiring new cultural knowledge and skills.
(4) *Role acculturation:* Adoption of new culturally defined roles.

All of these aspects involve cognitive, dynamic and performance processes in that the changes apply to the way that the person structures the world, as well as his skills, behaviour, goals, motives, emotions and attitudes. The first two aspects involve dynamic processes mainly, while the last two correspond to what is usually understood by *acculturation*, a combination of acquisition of competence in performing culturally relevant behaviour and the adoption of culturally defined roles and attitudes with respect to that behaviour. Full *integration* into the new group involves a combination of the three processes, cognitive, dynamic and performance, operating in an integrated manner with respect to all four aspects of adaptation.

The framework is intended to be generalizable to any situation in which a person is adapting to his contact with a new culture, but it will be illustrated specifically with respect to the situation of immigrants. Not all culture contact situations involve all of the four aspects in order for a person to cope.

Each of the aspects is represented by both a subjective and an objective side, the former referring to adaptation from the viewpoint of the person and the latter from that of an external observer. These "viewpoints" are presented in Table 2. The sub-divisions listed under "subjective" and "objective" are not intended fully to correspond with each other, but, in general, the "subjective" column refers to the attitude towards — or against — integration or even assimilation, and a reference to the newcomer's perception of the degree to which this has happened. The "objective" column refers to externally observable events and performances, such as social interaction, e.g. whether the newcomer has friends from the unfamiliar cultural group; or actual competence in using the host language.

The aspects of adaptation could be further sub-divided, but for the purposes of the present treatment, the four aspects divided into two viewpoints will suffice. In "From Stranger to Citizen" (Taft, 1966) a separate treatment of social interaction was suggested and this led to the discovery that, for certain immigrants, the perception that they are well accepted socially by informal social groups in the host culture plays a central role in their identification with the new country (Taft, 1966; Richardson, 1974), and in the case of those from non-English-speaking countries it leads to improved competence in English. In this 1966 work, the subjective viewpoint was further divided into a motivational aspect — what the person wanted to achieve — and a perceived achievement one — how successful he thought he was in achieving his goal. The objective viewpoint was also treated in two aspects: what actions the person actually took to try to achieve his wishes with regard to his adaptation; and some measure of his actual success. This multi-facet approach provides an opportunity to study the interrelationships between the various aspects of their sequences. (Further details of this approach to the study of the adaptation of immigrants are to be found in Taft, 1973.)

Measurements of the status of immigrants in Australia on these aspects were factor analysed (Taft, 1966, pp. 9-10) for several groups of different nationalities, and four relatively invariant factors emerged. The first, *primary integration* was fairly closely related to cultural adjustment and identification. It is not identical with primary socialization which involves basic values more directly, but it is close to it as it relates to self concept and feelings of identity which derive from the significant identifications made by the person with other individuals and groups. This factor refers mainly to the dynamic aspects of the cultural adaptation.

Table 2

Aspects of adaptation to new groups in their objective and subjective viewpoints

Aspect	Viewpoints	
	A. Subjective	B. Objective
1. CULTURAL ADJUSTMENT	Emotional comfort Feeling "at home" in the society Satisfaction with life	Socially acceptable behaviour Social interaction with host group Economic and social integration
2. IDENTIFICATION	New reference group Feeling of belonging Feeling of sharing "fate"	Formal membership (e.g. citizenship) Overt identity Actual common fate
3. CULTURAL COMPETENCE	Attitude towards learning about the new culture Self-perceived competence in the language and roles	Actual knowledge of the language and history of new society Actual competence in using the language and performing roles
4. ROLE ACCULTURATION	Self-perceived convergence of attitudes and values Desire to conform to culturally defined modes Culturally monistic versus pluralistic attitudes	Actual role behaviour (e.g. gestures, food habits, dress) Active use of the host language Full integration or assimilation

The second factor, *secondary integration* coincides fairly closely with what I have called "role acculturation". There were high loadings on the newcomer's adoption of the behavioural norms of the host group, and his active use of English. Unexpectedly, informal social integration with the host group loaded on secondary rather than primary integration, but perhaps this just means that such social contacts are rather superficial. This factor involves mainly the cognitive aspects of acculturation.

A third factor is related to *cultural competence*; the high loadings were registered on the person's knowledge of standard and colloquial English, and also on his general level of education, and related variables such as his occupational level and social class. It is not surprising that well educated immigrants score higher than the less well educated on measures of culture competence and also on secondary integration, but they are not higher on primary integration. Presumably education, and a related general sophistication, facilitates adaptation to the cognitive and performance aspects of a new culture, especially when the move occurs from a more traditional to a more modern one. (The review by David (1972) of the adaptation of American sojourners (mainly Peace Corps Workers) to a more traditional society, indicates that the evidence is inconclusive on the value for effective functioning of such factors as the level of education, intelligence, language skills and personality adjustment.)

There was also a fourth factor which was interpreted as *attitude towards the original reference group* and its culture. Although, on the whole, there was a negative correlation between scores on this factor and primary and secondary integration with the host country, the size of the correlation is a function of attitudes towards cultural pluralism in both the host and the original groups, and in the person himself (see Taft, 1966). If the attitude climate is in favour of cultural pluralism, this fourth factor could be independent of the others. For example, a technical aid expert from the USA to, say, Bangla Desh could become quite fully adapted to the latter culture in all of the four aspects set out in Table 2 — even in role acculturation — without becoming any weaker in his enculturation to his original American culture, and in fact he might even be strengthened in his "Americanism" as a result of his experience in the alien culture.

The aspects of the adaptation process are not unique to the newcomers who are described in Table 1 as "settlers", but they could apply just as well to anyone who is exposed for any length of time to contact with a new society, including those who are segregated in new communities (hospital, army, prison, etc.) or subjected to a changed social situation (for example in upward or downward social mobility). In each case, the newcomer's adjustment, identification or acculturation to the new society might become an issue. But whether such changes are likely to occur is partly dependent on

150   R. TAFT

the individual and partly on the society. The person may have no wish to go
beyond superficial contact with members of the new society, and in turn the
latter may or may not encourage the newcomer to become in any way
integrated with it; in fact it may not even permit any form of integration at
all. If the person is not motivated towards integration, or if the new society
does not permit it, it is not likely that he would start to feel that he belongs to
the new group (identification), although this is not impossible as can be seen
by the way that some sojourners, such as anthropologists and diplomats,
sometimes start to develop a proprietory interest in the particular society
with which they are associated. Similarly, without some integration, role
acculturation is likely to be quite limited.

   Nevertheless, when we posit a situation where a person has to cope with
an unfamiliar culture this implies that he is in some sort of communication
with it. The mere fact of such communication could conceivably lead to the
development of some of the aspects of adaptation to which we have referred,
even in the absence of any form of social interaction; let alone integration.
For example, a classicist may "fall in love" with an ancient culture, i.e.,
become satisfied and identified with it, and an intending sojourner may do
the same while studying a culture in anticipation of subsequent contact with
it (anticipatory identification). Subsequent contact could lead, at the very
least, to some social interaction ("objective adjustment") and, perhaps, to
the active use of the vernacular language and para-language of the new
society ("objective role acculturation"). In turn, such direct communication
with the new culture could lead to other aspects of the adaptation process.
Thus, a person who makes contact with a culture with the intention of
confining himself to superficial relationships might, in time, become
assimilated to it in spite of himself. This is the phenomenon of "going
native" well illustrated by the almost legendary instance of F. Hamilton
Cushing who went to study the Zuni in 1882 and stayed to become one of
them. Even persons who make contact with an unfamiliar group in order to
spy on it, or otherwise do it harm, can become assimilated to it in the end and
identify with the fate of the group.

   The explanation for this phenomenon probably lies in the cognitive area
— it results from the drive to reduce dissonance between behaviour values
and self concept, or merely perhaps, to reduce the complexity of
information processing. Satisfaction with the way of life of the group and a
feeling of relaxation in its presence could also play a major part in
"converting" an outsider into a fully participating member.

   Complete assimilation is one way of coping with an unfamiliar culture but
it is not always the appropriate way or even possible one. The form of coping
adopted will be a function both of the individual and the society and the
interaction between the two. In view of the complexities involved it would

be impossible at this stage to provide a universal model to account for all cases of culture coping, but the framework proposed here, based largely on the situation of the immigrant, may be generalizable to many of the other situations, particularly those that involve a long-term association with the new culture.

I will conclude, in any case, with a reiteration of my main point that there are communalities in the process of adapting to and coping with various types of unfamiliar cultures. An analysis of this process along the lines attempted here would enable more accumulation of common findings between the different bodies of studies than has hitherto occurred. Specifically it is suggested that the effect of all culture contact situations that evoke in individuals the need to cope with an unfamiliar culture can be analysed in terms of the employment of new cognitive, dynamic and performance mechanisms by the participants and their development of new coping repertoires.

ACKNOWLEDGEMENTS

This paper contains the fruits of many stimulating discussions over the past few years and owes a particular debt to the East-West Center (and through it to the generosity of the American Congress) for a senior fellowship at the Culture Learning Institute. In particular I thank Brian Bullivant, Harwood Fisher, Agnes Niyekawa Howard, Peter Kelvin, Anne Keppel, Alan Richardson, Richard Ripple, John Walsh and Neil Warren for their willingness to exchange ideas relevant to the topic.

REFERENCES

Adler, P. (1974). *In* "Topics in Culture Learning." Vol. II, pp. 23–40. East-West Center, Hawaii.
Argyle, M. (1967). "The Psychology of Interpersonal Behaviour." Penguin Books, Harmondsworth, Middlesex.
Bar-Yosef, R. (1968). *International Migration Rev.* 2, 27–45.
Bem, D. J. (1967). *Psychol. Rev.* **74**, 183–200.
Bennett, J. W., Passin, H. and McKnight, R. K. (1958). "In Search of Identity: The Japanese Overseas Student in America and Japan." University of Minneapolis, Minneapolis.
Berger, P. L. and Luckmann, T. (1967). "The Social Construction of Reality." Doubleday Anchor Books, New York.

Berry, J. W. and Annis, R. C. (1974). *J. Cross-cult. Psychol.* **5**, 382–406.
Bettelheim, G. (1943). *J. abnorm. soc. Psychol.* **38**, 417–452.
Bochner, S. and Wicks, P., Eds (1972). "Overseas Students in Australia." University of New South Wales Press, Sydney.
Brein, M. and David, K. H. (1971). *Psychol. Bull.* **76**, 215–230.
Brim, O. G. and Wheeler, S. (1966). "Socialization Through the Life Cycle." Wiley, New York and Chichester.
Brody, E. G. (1970). "Behaviour in New Environments." Sage, Beverly Hills.
Campbell, D. T. (1964). *In* "Cross Cultural Understanding: Epistemology in Anthropology" (Eds F. S. C. Northrup and H. H. Livingston), pp. 308–338. Harper, New York.
Carringer, D. C. (1974). *J. Cross-cult. psychol.* **5**, 492–504.
Castaneda, C. (1974). "Journey to Ixtlan." Penguin Books, Harmondsworth, Middlesex.
Coelho, G. C., Ed. (1972). "Mental Health and Social Change: An Annotated Bibliography." NIMH, Rockville, Maryland.
Coulter, F. and Taft, R. (1973). *Human Relations* **26**, 681–693.
Curle, A. (1947). *Human Relations* **1**, 42–86.
Curle, A. and Trist, E. L. (1947). *Human Relations* **1**, 242–288.
David, K. H. (1972). *Trends.* (Center for Cross-Cultural Training and Research, Hilo, Hawaii), **4**, whole of No. 3.
Davidson, G. (1974). *J. Cross-cult. Psychol.* **5**, 199–211.
De Sola Pool, I. (1958). *Antioch Rev.* **18**, 431–446.
De Vos, G. A. and Hippler, A. E. (1968). *In* "Handbook of Social Psychology" (Eds G. Lindzey and E. Aronson), Vol. IV, pp. 323–417. Addison-Wesley, Reading, Mass.
Dignam, M. H. (1966). *Rev. for Religious.* **25**, 669–677.
Dornbusch, S. M. (1955). *Social Forces* **33**, 316–321.
Eisenstadt, S. (1954). "The Absorption of Immigrants." Routledge and Kegan Paul, London.
Foa, U. G. and Chemers, M. M. (1967). *Int. J. Psychol.* **2**, 45–57.
Frankl, V. (1959). "From Death Camp to Existentialism." Beacon Press, Boston.
Gajdusek, D. C. (1970). *Engineering and Science* **33**, 26–33, 56–62.
Garabedian, P. C. (1963). *Social Problems* **11**, 139–152.
Gergen, K. J. (1968). *In* "The Self in Social Interaction" (Eds C. Gordon and K. J. Gergen), Vol. I, pp. 299–308. Wiley, New York and London.
Goffman, E. (1961). "Asylums." Doubleday Anchor Books, New York.
Guiora, A. Z., Paluszny, M., Beit-Hallahmi, B., Catford, J. C., Cooley, R. E. and Dull, C. Y. (1975). *Lang. Learning* **25**, 43–61.
Guthrie, G. (1975). *In* "Cross-cultural Perspectives in Learning." (Eds R. W. Brislin, S. Bochner and W. J. Lonner). Sage, Beverly Hills.
Hartley, R. (1960). "The Acceptance of New Reference Groups: Final Report." NR171-033. Office of Naval Research, Washington.
Inkeles, A. (1969). *In* "Handbook of Socialization Theory and Research" (Ed. D. A. Goslin), pp. 615–632. Rand McNally, Chicago.
Inkeles, A. and Smith, D. H. (1974). "Becoming Modern." Harvard University Press, Cambridge.
Kelvin, P. (1970). "The Bases of Social Behaviour." Holt Rinehart, London.
Kimball, S. T. and Watson, J. B. (1972). "Crossing Cultural Boundaries: The Anthropological Experience." p. 21. Chandler, San Francisco.

Lambert, W. E. (1967). *J. Social Issues.* **23**, 91–109.
Levine, S., Goldman, L. and Coover, G. D. (1972). *In* "Physiology, Emotion and Psychosomatic Illness" (CIBA Foundation Symposium No. 8), pp. 281–291. ASP (Elsevier), Amsterdam.
MacCannell, D. (1973). *Am. J. Sociol.* **79**, 589–603.
Malpass, R. (in press). *In* "Culture, Child and School" (Eds M. Maehr and W. Stallings). Brooks, Cole, Monterey, California.
Miller, G. A., Galanter, E. and Pribram, K. H. (1960). "Plans and the Structure of Behaviour." p. 93. Holt, New York.
Murphy, H. B. M. (1974). *International Migration* **12**, 333–350.
Newcomb, T. M. (1943). "Personality and Social Change." Dryden, New York.
Oberg, K. (1960). *Practical Anthrop.* **7**, 177–182.
Peal, E. and Lambert, W. E. (1962). *Psychol. Monogr.* **76**, whole of No. 546.
Richardson, A. (1974). "British Immigrants and Australia: A Psychosocial Inquiry." ANU Press, Canberra.
Riley, M. W., Foner, A., Hess, B. and Toby, M. L. (1969). *In* "Handbook of Socialization: Theory and Research" (Ed. D. A. Goslin), pp. 951–982. Rand McNally, Chicago.
Rogers, E. (1962). "Diffusion of Innovations." Free Press, Glencoe.
Rootman, I. (1972). *Sociol. of Educ.* **45**, 258–270.
Ruesch, J., Jacobson, A. and Loeb, M. B. (1948). "Acculturation and Illness." *Psychol. Monogr.* **62**, whole of No. 40.
Sanford, R. N., Ed. (1956). *J. Social Issues* **12**, 1–70.
Sarbin, T. R., Taft, R. and Bailey, D. E. (1960). "Clinical Inference and Cognitive Theory." Holt Rinehart, New York.
Schein, E. H. (1956). *Psychiatry* **19**, 149–172.
Schutz, A. (1964). *In* "Studies in Social Theory" (Ed. A. Brodersen), pp. 91–105. Martinus Nijhoff, The Hague.
Spiro, M. E. (1961). *In* "Studying Personality Cross-culturally" (Ed. B. Kaplan), pp. 93–128. Harper and Row, New York.
Taft, R. (1961). *Genetic Psychol. Monogr.* **64**, 309–384.
Taft, R. (1966). "From Stranger to Citizen." Tavistock, London.
Taft, R. (1973). *In* "Psychology and Race" (Ed. P. W. Watson), pp. 224–240. Penguin Books, Harmondsworth, Middlesex.
Taft, R. (1974). *In* "Readings in Cross-Cultural Psychology" (Eds J. L. M. Dawson and W. J. Lonner), pp. 268–276. University of Hong Kong Press, Hong Kong.
Triandis, H. C., Malpass, R. J. and Davidson, A. R. (1971). *In* "Biennial Review of Anthropology" (Ed. D. J. Siegel), pp. 1–84. Stanford University Press, Palo Alto.
Wardell, W. I., Hyman, M. and Bahnson, C. B. (1964). *J. Chronic Diseases* **17**, 73–84.
Wick, J. A. (1971). *Rev. for Religious* **30**, 19–35.
Wood, M. M. (1934). "The Stranger: A Study in Social Relationships." Columbia University, New York.

Are Cognitive Processes Universal? A Contribution to Cross-cultural Piagetian Psychology

5

PIERRE R. DASEN

I. INTRODUCTION

Are cognitive processes universal? After more than a century of controversies around this apparently simple question, we still have no simple answer. However, a wealth of data has now been accumulated and some convincing generalizations begin to appear. In one of the best introductions to "culture and thought", Cole and Scribner (1974) come to the conclusion that "we are unlikely to find cultural differences in basic component cognitive processes" (p. 193). However, cultural differences are found in the way these basic processes combine into "functional cognitive systems" for various purposes. In other words: "cultural differences in cognition reside more in the situations to which particular cognitive processes are applied than in the existence of a process in one cultural group and its absence in another" (Cole *et al.* 1971, p. 233).

The goal of this chapter is to ask the same overall question and look for similar generalizations in one specific area of cognitive psychology, the developmental theory of Jean Piaget and his co-workers. Are the structures described by Piaget in Swiss children (and since extensively documented in many Western countries) to be found in the cognitive development of children all over the world? Are the stages and their hierarchical ordering universal? Or are there aspects of the child's reasoning which are culturally determined? What are the situational components which determine whether a particular basic operation will be applied or not? These are some of the questions we will attempt to answer. We will come to no definite conclusion, but will find indications that some aspects of operational development are indeed universal (the "qualitative" or structural properties) whereas others are partly culturally determined (generally speaking the "quantitative" aspects, such as the rate of development).

Piaget's theory has given rise to a large number of cross-cultural studies. The purpose of this chapter is not to provide an extensive review of these studies, but rather to present in detail some empirical research within a general theoretical context. Most data reported will be drawn from the author's own work, and this choice should not be seen as a conceited selection of quality, but rather as a modest expression of egocentrism. A general review of the area has been previously provided by the author (Dasen, 1972). Other critical reviews of importance have been written by Levine (1970), Lloyd (1972), Cole and Scribner (1974), Carlson (1976) and Greenfield (1976). A selection of previously published papers on cross-cultural Piagetian psychology forms the third section of the reader compiled by Berry and Dasen (1974) and the author is editing a book of original reports which will provide a panorama of the most recent research in the area (Dasen, 1976). This chapter should be viewed in the context of this specialized literature. Those readers wishing to brush up on Piaget's theory in more general terms are referred to the short introduction by Ginsburg and Opper (1969) the classical compendium by Flavell (1963) or Furth's (1968) more theoretical introduction. Droz and Rahmy (1972) have prepared a guide to reading Piaget's original writings, and Modgil (1974) has compiled a monumental handbook of the research inspired by the Genevan school.

Our presentation will begin with the sensori-motor origins of cognitive development: a report on pilot studies and an on-going longitudinal research programme on the development of sensori-motor intelligence in African babies. These first results indicate that the structural properties and the ordering of the sensori-motor stages are identical in African and European children. The rates of development on the other hand are shown to vary according to the complexity and specific content of the problems presented. Compared to French norms, the African precocity usually found in postural and motor development seems to be present also in the early intellectual achievements.

Next we shall turn our attention to the concrete operational stage and its best-known index, conservation. We shall compare the rates of development of conservation reported by a large number of researchers in all parts of the world, and will discuss the generality of the processes involved, particularly in view of the apparent anomalies reported by Bovet (1974). We will also discuss the significance of the absence of conservation behaviour in some subjects, drawing on the data of a small learning experiment with

Eskimo children and on the competence/performance distinction introduced by Flavell and Wohlwill (1969).

Finally we shall examine some of the cultural factors which seem to influence the rate of development of concrete operations. Among the various possibilities, we shall document especially the importance of acculturation and the influence of eco-cultural demands. The results of a first series of studies with Australian Aboriginal children show a correspondence between the frequency of concrete operational behaviour and the degree of contact with Western values and life-style. Another study comparing the development of conservation and spatial concepts in Australian Aboriginal, Eskimo and African children suggests that the ecological demands placed upon a subsistence-level population, and the resulting economic activities (e.g. hunting vs agriculture), influence the development of some concepts over others.

II. THE STAGES OF SENSORI-MOTOR INTELLIGENCE IN THE AFRICAN BABY*

A considerable number of studies have examined the psycho-motor development of the African baby; they have been summarized by Warren (1972), Werner (1972), Zempléni and Zempléni (1972) and Dasen (1974b). Most of these studies have used so-called "baby tests" derived from Gesell's detailed observations and most have found the African baby to be advanced on Western norms at birth and up to the second year of life. Warren (1972) has produced an excellent critique of the methodology employed in most of these studies and has questioned the notion of African infant precocity. In still more recent studies, Super (1973) and Kilbride and Kilbride (1975) have demonstrated that there is no general precocity, but that some culturally valued skills (such as sitting, stepping, standing and smiling) develop relatively early because of deliberate teaching and incidental practice, whereas other less valued skills (such as crawling or rolling over) show no advance or develop later than in Western babies.

Piaget's (1936, 1937) early observations on the sensori-motor origins of cognition have recently received renewed attention. Some experimental studies, particularly of object permanency, have replicated and expanded Piaget's formulation (e.g. Décarie, 1967; Bell, 1970; Bower and Paterson, 1972), and ordinal scales of sensori-motor development have been

---

* Part of the results reported here and further details on the methods, subjects and experimental situation have been published in French by Bovet et al. (1974). The first stage of the project was reported in Dasen (1973a, b).

constructed (Uzgiris and Hunt, 1975; Corman and Escalona, 1969; Casati and Lézine, 1968). So far, however, there has been little cross-cultural work published in this area. Within Western samples, Golden and Birns (1968) failed to find social-class differences in object permanency in 18- and 24-month-old infants. Wachs *et al.* (1971) on the other hand found social-class differences at some ages on some of the items of the Uzgiris–Hunt scale. Paraskevopoulos and Hunt (1971) compared the ages at which infants living under differing conditions achieve levels of object construction and verbal and gestural imitation; they found a significant effect of the infant–caretaker ratio in two Athenian orphanages. Goldberg (1970) studied sensori-motor intelligence in urban Zambian infants, using the Corman–Escalona scale. She found an advance on American norms at 6 months and a slight retardation at 9 and 12 months. Performance on the S (space) scale was significantly better than on the OP (object permanency) scale at each age level, which is the reverse of Corman and Escalona's (1969) results with American babies.

The study which is to be reported here is an application of the Casati–Lézine scale to infants in a rural area of the Ivory Coast.

A. Method

1. The Casati–Lézine (1968) Scale of Sensori-motor Intelligence

The Casati–Lézine scale of sensori-motor development follows Piaget's observations and theory very closely; it concentrates on Piaget's sensori-motor stages 3 to 6 inclusive. Stages 4 to 6 are further sub-divided into sub-stages A and B, marking the beginning and the full accomplishment of each stage. The scale consists of seven series (or tasks, which are sub-divided into hierarchically ordered items):

1. Object permanency. The infant has to find an object hidden under a screen (cloth), either when it is still partly visible (stage 3B), or when it is completely hidden but the child has already started a grasping movement (4A). At stage 4B, the child searches for the object under one screen (without having started a grasping movement) but if it is moved behind a second screen, the child continues to search under the first. The "visible displacement" to a second screen is followed at stage 5A, whereas at stage 5B the child is able to follow the object through an "invisible displacement" under one screen (the object is hidden in a box, the box is hidden under the screen, and the object is released: the object remaining hidden under the screen, the empty box is shown to the infant). At stage 6A the infant follows the object through an invisible displacement to a second screen. At the end

of the sixth stage (6B) the infant is able to follow systematically an object through a series of invisible displacements in sequence, using three screens.
2. An object is placed out of reach, with a string attached to it. The level of development (stages 4A to 5B) is determined by the complexity of the situation (length, position and number of strings) in which the subject is able to solve the problem by pulling the string.
3. An object is placed out of reach on a cloth. The infant is able to get at the object by pulling the cloth. The complexity of the situation (e.g. cloth nearby or further removed) again determines the level of development (stages 4A to 5A). In a more difficult situation, the object is placed on a wooden board which can be rotated on a pin to move the object within reach. The child is placed at stage 6B if he solves the problem by "insight", at stage 6A if he solves it by trial and error, and at stage 5B if he can do it after a demonstration.
4. Use of an instrument. An object is placed out of reach, and the infant is given a toy rake or a ruler with which be may reach for the object. The way he solves this problem indicates his stage of development (4B to 6B).
5. Exploration of objects. The infant is given a small mirror and a matchbox and his level of development is judged from the way he handles these objects (3B to 6B).
6. Combination of objects: tube and rake. A small object wrapped in a piece of paper is placed inside a tube in such a way that it cannot be reached with the fingers. The plastic toy rake is placed within reach. The stage of development (5B to 6B) is judged from the way the child uses the rake to push the paper out of the tube.
7. Combination of objects: tube and small chain. The same tube is placed in front of the child at the same time as a small chain made of paper clips. The way the child discovers how to make the chain pass through the tube (almost all children attempt to do this, but a regrouping of the clips is necessary to solve the problem) determines his developmental stage (5B to 6B).

The details of the techniques and the assessment of the observed behaviours are described fully by Casati and Lézine (1968).

2. Subjects

In a first part of the study, 73 infants aged 6 to 24 months were tested, 39 in 1971 by Dasen and 34 in 1972 by Bovet and Othenin-Girard. Subjects were included only if their dates of birth were known. Subsequently a more extensive longitudinal study was arranged (1973-75) by Dasen, Lavallée and Retschitzki. This second part can be considered as a replication of the preliminary study, although it will eventually lead to much more extensive analyses.

The studies took place in villages in the Ivory Coast, about 200 km north-west of Abidjan, the capital city, in the area where tropical rain forest gives way to savannah. The inhabitants of the region are from the Baoulé tribe and live mainly from subsistence-level agriculture (yams, plantain, manioc) and from the production of some cash crops (coffee, cocoa). Although acculturation is well on its way, child rearing in these villages still follows the traditional patterns. The daily life and customs of the Baoulé have been described by Guerry (1970).

3. Experimental Situation

The infants were tested when sitting on their mother's lap in front of a table; constant personal contact with the mother and the possibility of reaching for the breast seem to be most important to insure a satisfactory testing situation. The examinations took place in familiar surroundings, in the children's own courtyards in the first part of the study, in a specially built straw observation-hut in the second part. Care was taken to create as natural a testing situation as possible: the children and mothers were quite familiar with the experimenters, and local assistants were trained to present the objects to the child and to serve as interpreters.

The administration of the scale took between 30 minutes and two hours, and often several sessions were necessary to complete the testing. Emotional reactions were taken into account: some children show aversion or apathy towards strangers (particularly in the second year of life) and their behaviour cannot be interpreted as a true indicator of their developmental level. Some records had to be discarded completely from the analysis for this reason (20 in 1971, 3 in 1972, 13 in 1973/75). With other subjects only partial results were obtained; these were retained in the samples. Generally speaking the number of "refusals" diminished as the skill of the experimenters in creating an adequate experimental situation increased. The fear of strangers seems to be especially marked in the African child (Ainsworth, 1967; Konner, 1972), but similar difficulties exist when testing Western infants (e.g. Lézine et al., 1969, p. 36), and the discarding of results presents a serious methodological problem (Lewis and Johnson, 1971).

B. Results and Discussion

1. First Study (Bovet et al., 1974)

The cumulative frequencies for the attainment of each sub-stage were calculated for each of the seven series in the scale, dividing the sample into five age-groups. These results are presented in detail in Bovet *et al.* (1974) and are compared with the French norms provided by Lézine *et al.* (1969). Such a comparison presents some methodological difficulties, especially since the European norms were not obtained by the same group of experimenters as the African data (Warren, 1972). Furthermore the number of subjects in the first study is quite small compared to the number of infants tested by Lézine *et al.* Our sample can be considered to be representative of the general Baoulé infant population, whereas Lézine's subjects were obtained in day-care centres of lower-class suburbs of Paris, and therefore may not be representative of the French population. Thus any comparison has to remain tentative, and we shall consider only overall trends.

On three series (both combinations of objects and the use of an instrument-series 4, 6 and 7) there is an obvious advance of the African results over French norms throughout the age-range and at each sub-stage. On all three tasks, the infant has at least one object within reach, the problem being to explore the possibilities of combining it with a second object, or to use it as a means for reaching a coveted object. The tasks call for exploration, active manipulation and the solving of a problem either by trial and error or with foresight.

On the other series (object permanency, object attached to a string or placed on a cloth, and exploration of objects, series 1, 2, 3 and 5) there is an advance over French norms in the first sub-stages (up to 5A). In the later sub-stages results are parallel to French norms on series 1 and 2, and a small delay occurs compared with French norms on series 3 and 5.

It seems that the advance occurs when the objects are close at hand or can be manipulated directly: on object permanency (series 1) as long as the object is not displaced to a second screen, as long as the string (2) is placed in direct line with the object (as opposed to being placed in a "Z" shape), when the object is placed on a cloth (3) near the child but not when it is further removed, or when the exploration of an object (5) requires only simple motor schemes. The development seems to parallel that of French children when the situations are spatially or temporally more complex, when the object is hidden (1) under a second screen or under two superimposed screens or is moved in succession, or when the object is placed far away (2, 3) and a complex scheme of actions is necessary to retrieve it.

The slight lag which occurs in two situations (the second parts of series 3 and 5) seems to be quite directly linked to the content of the problem: they require the manipulation of some bizarre apparatus such as rotating a wooden board or opening a match box. It is probably not the lack of familiarity with the test material as such which causes the difficulty; the plastic tube and rake, the toy cars and other objects used for further tasks are quite unfamiliar to the infants of the study, and despite this they manage to use them very satisfactorily. Rather it seems to be the type of manipulation, the rotating around an axle, or sliding the inner part of the box, which is not culturally relevant. Few objects exist in the child's environment which would require such actions, whereas the European child would usually have plenty of occasions to observe or manipulate toys, furniture, or other objects which involve a rotation (wheels of toy cars, spinning-tops) or a sliding movement (opening a drawer, nesting boxes).

At this stage we cannot "explain" the precocity of the African infants on some of our sensori-motor tasks, but we can speculate on some of the cultural characteristics which may produce it. The Baoulé neonate and his mother remain inside the house for the first two weeks after birth; immediately thereafter, the mother returns to normal life, carrying the baby on her back. Compared with an infant lying in a crib for most of the day, the African baby thus receives an enormous amount of proprioceptive, tactile and visual stimulation which enhances its psycho-motor and postural development. The baby may take advantage of this motor precocity to explore his environment, and build up the schemes which lead to the kind of sensori-motor structures of intelligence we have been studying.

Furthermore the Baoulé infant is breast-fed on demand until weaning occurs at about 18 months. The infant seems to be quite active in this process: he may get immediate satisfaction by crying, but we have also observed many occasions when he actively searched for the breast. Even when he is attached to the mother's back, he wriggles to the side until he can reach for it. This early experience in searching actively for the breast, and in finding that he can build up motor schemes which will lead to satisfaction, may explain at least part of the precocity in object permanency and in the handling of objects which are within easy reach.

However much more detailed observation of the infants' spontaneous behaviour is required to reach more definite conclusions. For example it seems, at first sight, that being attached to the back with arms and legs separated on each side of the mother (which prevents the child from touching one hand with the other) would hinder the development of object manipulation, particularly in the case when two objects, each held in one hand, have to be combined. Lézine (personal communication) suggests that this position may in fact foster an early lateralization, which would in turn favour the manipulation and combining of objects; this hypothesis is open to verification. It has also been suggested that object-manipulation is not generally valued in African cultures, whereas social interactions are highly stressed (Zempléni, 1970; Valantin, 1970). However it is possible that these social interactions, which also involve the active participation of the infant, may foster the same sensori-motor structures as physical actions would (Piaget, 1965). In any case, no detailed ethological study of the African infant's spontaneous behaviour and object manipulation has yet been published. We are currently involved in such a study, and seem to find more object manipulation than expected, especially since the infant is left very free to explore his environment and to take any objects he likes (even dangerous ones).

2. Second Study (Dasen, Lavallée and Retschitzki)

More extensive data have been obtained in an on-going, longitudinal project. For the moment, pending further analysis, we can consider this new set of results as a cross-sectional replication of the first study. Such a replication is not without interest, since the first results were based on relatively few subjects and were obtained by two different groups of experimenters.

The results calculated on 254 observations are presented in Table 1 for object permanency only, together with the previous results of the first study and the French norms of Lézine et al. (1969). The results of the two studies are notably similar. Compared with the French norms, there is a marked precocity of stage 4 (A and B). In both cases, this precocity is also found in stage 5A at 9 to 12 months, but disappears after that age; neither is it significant for stages 5B and 6A. On stage 6B, however, a significant advance over French norms appears in the second study, whereas this was not the case in the preliminary work. On the whole it is not the small differences but the striking similarity in developmental curves which is the remarkable feature of these results.

On object permanency, all subjects have attained the upper stage (6B) at 20 months, whereas on all other series (except series 4, the use of an instrument) this is the case at 22–26 months only. However item 7 of this series may in fact be too easy to mark the end of stage 6: since the object is shown between displacements, it corresponds to item 8 in the Uzgiris–Hunt (1975) scale, which is a stage 5 item. Thus items 14 (serial, systematic displacement under three screens; the object is not shown during displacement) and 15 (as 14, but the object is left under the first screen) of the Uzgiris–Hunt scale were administered to examine the upper limit of stage 6. The results for item 14 are comparable to those of item 7 in the Casati–Lézine scale, whereas item 15 is slightly more difficult (as well as more difficult to score), 100% success being attained at 26 months.

C. Conclusion

The most important conclusion to be drawn from this set of studies may have been overlooked because we have paid attention to cultural variations and

Table 1
Object permanency. Cumulative percentages of subjects attaining sub-stages as a function of age.

French norms, from Lézine et al., 1969, p. 17[a]

Age in months		6	7	8	9	10	11	12	13	14	15	16	17–18	19–20	>21
N		8	22	29	30	29	23	17	28	19	32	16	24	16	12
Stages	Items														
3B	1	25	82	93	100	100	100	100	100	100	100	100	100	100	100
4A	2	0	14	31	60	83	91	94	96	100	100	94	100	100	100
4B	3	0	5	17	30	62	70	76	93	100	94	94	100	100	100
5A	4	0	5	0	3	21	30	41	71	84	84	81	100	94	100
5B	5	0	0	0	0	0	0	24	29	47	50	63	92	94	100
6A	6	0	0	0	0	0	0	0	11	40	38	38	67	94	100
6B	7	0	0	0	0	0	0	0	0	0	11	16	6	58	94	92

[a] Reproduced by permission of Les Editions du Centre de Psychologie Appliquée, Paris, from their Monographie No. 1, "Les Étapes de l'Intelligence sensori-motrice de l'Enfant", by I. Lézine, M. Stambak and I. Casati, 1969, p. 17.

Baoulé infants, Ivory Coast (Dasen, Lavallée and Retschitzki) (second study)

Age in months		6	7	8	9	10	11	12	13	14	15	16	17–18	19–20	>21
N		5	4	14	11	11	10	16	18	16	11	13	28	31	66
Stages	Items														
3B	1[a]	60	75	100	90	100	100	100	100	100	100	100	100	100	100
4A	2[a]	40	50	57	90	100	100	100	100	100	100	100	100	100	100
4B	3[a]	0	25	42	54	90	100	100	94	100	100	100	100	100	100
5A	4[b]	0	0	0	36	54	70	68	44	93	81	84	100	100	100
5B	5[b]	0	0	0	9	9	0	25	11	68	72	76	100	100	100
6A	6[b]	0	0	0	0	0	0	6	0	43	63	76	89	97	100
6B	7[c]	0	0	0	0	0	0	6	0	12	36	38	68	94	100

Significance level of Baoulé/French comparison, using the Kamara and Easley (1976) statistic: [a]NS [b]NS (0·10) [c]0·05 [d]0·01.

Baoulé infants, Ivory Coast (Bovet et al., 1974), p. 372 (first, preliminary study)

Age in months		6–8	9–12	13–16	17–20
N		12	15	17	10
Stages	Items				
3B	1	72	100	100	100
4A	2	55	100	100	100
4B	3	33	85	100	100
5A	4	6	48	70	100
5B	5	0	18	44	94
6A	6	0	0	26	94
6B	7	0	0	9	60

differences in the rate of development of the various sub-stages on different tasks: it is, in fact, that the qualitative characteristics of sensori-motor development are quite similar or even identical in French and Baoulé infants, in spite of vast differences in their cultural environment. Not only are the structural properties of the stages, and therefore their order of appearance, identical in both groups, but even the actions and schemes, and the way these are slowly built up into more complex action-patterns which eventually enable the infant to solve rather difficult problems, seem to be identical.

For example, the last series in the Casati–Lézine scale (the combination of a tube and a small chain) is, at first sight, a quite impossible task. For one thing, why should the infant wish to combine these two objects? He may just as well look through the tube, roll it on the table, put the chain around his fingers, or throw it at the experimenter. Yet, after stage 5A, almost every infant starts to search for some way of making the chain pass through the tube. When this task is presented to a Baoulé infant, it seems even more ludicrous, since the subject will never have seen a plastic tube or paper clips before. Yet he takes these two strange objects, and combines them exactly as the infants in the day-care centre of Paris did; not only does he get the idea of combining them, but he does this following the same steps, with the same errors, and finding the same successively more and more adapted solutions. (On average, he even finds them significantly earlier than his French age-mate.)

These striking similarities, which we dare not call universals after a comparison of only two populations, seem to show that there may be generalities in the way the human infant interacts with his environment, builds up knowledge of this environment and develops the basis of his later reasoning processes.

Yet, the cultural variations in the rate of development show that sensori-motor intelligence is not completely determined by biological factors (genetics or maturation) but also depends on particular stimulations. We have not found an overall precocity, but advances in some respects, parallel results in others, and a few delays, which reminded us of Super's (1973) results for motor development in Kenyan infants. These differential rates of development seem to be linked to cultural characteristics, to the predominant mode or quantity of stimulation, to the cultural value placed on certain skills over others. We are not in a position to specify the details of this link or to describe the mechanism of the cultural influence on cognitive development. Detailed observations on the spontaneous behaviour of the same infants in their "home" situation should provide part of the missing information. However this type of correlational research is not fit to prove causal links.

As we move, in the next section, to a discussion of the next stage, that of concrete operations, we shall come to much the same conclusion: the qualitative aspects of development, the structure of the stages, their ordering and the type of answers the children give to Piagetian tasks, seem to be quasi-universal, whereas the rates of development seem to vary under the influence of socio-cultural factors. However, we shall also find that the rates of development are not uniform across conceptual domains within a cultural group, but are dependent to some degree on the cultural value placed on some concepts over others.

III. THE STAGE OF CONCRETE OPERATIONS

A. Qualitative Aspects: the Sequence of Stages

Among the many aspects of concrete operational development which Piaget and his colleagues have described, conservation behaviour has received an unduly large amount of attention. To apprehend the invariance of certain characteristics of an object across the transformation of its perceptual aspects is an important step in cognitive development, although its precise mechanisms are still being debated; it is often considered a sort of "marker" of concrete operational development, whereas other interesting indices are neglected. The same emphasis on conservation has been evident in cross-cultural studies; since so much information has been accumulated on a single aspect of development, we were tempted to follow the general trend, and chose it as the example for our discussion.

There are strong indications that conservation (be it of quantity, weight, volume, number, length or area) is a universal, insofar as it has been found in at least some of the subjects in every population studied. Flavell and Wohlwill (1969, p. 84 f.n.) have made a distinction between "strong" and "weak" sequential invariance, or what may be called strong and weak universals.

"A sequence is strongly invariant if it is both universally present and universally fixed in the childhoods of undamaged human beings. For instance, we imagine that all intact human infants achieve primary and tertiary circular reactions, and achieve them in that order only. A sequence is weakly invariant if, when present, it is universally fixed. One may be able to find children who do not attain A, or B, or both; but for all children who do attain both, the order of attainment is the same."

Thus, following this definition, concepts of conservation (as well as most other concrete operational concepts) could be viewed as "weak" universals, whereas sensori-motor development would be a case of a "strong" universal.

The variations among cultural groups or sub-groups in the proportion of subjects displaying conservation on a particular concept will be discussed later. Since this proportion usually increases with age, it is often referred to as a measure of the "rate" of development. It is this quantitative aspect of conservation behaviour which seems subject to cultural variations. The qualitative aspects of conservation, the succession of non-conservation, transitional and conservation answers, and the type of reasons given to explain either a non-conservation or a conservation judgment, are usually reported to be identical with those described by Piaget and verified by many others in Western children. There are, however, some exceptions to this general rule, and these deserve special attention.

Bovet (1974) for example has reported a "deviation" from the usual sequence of stages in the acquisition of conservation of quantity (liquids) in illiterate Algerian children. Very young children (5 to 6 years old) gave undifferentiated non-conservation answers, based on the action of pouring the liquid from one glass to another rather than on the dimensions of the containers. Somewhat older children (7 to 8 years) gave conservation answers, but were unable to give a proper reason for the judgment. Still older children gave dimensional non-conservation or transitional answers (8 to 11 years) or conservation answers justified by the usual identity, compensation or reversibility arguments (10 to 12 years).

The same children were then subjected to two additional situations, one in which they were to pour water from one container to the next of a different shape, predicting each time where the water level would be (usually solved correctly before conservation is achieved), the second in which they were asked to pour quantities of liquid as equal as possible into pairs of glasses which differed either in diameter or in height or in both dimensions (usually solved correctly at about the same age as conservation problems).

The 7- to 8-year-old "conservers" could not solve these additional tasks correctly: they were obviously not taking into account the dimensions of the glasses, although their attention must have been gradually drawn to the perceptual aspects of the situation, for when presented with the initial conservation task again, they now gave dimensional non-conservation answers. This apparent "regression" led Bovet to conclude that these children were still at the pre-operational stage in spite of their initial conservation answers; in other words, they were not "conservers" but "pseudo-conservers". The same "additional" stage characterized by non-operational conservation answers occurred in conservation of quantity using plasticine balls, and in conservation of weight, but not in conservation of length.

Bovet emphasizes the fact that this additional stage is a temporary departure from the usual sequence: with increasing age, the pseudo-conservation gives way, first to non-conservation and then to intermediate and finally conservation answers. Greenfield (1976), in a discussion of Bovet's paper, suggests that pseudo-conservation may have occurred also in her Wolof study (Greenfield, 1966) but has gone unnoticed because of procedural differences. Greenfield's conservation task had two parts: first the water was poured from the initial container into a single narrower glass, and on the second part it was poured from the initial container into six shorter, narrower glasses. Most subjects classified as non-conservers in the 8 to 9 and 11 to 13 year-old groups made conservation judgments in the first part but not in the second part of the procedure. These children may have been "pseudo-conservers". In this case, the pseudo-conservation pattern seems to persist among unschooled Senegalese children until a much later age than reported by Bovet for Algerian unschooled children, and it can no longer be considered as a temporary discontinuity, occurring only in young children before the usual sequential development takes place.

However Greenfield's "pseudo-conservers" may also have been at the intermediate stage of fluctuating answers. In the absence of data on the justifications given by these subjects and since the situational variations suggested by Bovet had not been used, it is impossible to decide. Similarly the early rise and subsequent decline of conservation answers reported by de Lemos (1966) in a sample of Australian Aboriginal children (Hermannsburg), and found again five years later by Dasen (1970, 1974a), may have been due to pseudo-conservation. Seagrim and Lendon (personal communication) are conducting longitudinal research in the same location which should clarify the issue. There are no reports of pseudo-conservation in other populations; the question also remains open whether it could be found in very young Western children.

B. Quantitative Aspect: Cross-cultural Comparison of Rates of Development

The results obtained with Piagetian tasks are often reported in the form of a percentage of subjects classified at each stage (or sub-stage) within each age group. In graphical form, a curve resembling the normal ogive is usually obtained, although other polynomials may also be adequate (Kamara and Easley, 1976). These curves can be considered to represent the "rate" of development of the particular concept in the population studied but of course *not* the rate of development in any individual child.

To provide some idea of the large cross-cultural variability, we have chosen to present on one single graph (Fig. 1, reprinted from Dasen, 1973a, p. 157) the developmental curves for conservation of continuous quantities (liquids) from all cross-cultural studies until 1972 for which percentage data were available to us. Such a comparison is methodologically imperfect, since nothing guarantees the comparability of the studies. The various curves are affected by differences in task administration, scoring, language and communication difficulties, age determination or any other aspects of the testing situation and the method used. Such recently described phenomena as pseudo-conservation (discussed previously) or the competence/performance distinction (to be discussed later) may also interfere with such a comparison. In any case, the curves should not be taken as comparative measures of cognitive capacity in the groups compared.*

With all these precautions, and looking only at the general trends indicated by these curves, it remains obvious that the cross-cultural variability in the proportion of individuals attaining this concept of conservation is very large. The rate of development seems to be determined by cultural factors to a large extent; we shall discuss some of these factors, and their effect, in a later section. Of interest are those developmental curves which do not reach 100% (described by Dasen, 1972, 1973a, 1975c, as asymptotic), particularly if the study included adolescents or adults. These curves indicate that there is a large proportion of individuals who do not acquire (or at least, display) this particular set of concrete operations. This is a serious limitation to the universality of Piagetian stages.†

What is the significance of this phenomenon? In Cole and Scribner's words, "Until we have some better idea of what induces some members of traditional societies to solve conservation problems while their neighbours do not, we cannot be certain about the significance of conservation tests as a tool for understanding the relation between culture and cognitive development" (1974, p. 156). Elsewhere in the same chapter they write, "Can we imagine an adult who would pour water from a small bucket into a larger one

---

* It seems that the following interpretation of such curves may sometimes be made (quoted by Cole and Scribner, 1974, p. 156): "Tribe X does not mature past the European 11-year stage if 50% of the members of tribe X conserve and 50% do not." We personally know of no such silly statement in print, but it seems not impossible that it may occur, since Porteus (reviewed in Kearney, 1973) has had the effrontery to establish a "hierarchy of races" according to the results on his maze test, expressed in terms of mental age. Maybe it is only wishful thinking to believe that cross-cultural psychology has now moved beyond this stage of naïve ethnocentrism.

† After Flavell and Wohlwill's (1969) definition, a concept characterized by an asymptotic developmental curve would be a "weak" universal (if those who do acquire it follow the same sequence of sub-stages).

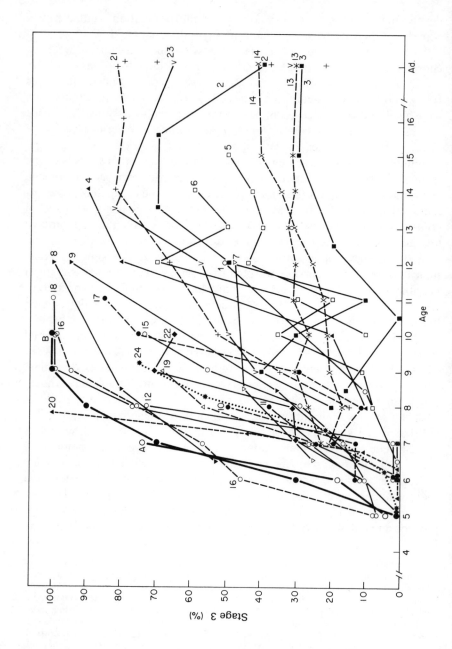

Fig. 1. Conservation of quantity (liquids). Percentage of subjects attaining full conservation. Reprinted from Dasen (1973a). Reproduced by permission from *Psychologie Canadienne/Canadian Psychological Review*, University of Calgary, Alberta, Canada.

A	Europeans, Geneva	(Piaget and Inhelder, 1963)
B	Europeans, Canberra	(Dasen, 1974a)
1	Algerians, unschooled	(Bovet, 1974)
2	Australian Aborigines	(Dasen, 1974a)
	(Hermannsburg), medium contact	
3	Australian Aborigines	(Dasen, 1974a)
	(Areyonga), low contact	
4	Ebrié, Ivory Coast (Adiopodoumé)	(Dasen, 1975a)
5	Australian Aborigines (Hermannsburg)	(de Lemos, 1969)
6	Australian Aborigines (Elcho Island)	(de Lemos, 1969)
7	Wolof, Senegal, rural, unschooled	(Greenfield, 1966)
8	Wolof, Senegal, rural, schooled	(Greenfield, 1966)
9	Wolof, Senegal, Dakar, schooled	(Greenfield, 1966)
10	Aden, Arabs	(Hyde, 1970)
11	Aden, Indians	(Hyde, 1970)
12	Aden, Somali	(Hyde, 1970)
13	Papua-New-Guinea, unschooled	(Kelly, 1970)
14	Papua-New-Guinea, schooled	(Kelly, 1970)
15	Iran, rural	(Mohseni, 1966)
16	Iran, urban	(Mohseni, 1966)
17	Thailand, rural	(Opper, 1971)
18	Thailand, urban	(Opper, 1971)
19	Rwanda, rural, schooled and	(Pinard et al., 1973)
	unschooled	
20	Tiv, Nigeria, rural, unschooled	(Price-Williams, 1961)
21	Papua-New-Guinea, schooled	(Prince, 1969)
22	Oglala Sioux	(Voyat, personal communication)
23	Papua-New-Guinea, schooled	(Waddell; personal communication)
24	Lebanon, Beirut, schooled	(Za'rour, 1971)

and believe that the amount of water has been decreased by this act? In desert communities where water is a treasured commodity, everyone can be expected to conform to certain laws of conservation" (pp. 151–52). Yet de Lemos (1969, p. 262) mentions a practical situation in which adult Aboriginal women in central Australia could choose between one measure of sugar poured into a tall and narrow container and two measures poured into a larger one; of 12 women, eight chose the one with less sugar, but where the level was higher. Thus non-conservation seems to occur even in situations more natural than the usual task administration; but there is still no study testing conservation in a completely natural, culturally relevant situation.

Does being a conserver or non-conserver have any practical significance? Heron (1971) found no relation between a non-verbal measure of conservation of weight and the scores on a non-verbal reasoning test. The reasoning test scores, but not the results of the conservation task, were related to school achievement. A similar lack of correlation between conservation of weight and multiple classification and other operational tasks was further demonstrated by Heron and Dowel (1973, 1974) in Papuan children and in Yugoslav child immigrants to Australia, leading Heron (1974, p. 100) to propose "a *clear separation* of conservation from other cognitive behaviours".

However, the problem of the interpretation of "asymptotic" curves is not limited to conservation alone, for they also occur in other areas of concrete operational development. Part of the answer may come from the suggestion that we may have been measuring a "performance" which is only a poor indicator of the underlying "competence". It is to a discussion of this important distinction that we will now turn our attention.

C. The Performance/Competence Distinction

Recurrently, there have been indications that the initial answer a child gives in a Piagetian task may not reflect his "true" level of reasoning, i.e. the underlying structure or competence. In some cases, with very little "help" (either further questioning, or additional task situations, or exposure to other operational tasks, or training procedures), they seem to be able to "actualize" the latent structure.

De Lemos (1969, pp. 264–65) for example states that "because the Aboriginal society does not appear to recognize or encourage the development of concepts of conservation, these may not be clearly formulated even when the operational capacity is present. In this case it is likely that a little experience with the test situation would be sufficient to develop the concepts."

Bovet (1974) reports the following "Aktualgenese" in Algerian illiterate adults, when testing for conservation of weight:

". . . in several instances, the initial response was a conservation one. Then when the experimenter, in an attempt to obtain a justification for this response, pointed out the differences in appearance of the two objects, the subjects would no longer give a conservation response. In the course of the dialogue, however, the subjects would return to a conservation judgement, and would be able to relate the various dimensions of the objects by means of reasoning based on compensation. These adults' reactions seem to replicate in a condensed sequence the developmental trends noted in the children where an initial non-operational conservation finally becomes, at a later stage, an explicit conservation judgement.

For some of the nonconserving subjects, all that was required for them to grasp the notion of conservation was to weigh the two pieces of clay once on a pair of scales in front of them. They then accompanied their judgements by logical justifications and, what is more, generalized their conservation responses to various changes in shape." (pp. 324–25)

"It is interesting to observe therefore the existence of two concomitant ways of approaching the problem, with an intuitive approach characteristic of everyday practical use being the spontaneous response, and at the same time the logical approach being latent." (p. 330)

"The use of learning situations therefore seems essential in any cross-cultural study, in order to try and reach the potential reasoning capacity of the subjects. A number of precautions must, however, be taken. If these learning techniques are related to the Piagetian type of concepts, they need to come within the framework of Piagetian theory, that is to say, they should consist of 'exercises in operativity.' " (pp. 333–34)

Such a learning study was carried out by Pinard et al. (1973) on three groups of 16 7-year-old children, respectively French Canadian, unschooled Rwandan and schooled Rwandan (5 to 6 months of schooling), with the corresponding control-groups. All these children were completely pre-operational on a pre-test comprising eight tasks of conservation of quantity. Thereafter the experimental groups were subjected to a training procedure using anticipation and compensation situations. Two post-tests were administered, at 15 days and 2 months after the pre-test. The induced acquisition of conservation in the experimental groups was stable over both post-tests, generalized to a variety of situations, and the conservation answers were justified by the usual identity and some compensation and reversibility reasons.

The number of training sessions to induce conservation was not significantly different among the three groups. Whereas there seems to be a small time-lag in the spontaneous acquisition of conservation of quantity in the Rwandan samples compared to the French Canadian children, the capacity to learn the concept seems to be identical, and the learning procedures are able to reduce or suppress the time-lag. The only difference found between the three groups was in the number of children successful on the compensation exercises after one single session: there were none in the French Canadian group, three in the Rwandan group with schooling, and seven in the unschooled group. One possible interpretation of this rapid learning is that these children already had a latent competence for conservation of quantity, which, for some unknown reason, did not manifest itself in the performance on the pre-test, but was then "activated" by a minimum of operational exercises.

In this experiment all the subjects were at an age when conservation is acquired spontaneously by most children within a short time. What effect would the learning procedures have on children (in those populations where the developmental curve is asymptototic) who have not acquired the concept even at a much later age? Would their learning be even faster, since

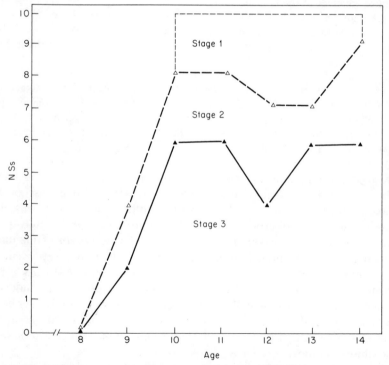

Fig. 2. The development of conservation of quantity in Cape Dorset Eskimo children. Stages: 1 = non-conservation; 2 = transitional; 3 = full conservation.

they are older? or would it be slower, since they may have missed the "critical period" in which the concept is usually acquired? A small training experiment which we carried out as part of a study with Eskimo children (Dasen, 1975b) may give us some preliminary indications.

The study was conducted at Cape Dorset, on Baffin Island (Canada), with Central Eskimos. Ten schooled children were examined at each age from 8 to 14 years for conservation of quantity (liquids) as well as for a variety of other Piagetian concepts (for a detailed report on procedures and results, see Dasen, 1975b). Figure 2 presents the results of the initial testing ("pre-test 1"). The stage 3 curve (full conservation) shows an "asymptote" at 60% beginning with age 10. Among the 50 children aged 10 to 14 years, there were 11 who gave non-conservation answers (stage 1); all except two explained their judgments by perceptual (dimensional) reasons. More than half of these children had less than average school attendance and below average school achievement; their results on other Piagetian tasks (elementary logic and space) were average for their age, except for below-average performance on mental imagery tasks.

These 11 children were subjected to the task of conservation of quantity (liquids) for a second time ("pre-test 2"), on the average 12 days (2 to 27 days) after the first pre-test. The results of the pre-tests are shown in Fig. 3, each subject being identified by a number, the first two digits of which indicate his age. On the second pre-test, four subjects have attained stage 3, and three subjects give transitional answers (stage 2). For these children, it seems that a mere exposure to other operational tasks, and/or becoming more familiar with the testing situation, has been sufficient to produce a learning effect.

The eight subjects situated at stages 1 and 2 on the second pre-test were then subjected to a learning procedure developed by Lefebvre and Pinard (1972). On a first session, a conflict is produced by showing the inefficiency of the child's predominant notional rule based on the height of the liquid in the container. Thereafter the child is subjected to operational exercises based on compensation and addition/subtraction operations. After each set of exercises, the child is asked to pour in a second glass of different shape the same quantity of liquid as contained in a standard glass. If the child succeeds on a complete set of exercises and on the anticipation task, he is subjected to a post-test (the usual conservation of quantity task), but training is continued if he does not give full conservation answers. The results on the post-tests are shown in Fig. 3.

The three subjects who started at stage 2 moved to stage 3 after two or three training sessions. The subjects starting at stage 1 moved to stage 2 after two to four sessions; because of time limitations, the experiment had to be discontinued, and it is not known whether these subjects would also have attained stage 3, and how many training sessions would have been required. The only subject showing absolutely no learning in spite of five training sessions was an additional subject aged 12 years, who was partly deaf and probably mentally retarded.

This small experiment lacks the elaborate pre-tests, the control groups and large number of subjects, the post-tests checking generalization and stability, which are the usual requirements of this type of study (cf. Inhelder *et al.*, 1974). However, its limited results give us some additional clues as to the competence/performance distinction. All subjects who showed rapid

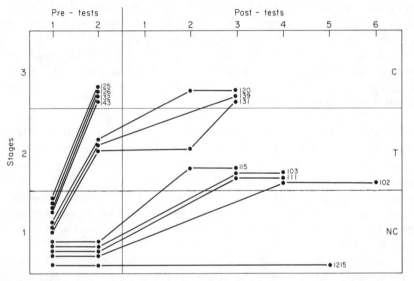

Fig. 3. Training conservation of quantity, Cape Dorset Eskimo children. Stages: 1 = non-conservation; 2 = transitional; 3 =full conservation.

learning and moved to stage 3 were aged 12 to 14 years; it is difficult to believe that these children did not already have the operational structures for conservation of quantity on the first pre-test. But for some reason their (supposed) latent competence did not manifest itself in their performance. On the other hand, those subjects ramaining at stage 1 on the second pre-test and moving to stage 2 after the training sessions, were all aged 10 and 11. It is likely that these children had not acquired the necessary operational structures for conservation, but that these were being built up during the training procedure.

The competence/performance model was first proposed for cognitive-developmental phenomena by Flavell and Wohlwill (1969, pp. 71–5) who derived it from Chomsky's linguistic model.

"The competence model gives an abstract, purely logical representation of what the organism knows or could do in a timeless, ideal environment, whereas the automaton model has the job of describing a real device that could plausibly instance that knowledge or skill, and instance it with the constraints (memory limitations, rapid performance, etc.) under which human beings actually operate" (p. 71).

Similarly, Cole and Bruner (1971) are drawing on the work of another linguist, Labov, to suggest that a competence/performance distinction should be introduced in comparative studies of cognition, and that the "deficit" interpretation ought to be replaced by a "difference" interpretation.

"The crux of the argument, when applied to the problem of 'cultural deprivation', is that those groups ordinarily diagnosed as culturally deprived have the same underlying competence as those in the mainstream of the dominant culture, *the differences in performance being accounted for by the situations and contexts in which the competence is expressed*" (Cole and Bruner, 1971, p. 238).

Similarly, Cole *et al.* (1971) concluded from a large set of cross-cultural studies in experimental anthropology that "cultural differences in cognition reside more in the situations to which particular cognitive processes are applied than in the existence of a process in one cultural group and its absence in another" (p. 233). Or, in other words (Cole and Scribner, 1974), "we are unlikely to find cultural differences in basic component cognitive processes" (p. 193). Cultural factors however influence the way basic processes are organized into "functional systems" and how these are applied in any given situation.

"If cultural differences are assumed to be reflected in the way functional systems are organized for various purposes, then a double line of research becomes important: the first is to uncover the culturally determined experiential factors that give rise to different dominant functional systems . . .; the second is to determine which situational features — content domain, task requirements — call out which functional organizations" (p. 194).

These formulations were not specifically aimed at cross-cultural Piagetian psychology, but they may well apply to this area as well. This is explicitly stated by Heron (1974; Heron and Dowel, 1973, 1974), who cites Flavell and Wohlwill (1969) and Cole and Bruner (1971) to explain the discrepancy in performance on tasks regarded as characteristic of the same stage. Possibly the absence of conservation of weight in some of his Zambian or Papuan subjects may be attributed to the "Labov effect": maybe the weight conservation task was not "their problem".

In this respect, Heron (first in Heron and Simonsson, 1969) calls attention to what he has termed "cognitive ambience":

"By this term I mean the 'values with cognitive relevance that are *implicit* in the total pattern of adult and older sibling behaviour within which (early) development takes place . . . the total pattern of implicit cognitively-relevant cultural values communicated through linguistic and other behaviour by adults and older children'. I must re-emphasise what is the vital feature of this 'communication of cognitively-relevant cultural values': it is *the unintentionality, the day-by-day usualness, the taken-for-granted assumptions about what is and what is not important in life"* (Heron, 1974, p. 97).

For example, Heron and Simonsson (1969, p. 290) suggest that precise comparisons of quantity are not culturally relevant to Zambian children: "Questions of amount or quantity are not dealt with in the terms of precision and exactitude with which they are invested in other cultures; the probability of a Zambian preschool child becoming aware of any importance being attached by his elders to exact identity or equivalence is effectively zero." Much the same observations have been made by Waddell (personal communication) for Papuan children.

All this seems to indicate that *performance* on conservation tasks, and possibly on other Piagetian tasks as well, is partly culture-bound. If this is so, and since these concepts are obviously relevant in the Western technological culture in which Piaget's theory was developed, performance should increase with acculturation. This is the question we will examine next, as we turn to a discussion of some of the factors which may influence concrete operational development.

D. The Influence of Acculturation*

Most quasi-experimental cross-cultural Piagetian studies comparing two or more sub-groups of the same ethnic group have attempted to assess some aspect of acculturation, or factors which are usually linked to acculturation, such as schooling or urban/rural residence, the use of a second language being often associated with these variables. The first study we are summarizing here differs from most previous ones insofar as both groups compared live in isolated locations in the semi-desert of Central Australia, both have kept their ethnic identification and speak their vernacular, although both groups are attending school and learning English; the main difference between the two groups lies in the length and amount of contact

* The studies reported in this section were carried out under the guidance of Professor Gavin N. Seagrim (Australian National University).

they have had with the dominant European culture, and in the extent to which traditional values and activities have persisted.

1. Study 1 (Dasen, 1970, 1974a)

One hundred and forty-five children, aged 6 to 16 years, and 20 adults, were tested in two different locations in Central Australia, both west of Alice Springs. The low-contact group consisted of the total school population at Areyonga Settlement (N = 55); the high-contact group was selected from the Hermannsburg Mission school (N = 90).

The following is a description of the history and present situation of the two groups to be compared:

"The low-contact group consists of Pitjantjara (Pitjantjajara) Aborigines living at the Areyonga Government Settlement, which was established as a ration depot in 1944 and which has included a school since 1950 and a medical dispensary since 1952. Some contact between the Western Desert tribes and European missionaries had existed since 1920, but even when Areyonga was established, contact with European culture was only sporadic, and mainly limited to the distribution of goods, the Aboriginal population remaining mainly nomadic. In later years, some Aborigines became more sedentary, but traditions and customs were constantly revived by the arrival of new groups from the desert (up until about 1965). In 1969, when this study was carried out, the Aboriginal population at Areyonga had become sedentary for part of the year, although most families did not use the houses provided by the settlement, but lived in tin shacks resembling the traditional shelters and which could be moved from time to time. For about four months each year, however, most of the population still leaves on 'walkabout', visiting their ancestral sacred grounds and performing ceremonies, travelling over wide distances in the Western Desert, and living mainly from hunting and gathering. During the sedentary months, the children attend school more or less regularly and most adults have some form of employment, although these jobs tend to be rather artificial because there is no real economic reason for them, except welfare. Access to the settlement, which is situated on Reserve 1028, is restricted and is subject to a permit issued by the welfare administration; access is further hindered by distance (approximately 140 miles from Alice Springs) and poor road conditions.

The medium-contact group consists of Aranda (Arunta) Aborigines living at Hermannsburg Mission, which was established in 1877. with school activities dating back to 1880. Schooling was initially conducted in Aranda, but from the 1930s onward English became more important, and finally the sole language of instruction; the curriculum and facilities were extremely basic until the 1950s. In 1969, the schooling conditions in Areyonga and Hermannsburg tended to be quite similar, although Hermannsburg had slightly better equipment and a more stable staff. The Aboriginal population at Hermannsburg still uses the vernacular almost exclusively, but Aboriginal values and traditions have been abandoned to some

180   P. R. DASEN

extent, without being necessarily replaced by their European equivalents. Housing tends to be of a better standard than at Areyonga, although this is a recent achievement and a few families are moving back into tin shacks. The population is more stable than at Areyonga; there is no annual 'walkabout', although many Aborigines tend to travel frequently to other settlements. Adults are employed on the same type of jobs as at Areyonga, but the mission also has a productive cattle industry and a tannery, and a cash economy is promoted by a well-equipped store. Access to Hermannsburg is free, and tourist buses pay regular visits to the mission; the station is linked to the nearest European centre by 70 miles of a relatively good road." (Dasen, 1974a, pp. 382–83).

The following Piagetian tasks were used: conservation of quantity, weight, volume and length, seriation of lengths. These tasks are widely known and their description need not be repeated here (the detailed procedures are reported in full in Dasen, 1970, and with some detail in Dasen, 1974a). In addition three tasks assessing the development of topological, projective and Euclidean spatial relationships (Piaget and Inhelder, 1948) were used:
(1) *Linear, reverse and circular order.* The subject has to copy a linear display of nine objects, reverse this order and finally change a circular display into a straight line. The task assesses topological spatial relationships of neighbourhood, order, and one-to-one correspondence.
(2) *Rotation of landscape models.* (Localization of topographical positions.) The subject has to locate on one landscape model rotated by 180°, seven successive positions and orientations of a corresponding object placed on an unrotated landscape model. The models and objects used were adapted to the local landscape, but retain the same spatial features as originally used by Piaget and Inhelder (1948; 1956, p. 421). The task assesses topological, projective and Euclidean (metric) spatial relationships, the construction of a coordinate system and the flexibility of spatial operations.
(3) *Horizontality.* This task assesses the coordination of two spatial (Euclidean) reference systems. The subject is required to draw, on corresponding outline figures, the level of water in a half-filled bottle tilted into various positions. The complete task consists of three parts: (a) the water level is hidden (anticipation); (b) the water level is visible (copy); (c) the level is hidden again (anticipation after copy). However, results will be reported for part (a) only, reflecting the spontaneous performance level, as with the other tasks, without any additional learning effect.

Results

The comparison of the number of subjects classified as having attained concrete operations (stage 3) in the Hermannsburg and Areyonga samples is presented in Table 2. The chi-squares were calculated according to a method recently proposed by Kamara and Easley (1976) which takes into account not only the total frequencies, but cumulates the p values for each age level. The differences are statistically significant beyond the 0·05 level for six of the tasks, favouring the Hermannsburg group and thus indicating a strong effect of European contact. Only one of the differences is significant for the spatial tasks, indicating that the influence of acculturation is more marked on concepts, such as conservation, which are less relevant to Aboriginal culture.

Table 2
The influence of acculturation (study 1). Comparison of the attainment of concrete operations (stage 3) in the Hermannsburg and Areyonga samples.

Task	V (Chi-square)	d.f.	p (1 tail)
Quantity	26·735	10	0·001
Weight	17·763	10	0·05
Volume	9·781	10	NS
Length 1	16·519	8	0·05
Length 2	16·145	8	0·05
Seriation	27·592	10	0·001
Orders	11·672	10	NS
Rotation	19·179	10	0·05
Horizontality			
Stage 3A+3B	−0·141	12	NS
Stage 3B only	11·339	12	NS

2. Study 2 (Dasen et al., 1973)

Thirty-five children, aged 5 to 14, were tested in their homes in the vicinity of Adelaide, South Australia. These children had been adopted or were being fostered by European families; since it is quite difficult to locate such children, our sampling suffers from various deficiencies. The most important of these is probably the age at which the children were adopted or first fostered: although this occurred in the first year of life for 21 children, the mean age at adoption was 18·5 months for the total sample, and many children had changed families several times. The tribal origin of most of the children was not known, and only seven were of full Aboriginal descent (the mode, 17 children, being of half Aboriginal ancestry). Early medical histories were sketchy, but it seems that early malnutrition and severe illnesses were quite common. Three of the five oldest children (13 to 14 years) had very bad early medical histories; their results on the cognitive tasks were completely out of line with the results of the rest of the sample.

Thus this age group was not included in the statistical analyses reported below. The following Piagetian tasks were used: conservation of quantity (liquids), conservation of weight, seriation of lengths, reclassification, horizontality. The procedures were identical with those described previously; the reclassification (Nixon) task has been described by de Lacey (1970).

Results

The number of subjects classified as having attained concrete operations (stage 3) in the Adelaide sample is compared with the results obtained previously with Aboriginal children living on an isolated mission station in Central Australia (Hermannsburg) and with European children living in Canberra. (Full results of these two comparison groups are available in Dasen, 1970, 1974a.) The results on the reclassification task are compared with results obtained at Hermannsburg in a subsequent longitudinal study (unpublished) and with the results reported by de Lacey (1970) for Europeans of high social status living in Sydney. The p values of chi-squares calculated according to the method proposed by Kamara and Easley (1976) are reported in Table 3.

Table 3

The influence of acculturation (study 2): comparison of the attainment of concrete operations (stage 3) in the Adelaide sample of adopted children and the Canberra and Hermannsburg samples. P values of chi-squares.

Task	Adelaide/Canberra p	Adelaide/Hermannsburg p
Quantity	0·01	0·001
Weight	NS	NS
Seriation	NS	0·001
Reclassification (Nixon)	NS [a]	0·001
Horizontality	NS	0·001

[a] Comparison of Adelaide children with Europeans of high social status living in Sydney (data from de Lacey, 1970).

The results obtained by these adopted and fostered Aboriginal children are identical to those of European children on the tasks of seriation, reclassification and horizontality (as well as on the Peabody Picture Vocabulary Test, Form A). In each case, the number of children classified at stage 3 is significantly larger than in the Hermannsburg sample. On the conservation of quantity, the number of children attaining stage 3 is intermediate between the frequencies obtained at Hermannsburg and at

Canberra. It has not been possible to ascertain why the results on this conservation task differ from those on the other operational tasks. There is a possibility that the conservation tasks demand a more advanced level of verbal competence than the other tasks, because a verbal judgment is required (despite the fact that adequate reasons were not required in the scoring), whereas the response to the other tasks is mainly non-verbal (although the subject has to specify the dimension of reclassification on the Nixon task). Possibly the language models provided by the families of the two samples compared were somewhat different (although performance on the Peabody Picture Vocabulary Test, Form A, was comparable to European norms taken from the instruction manual). Possibly conservation tasks may be more sensitive to adverse conditions in the early environment. We may also take into account Lefèvre's (1970) suggestion that conservation concepts may present particular problems to the adopted child because of emotional difficulties: the possible difficulty in "conserving" a stable image of himself and of his parents as objects of identification. This hypothesis is open to experimental verification. The study is being replicated in Britain by Sohan Modgil (personal communication) with apparently very similar results.

3. Conclusion

Drawing together the results of these two studies, it seems that the variable of "European contact" may form a continuum which is directly related to the "rate" of development of concrete operations (or at least to the performance on concrete operational tasks).

A first interpretation of these findings could be phrased in terms of the "deficit hypothesis" (Cole and Bruner, 1971): our measures would be a direct reflection of cognitive competence, and Aboriginal culture, for whatever reason (lack of early stimulation, deficient linguistic models, disorganized communities and social interactions, etc), would be deficient in its ability to foster this cognitive competence. With increasing contact with the dominant culture, the proportion of children being able to display the proper competence would increase.

A second interpretation could be phrased in terms of the "Labov effect": our experiments being inadequate, their results are meaningless. The differences we have found in the performance levels simply reflect the fact that the tasks were not "their problem". With increasing contact with the dominant culture, the proportion of children being able to display the proper performance would increase simply because the experimental situation becomes more adequate.

Neither of these extreme positions seems satisfactory, although the second interpretation is certainly safer than the first in our present state of knowledge. However a third, intermediate interpretation is possible and preferable, which we could phrase in terms of the "difference interpretation" (Cole and Bruner, 1971): there is a true difference in cognitive performance (but maybe not in competence) between the two cultural groups. This difference results from the fact that the two cultures value different areas of cognitive development. The "cognitive ambience" in Heron's terms may not be favourable within Aboriginal culture for the development of such concepts as conservation or number, although it is quite adapted to produce other skills (e.g. hunting and tracking, spatial orientation, knowledge of kinship structures*). As contact with the dominant culture increases, the value orientation and "cognitive ambience" changes. This cultural difference is not to be seen as a deficiency in one culture; there ought to be no values applied to cultural differences. However cultural variations are certainly more than experimental artefacts; there may be real differences which cannot be neglected.

In the next section, we shall give an extensively documented example of how different cultures may foster the development of certain areas of cognitive development over others. In the study to be reported, the results of Canadian Eskimos, Australian Aborigines and Ebrié Africans are compared on selected Piagetian tasks; no reference is made to a Western "norm". The three subsistence-economy populations are placed on an eco-cultural scale, with low food-accumulating, nomadic, hunting groups at one extreme, and high food-accumulating, sedentary, agriculturalist groups at the other extreme, following a model proposed by Berry (1966). In the nomadic groups, spatial concepts are expected to be valued and to develop more rapidly than in the sedentary groups. In the latter, on the other hand, concepts of conservation of quantity, weight and volume are expected to be valued and to develop more rapidly than in the nomadic groups. In other words, each cultural group is expected to develop specifically those skills and concepts which it most needs. These cultural differences do not exclude the universality of the underlying cognitive competence.

E. The Influence of Ecological Demands†

Within the renewed tradition of ecological cultural functionalism, Berry (1966, 1971) has suggested a model linking individual behavioural develop-

---

* The cognitive "operations" underlying these skills ought to be studied more extensively; cf. the attempts at more "emic" studies by Gladwin (1970), Levine and Price-Williams (1974), Price-Williams *et al.* (1976), Greenfield and Childs (1976).

† This study has been reported previously in the *Journal of Cross-Cultural Psychology* (1975), **6**, 156-172.

ment to the "ecological demands" placed on a group of people, partly through the mediation of cultural adaptation to this ecology ("cultural aids").

"Specifically, it is argued, persons who inhabit ecologies where hunting is the mode of sustenance should develop perceptual discrimination and spatial skills adapted to the ecological demands of hunting. . . . Their cultures are expected to be supportive of the development of these skills through the presence of a high number of 'geomentrical-spatial' concepts, a highly developed and generally shared arts and crafts production, and socialization practices whose content emphasises independence and self reliance, and whose techniques are supportive and encouraging of separate development. Implicit in this argument is the expectation that as hunting diminishes in importance across samples ranked in terms of this ecology dimension, the discrimination and spatial skills will diminish, as will each of the three cultural aids" (Berry, 1971, pp. 328–29).

Thus, an ecology dimension was defined by placing low food-accumulating, migratory, hunting and gathering, low population density groups at one end of the scale, and high food-accumulating, sedentary, agricultural, high population density groups at the other extreme. Socio-cultural characteristics which are known to vary fairly consistently with this ecological dimension are socialization practices, family structure, social structure and social relations (Berry, 1975a).

This model was largely supported by a comparative study (Berry, 1966) of Temne (Sierra Leone) and Eskimos (Baffin Island), which was later expanded (Berry, 1971) to include two populations considered to be at intermediate positions on the ecology dimension: Australian Aborigines and Melanesians (New Guinea). Both traditional and transitional samples were included and their results were analysed separately. The rankings of the dependent variables (scores on perceptual discrimination, Embedded Figures Test, Kohs Blocks and Raven's Matrices) followed the rankings on the ecology dimension with only one exception.

Still more recently, the model was considerably expanded (Berry, 1975a), and eco-cultural, socialization and acculturation indices were developed which enable a precise ranking of the populations on the eco-cultural scale. The model was then retested, using 17 different samples (Berry, 1975b).

The extension of Berry's model to the Piagetian area suggests that, although the sequence of stages in the development of concrete operations may prove to be universal, the rate of development may be partly determined by ecological and cultural factors. Thus the first of two hypotheses is advanced: if three subsistence-economy populations are placed on an eco-cultural scale, with low food-accumulating, nomadic, hunting groups at one extreme (e.g. Eskimos and Australian Aborigines), and high-food accumulating, sedentary, agriculturalist groups at the other extreme (e.g. Ebrié of the Ivory Coast), the former are expected to develop spatial concepts more rapidly than the latter. The choice of tasks assessing the development of spatial concepts would be based on Piaget and Inhelder's (1948) analysis of topological, projective and Euclidean spatial representation in children.

Furthermore, it seemed reasonable to expect that the African group, under the pressure of its own eco-cultural milieu, would develop other concepts more rapidly than the Eskimo and Aboriginal groups. This leads to the second hypothesis: because of the agricultural production, accumulation and exchange of food in the African group, its members are expected to attain concepts of conservation of quantity, weight and volume (Piaget and Inhelder, 1941, 1963) more rapidly than do Eskimos and Aborigines. A similar hypothesis could be formulated for the concept of number, but will not be tested here.

These hypotheses deal with the quantitative aspects of cognitive development, the differential rate of development of various areas of concrete operational reasoning, and not with the qualitative aspects of structure and hierarchical ordering of stages. Note also (see Berry, 1971) that the model is functional, emphasizing interactions rather than causal sequences, and that it applies only to subsistence-economy populations, for which the "ecological demands" are expected to be more uniform than in technological societies. For these and other methodological reasons, any comparison with a Western "norm" will be avoided.

Earlier support for a hypothesis stemming from the combination of Berry's model and a Piagetian framework came from the finding that Australian Aborigines, in two specific samples, acquired a particular set of spatial operations before they acquired a particular set of conservation concepts, whereas the reverse was found to be true in a European sample (Dasen, 1970, 1974a). This demonstration, however, required the use of an arbitrary scoring system in order to combine the results of several tasks into a single measure, and it had the drawback of using a Western comparison group. Later (Dasen, 1973a), these inconveniences were overcome by comparing directly the results of the Aboriginal sample with those of an Ebrié African sample (Adiopodoumé). However, the design was not yet judged to be satisfactory, in view of Campbell's (1961) suggestion that three points are required to make meaningful cross-cultural comparisons.

However, the above hypotheses do not clearly specify the ranking of the Eskimo and Aboriginal samples on the independent variable. Berry (1971) has placed his Eskimo samples at one extreme of the ecology scale, and the Australian Aboriginal samples at a more intermediate position, but definitely on the nomadic/hunting/low food-accumulating side; his results clearly support this ranking. We could therefore add to our first hypothesis the prediction that the rate of spatial concept development should be greater in the Eskimo than in the Aboriginal sample. Anthropological evidence in regard to this ranking seems to be equivocal, however, particularly if we wanted to include a similar distinction in the second hypothesis.

F. Method

1. Subjects

The subjects were 6- to 14-year-old schooled rural children drawn from three cultural groups.

(1) *Central Eskimos.* The settlement of *Cape Dorset* is situated on the south-west tip of Baffin Island, in the Northwest Territories of Canada. Its population is about 600. Cape Dorset Eskimos are well known for their artistic achievements: stone carvings and prints provide a large part of their income, together with local service jobs and welfare. But part of the food is still provided by hunting and fishing. Every family owns a house in the village, but while on hunting expeditions they may still live in igloos during winter and in tents during summer. Some families live for part of the year in isolated hunting camps. An excellent study of the village of Sugluk, very similar to Cape Dorset, has been provided by Graburn (1969).

(2) *Australian Aborigines.* The results to be reported here are those of the *Hermannsburg* sample, which has been described above (cf. pp. 179-180).

(3) *Ebrié Africans.* The village of *Adiopodoumé* is situated 17 km west of Abidjan, the capital city of the Ivory Coast. Its populaton is about 2,000. Most of its inhabitants are Ebrié, although some other ethnic groups are also present. The main activity is the growing of staple food (yams, plantain and various vegetables) as well as cash crops (coffee, cocoa and bananas). There is also some fishing in the lagoon, and a number of paid jobs are available in the city or at a nearby research station.

It should be noted that the cultural characteristics of the three samples come close to the requirements of Berry's model, but are not absolutely ideal. The Eskimos and Aborigines no longer rely exclusively on hunting and gathering and have become partly sedentary, whereas the African sample is somewhat heterogeneous as to ethnic background and parents' occupations.

The three samples will be labelled by the names of the locations in which

Table 4
The influence of ecological demands. Sample characteristics.

Age groups (years)	Central Eskimos of Cape Dorset Baffin Island				Australian Aborigines of Hermannsburg Central Australia				Ebrié Africans of Adiopodoumé Ivory Coast			
	Sex		Mean	Range	Sex		Mean	Range	Sex		Mean	Range
	M	F	(years and months)		M	F			M	F		
6	5	5	6; 0	5;10- 6;5	5	5	6; 3	5; 7- 6;5				
8	6	4	8; 1	7; 7- 8;4	5	5	8; 1	7; 8- 8;6	4	6	8; 1	7;7- 3;6
9	6	4	8;11	8; 7- 9;6	5	5	9; 1	8; 7- 9;5				
10	5	5	10; 2	9;10-10;5	5	5	10; 1	9; 7-10;6	5	5	9;11	9;7-10;4
11	4	6	11; 1	10; 8-11;6	5	5	10;11	10; 7-11;4				
12	5	5	12; 0	11; 7-12;4	5	5	12; 0	11; 8-12;6	6	4	12; 1	11;7-12;6
13	5	5	13; 1	12; 8-13;6	5	5	13; 7	12;11-14;6				
14	5	5	14; 0	13; 7-14;7					5	5	14; 1	13;7-14;6
n	41	39			35	35			20	20		

they were obtained, to indicate that they are not necessarily representative of each ethnic group as a whole. In particular, as we have seen in the previous section, results may be influenced by acculturation; the three samples were chosen to represent approximately equal levels of acculturation, as far as this could be done across different historical and cultural backgrounds. However, no measure of acculturation, other than the author's casual observations, can be offered.

In each sample, ten subjects (as nearly as possible five of each sex) were sampled randomly within each given age group. All subjects attended the local primary school, where teaching took place in a second language, and their ages were known from reliable school records. The sample characteristics are summarized in Table 4.

2. Tasks

The results of the following tasks will be reported in this section; they have been described or referred to previously (cf. p. 180).

Space:
(1) Linear, reverse and circular order.
(2) Rotation of landscape models (localization of topographical positions).
(3) Horizontality (water-level in tilted bottle), Part 1.
Conservation:
(4) Conservation of quantity (liquids).
(5) Conservation of weight (plasticine).
(6) Conservation of volume (water displaced by plasticine).

Concurrently, other tasks which are not relevant to the present hypothesis were used with some of the samples. These included conservation of length, mental imagery and optico-geometrical illusions. The only other tasks administered to all three samples were seriation of lengths and reclassification (Nixon test, cf. de Lacey, 1970); on both tasks the rate of attainment of concrete operations was fastest in the Cape Dorset sample, followed by the Hermannsburg and Adiopodoumé samples. The differences are statistically significant beyond the 0·05 level, except for the Hermannsburg/Adiopodoumé comparison on reclassification.

3. Procedure

The testing took place in the second language used in the subjects' schools (English for Eskimos and Aborigines, French for Ebrié). Adequate communication was ensured through check-items preceding each task; if communication was judged to be inadequate, results were classified separately. The testing was carried out by the author and his wife at Hermannsburg and Adiopodoumé, and by the author and Serge Rioux at Cape Dorset. The order in which the tasks were administered was randomized, except for the order of the tests of conservation of quantity, weight and volume, which was counterbalanced within each age group. For various reasons all tasks were not administered to all age groups; this appears clearly in the presentation of the results, each percentage being calculated on an age group of ten subjects.

G. Results

The structural properties of the stages and their hierarchical ordering were verified in each sample. Detailed analyses of the results, including frequencies of each sub-stage, are presented elsewhere (Dasen, 1970, 1974a, 1975b). For the purpose of the present argument, only the rate of development of stage 3 (the final stage of attainment of concrete operations) will be considered.

Hypothesis 1: Space

Results on the three tasks of a spatial operations are presented in Figs 4, 5 and 6 in the form of percentages of children, at each age group tested, attaining stage 3 in the three samples. The results clearly support hypothesis 1. On all three tasks, the rate of development is faster in the Cape Dorset and Hermannsburg samples than in the Adiopodoumé sample. The statistical significance of the differences in the proportions of children in each age class reaching the concrete operational stage was computed according to the scheme proposed by Kamara and Easley (1976). The corresponding p values appear in Table 5. For the spatial tasks, the developmental curves are all significantly different beyond the 0·05 level, except for the Hermannsburg and Cape Dorset samples on task 1 (linear, reverse and circular order), topological relations being acquired early in both these samples. On the two other tasks, the rate of development is significantly faster for the Cape Dorset sample than for the Hermannsburg sample, which confirms Berry's placing of these two populations on the ecology scale.

On the most difficult task, namely horizontality, the frequency of attainment of stage 3 is generally low. However the intermediate stage

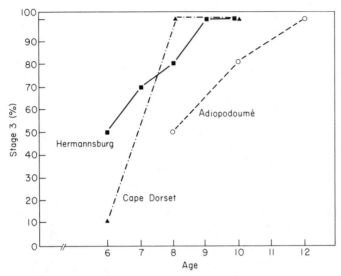

Fig. 4. Orders: percentages of subjects at stage 3 (full concrete operations).

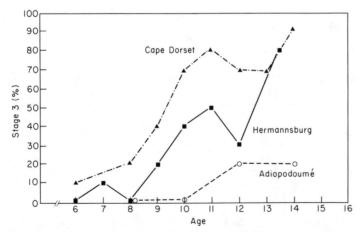

Fig. 5. Rotation: percentages of subjects at stage 3 (full concrete operations).

immediately preceding stage 3 already reflects the emergence of concrete operations. If this intermediate stage is combined with stage 3 (cf. Fig. 6), the differences between the three samples become even more marked, and are all statistically significant beyond the 0·0005 level.

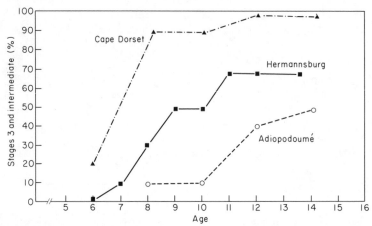

Fig. 6. Horizontality: percentages of subjects at stage 3 (full concrete operations) and intermediate stage, combined.

Table 5
The influence of ecological demands.

Level of significance of the differences in the proportions of children reaching stage 3
(p values)

| | Tasks | | | | | | | | |
| | Space | | | | | | Conservation[b] | | |
	Orders	Rotation	Horiz.	Q	W	V	Q	W	V
Age range	6–14 years			8–14 years			12–14 years		
Samples compared[a]									
A/H	0·01	0·05	0·05	NS	0·025	NS	0·025	0·001	0·025
A/C.D.	0·005	0·0005	0·0005	0·025	NS	NS	0·005	0·005	0·05
C.D./H	NS	0·0005	0·01	NS	NS	NS	NS	NS	NS

[a] A = Adiopodoumé; H = Hermannsburg; C.D. = Cape Dorset.
[b] Q = Quantity (liquids); W = Weight; V = Volume.

Hypothesis 2: Conservation

The results on the three conservation tasks are presented in Figs 7, 8 and 9 and the corresponding p values in Table 5. The second hypothesis receives only partial support from the data. If the age range 12 to 14 years is considered alone, the order of the developmental curves is as expected from the hypothesis: the rate of development in the Adiopodoumé sample is significantly faster than in the two other samples on all three tasks. On the other hand if the complete age range is considered, the differences are statistically significant in two cases only, because several discontinuities

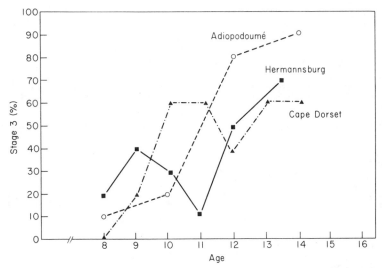

Fig. 7. Conservation of quantity: percentages of subjects at stage 3 (full conservation).

occur below age 12 which are·not in accordance with the hypothesis. On conservation of quantity, the percentage of conservers in the 8-, 9- and 10-year-olds appears to be exceptionally high when compared with the results of the older children; it has not been verified whether pseudo-conservation (Bovet, 1974) might have ·occurrred at these ages in the Hermannsburg sample. In any case, high percentages of conservation also occur in the Cape Dorset group at 10 and 11 years; in this case, the operational character of these conservation answers has been clearly established.

On conservation of weight, no clear differences occur between the three samples in the results of the 8- to 10-year-old children. On conservation of volume, the frequencies of stage 3 answers are higher in the Cape Dorset

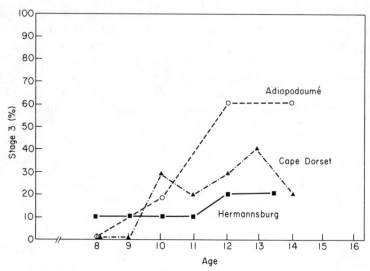

Fig. 8. Conservation of weight: percentages of subjects at stage 3 (full conservation).

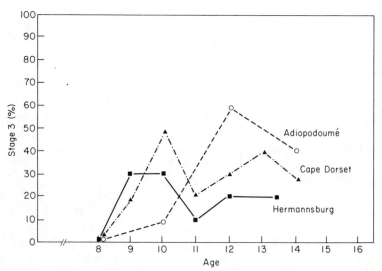

Fig. 9. Conservation of volume: percentages of subjects at stage 3 (full conservation).

and Hermannsburg samples than in the Adiopodoumé sample, at ages 9 and 10. It must be concluded that the ordering of the three samples does not occur as expected in these lower age groups: there is either no clear ordering, or it is even reversed. In the older age groups, however, hypothesis 2 is supported.

More recently we have had the opportunity to repeat the tasks of horizontality and conservation of quantity (liquids) in a sample of Baoulé children. This new sample would be placed even more to the extreme (sedentary, agriculturalist) end of Berry's eco-cultural scale. The results on the spatial task are exactly as those obtained in Adiopodoumé, whereas the developmental curve for conservation of quantity (stage 3) rises steeply from age 7 to reach 100% conservation at age 10, and there is no overlap at all with the other curves. If this Baoulé sample had been used for the original comparison, the second hypothesis would have been supported (at least for conservation of quantity) over the whole age range.

H. Discussion

Clear support for the model comes from our data on spatial concept development (hypothesis 1), since the rankings of the dependent variables occur according to expectation over the whole range of development. Further support comes from the results on the conservation tasks (hypothesis 2), if the age range 12 to 14 years is considered. Not only do these data support the model, they also indicate that the relationship between ecology and culture is positive at both ends of the ecological scale, in different areas of operational development. The results are equivocal, however, insofar as the expected relationship does not occur in the younger age groups. Several alternative explanations have been proposed by Dasen (1975a). However these *post-hoc* explanations are not very convincing, and the question is best left open to future research, which ought to attempt to specify the mechanisms by which these cultural and ecological factors influence cognitive development.

A further important question which this research cannot answer in its present state has to do with the previously discussed competence/performance distinction. Do the eco-cultural factors determine both or only one of these? Our hypothesis is that the tasks, as they have been applied here, measure the spontaneous use of the concepts; the results could be seen as measures of the probability with which these particular concepts would be used in everyday situations, and are thus meaningful. They would not necessarily be measures of the cognitive "competence" to use the concepts involved, nor to use concrete operations in general. In particular, the eco-cultural factors would determine the final levels of spontaneous use of the concepts (the levels of the asymptotic curves), whereas competence may be either universal or under the influence of other cultural factors.

Further research is needed to clarify this distinction. The present results demonstrate that the rates of development (at least of performance) are not uniform across different areas of concrete operations, and that these rates may reflect the adaptive values of the concepts concerned.

IV. CONCLUSION

This chapter started with a question concerning the universality of cognitive processes; subsequently we have continually switched back and forth between data arguing in favour of universality and other facts favouring cultural relativism. The initial warning, that we would not reach a definite conclusion, should now make sense.

Already in the first stage of cognitive development, that of sensori-motor intelligence, we have seen that culture seems to influence the rate of development to some extent, although the similarity in structure and process is certainly more striking than the differences. No doubt the initial interaction between the human organism and its environment follows universal paths, even though the content of the structures and interactive mechanisms may vary a great deal. Content seems to be of little relevance to the activation of sensori-motor schemata.

During the move from pre-operational to concrete operational thinking, on the other hand, content does become important; and even more important seem to be the functional aspects of concrete operational concepts. The underlying structures, the mechanisms, or "operations" in Piagetian terms, seem to be universal, but whether and at what rate they become functional seems to be determined to a large extent by cultural patterns. This may be why the results of cross-cultural Piagetian studies are often less than clear. This may also be why most, but not all, studies find large effects of acculturation, schooling and urbanization, and why large but often unexplained differences occur in the rate of development of concrete operational concepts. Future research ought to attach more importance to these functional aspects and in particular to the competence/performance distinction. The study we have presented on the verification of Berry's eco-cultural model within Piagetian psychology is a first step in this direction; it is one of the first quasi-experimental studies in this area, but its scope is still limited. In particular, the link with the competence/

performance model could only be suggested and not fully substantiated, and the precise mechanisms through which eco-cultural variables may influence cognitive processes remain to be demonstrated. On the one hand we feel that we have already accumulated a wealth of data, on the other it becomes obvious that the most important and most difficult research is still to be done.

Future research may possibly be more fruitful if it is no longer conceived as a verification of Piaget's theory, but is able to go beyond, to a search for mechanisms. Constant vacillation between consideration of universality and of cultural relativism has been a feature of this chapter: neither interpretation is true in itself, and choosing one over the other seems to be mainly a matter of personal preference; in any case neither "proves" or "disproves" Piaget's theory. If anything, the cultural variations simply expand the theory to encompass functional aspects which have been neglected in Piaget's earlier work, but which have since come to attention also in Western Piagetian research.

For example, Piaget's last stage of intellectual development, that of formal operations, has recently come under closer scrutiny, and it is often reported that large proportions of the population do not display formal operations (e.g. Lovell, 1961). Piaget (1972) still believes that all normal individuals are capable of reaching the stage of formal operations, if not between 11 and 15 at least between 15 and 20. "However, they reach this stage in different areas according to their aptitudes and their professional specializations" (p. 10). Thus the tasks initially devised to assess formal operational reasoning (Inhelder and Piaget, 1958) may be adequate for testing adolescents undergoing higher schooling but are not applicable to individuals in manual occupations, nor to those who are more interested in languages or law than in physics and mathematics. Little cross-cultural research has been published on formal operations, probably because it is obvious that the standard tasks would be culturally inadequate in most situations. New tasks have to be devised which test the same cognitive structures, but which are directly relevant to the daily activities and interests of the subjects.

The same programme could also be usefully carried out for concrete operations. Greenfield (1976) rightly suggests that cross-cultural researchers ought to follow Piaget's theory rather than his procedures. Ideally, one would wish to see a Piagetian-type study carried out in a cultural group by a member of that group, using situations and tasks entirely relevant to that culture. Piaget's theory would at last become emic rather than etic (Berry, 1969). In the meantime, however, there is still room for less ambitious but worthwhile cross-cultural Piagetian research.

REFERENCES

Ainsworth, M. D. (1967). "Infancy in Uganda: infant care and the growth of love." Johns Hopkins University Press, Baltimore.

Bell, S. M. (1970). *Child Dev.* **41**, 291–311.

Berry, J. W. (1966). *Inter. J. Psychol.* **1**, 207–229.

Berry, J. W. (1969). *Int. J. Psychol.* **4**, 119–128.

Berry, J. W. (1971). *Can. J. behav. Sci.* **3**, 324–336. (Reprinted in Berry and Dasen, 1974).

Berry, J. W. (1975a). *Ned. Tijdschr. Psychol.* **30**, 51–84.

Berry, J. W. (1975b). Nomadic style and cognitive style. Paper presented to the I.S.S.B.D. Conference, Surrey, England, July 13–17, 1975.

Berry, J. W. and Dasen, P. R. (1974). "Culture and Cognition: Readings in cross-cultural Psychology." Methuen, London.

Bovet, M. C. (1974). *In* "Culture and Cognition" (Eds J. W. Berry and P. R. Dasen), pp. 311–334. Methuen, London.

Bovet, M. C., Dasen, P. R. and Inhelder, B. (1974). *Archs Psychol.* **41** (Vol. 1972), 363–386.

Bower, T. G. R. and Paterson, J. G. (1972). *Cognition* **1**, 47–65.

Campbell, D. T. (1961). *In* "Psychological Anthropology" (Ed. F. L. K. Hsu), pp. 333–352. Dorsey, Homewood, Illinois.

Carlson, J. (1976). *In* "The developing individual in a changing world" (Eds K. Riegel and J. Meacham). Mouton, The Hague. In press.

Casati, I. and Lézine, I. (1968). "Les étapes de l'intelligence sensori-motrice. Manuel." Centre de Psychologie Appliquée, Paris.

Cole, M. and Bruner, J. S. (1971). *Am. Psychol.* **26**, 867-876. (Reprinted in Berry and Dasen, 1974).

Cole, M. and Scribner, S. (1974). "Culture and thought: a psychological introduction." Wiley, New York.

Cole, M., Gay, J., Glick, J. and Sharp, D. W. (1971). "The Cultural Context of Learning and Thinking." Basic Books, New York.

Corman, H. H. and Escalona, S. K. (1969). *The Merrill-Palmer Quarterly* **15**, 351–361.

Dasen, P. R. (1970). "Cognitive development in Aborigines of Central Australia." Unpublished PhD thesis. Australian National University, Canberra.

Dasen, P. R. (1972a). *J. Cross-cult. Psychol.* **3**, 23–39.

Dasen, P. R. (1973a). *Can. Psychol.* **14**, 149–166.

Dasen, P. R. (1973b). *Early Child Development and Care* **2**, 345–354.

Dasen, P. R. (1974a). *In* "Culture and Cognition" (Eds J. W. Berry and P. R. Dasen), pp. 381–408. Methuen, London.

Dasen, P. R. (1974b). *Archs Psychol.* **41** (Vol. 1972), 341–361.

Dasen, P. R. (1975a). *J. Cross-cult. Psychol.* **6**, 156–172.

Dasen, P. R. (1975b). *Int. J. Psychol.* **10**, 165–180.

Dasen, P. R. (1975c). *In* "Dips in Learning and Development Curves" (Eds J. Mehler and T. Bever). In press.

Dasen, P. R. (1976). "Piagetian Psychology: Cross-Cultural Contributions." Gardner Press (Halsted, Wiley), New York. In press.

Dasen, P. R., de Lacey, P. R. and Seagrim, G. N. (1973). *In* "The Psychology of

Aboriginal Australians" (Eds G. E. Kearney, P. R. de Lacey and G. R. Davidson), pp. 97–104. Wiley, Sydney.
Décarie, T. (1967). "Intelligence et affectivité chez le jeune enfant." Delachaux et Niestlé, Neuchâtel.
de Lacey, P. R. (1970). *J. Cross-cult. Psychol.* **1**, 293–304.
de Lemos, M. M. (1966). "The development of the concept of conservation in Australian Aboriginal children." Unpublished PhD thesis. Australian National University, Canberra.
de Lemos, M. M. (1969). *Int. J. Psychol.* **4**, 255–269.
Droz, R. and Rahmy, M. (1972). "Lire Piaget." Dessart, Bruxelles.
Flavell, J. H. (1963). "The Developmental Psychology of Jean Piaget." Van Nostrand, Princeton, New Jersey.
Flavell, J. H. and Wohlwill, J. F. (1969). *In* "Studies in cognitive development" (Eds D. Elkind and J. H. Flavell), pp. 67–120. Oxford University Press, New York and London.
Furth, H. G. (1968). "Piaget and knowledge: Theoretical foundations." Prentice-Hall, Englewood Cliffs, New Jersey.
Ginsburg, H. and Opper, S. (1969). "Piaget's theory of intellectual development: an introduction." Prentice-Hall, Englewood Cliffs, New Jersey.
Gladwin, T. (1970). "East is a Big Bird." Harvard University Press, Cambridge, Mass.
Goldberg, S. (1970). *H.D.R.U. Reports.* **15**, Lusaka, Zambia.
Golden, M. and Birns, B. (1968). *Merrill Palmer Quarterly* **14**, 139–149.
Graburn, N. H. H. (1969). "Eskimos without Igloos." Little, Brown, Boston.
Greenfield, P. M. (1966). *In* "Studies in cognitive growth" (Eds J. S. Bruner, R. R. Olver and P. M. Greenfield), pp. 225–256. Wiley, New York.
Greenfield, P. M. (1976). *In* "The developing individual in a changing world" (Eds K. Riegel and J. Meacham). Mouton, The Hague. In press.
Greenfield, P. and Childs, C. (1976). *In* "Piagetian Psychology: Cross-Cultural Contributions" (Ed. P. R. Dasen). Gardner Press, Halsted, Wiley, New York. In press.
Guerry, V. (1970). "La vie quotidienne dans un village baoulé." INADES, Abidjan.
Heron, A. (1971). *J. Cross-cult. Psychol.* **2**, 325–336.
Heron, A. (1974). *In* "Readings in cross-cultural psychology" (Eds J. L. M. Dawson, W. J. Lonner), pp. 94–101. Hong Kong University Press.
Heron, A. and Dowel, W. (1973). *J. Cross-cult. Psychol.* **4**, 207–219.
Heron, A. and Dowel, W. (1974). *Int. J. Psychol.* **9**, 1–9.
Heron, A. and Simonsson, M. (1969). *Int. J. Psychol.* **4**, 281–292.
Hyde, D. M. G. (1970). "Piaget and conceptual development." Holt, Rinehart and Winston, London.
Inhelder, B. and Piaget, J. (1958). "The growth of logical thinking." Routledge and Kegan Paul, London.
Inhelder, B., Sinclair, H. and Bovet, M. (1974). "Les structures de la connaissance: apprentissage et développement." P.U.F., Paris. ("Learning and the development of cognition." Harvard University Press, Cambridge, Mass., 1974.)
Kamara, A. and Easley, J. A. Jr. (1976). Is the rate of cognitive development uniform across cultures? A methodological critique with new evidence from Themne children. *In* "Piagetian Psychology: Cross-Cultural Contributions" (Ed. P. R. Dasen). Gardner Press (Halsted, Wiley), New York. In press.

Kearney, G. E. (1973). *In* "The Psychology of Aboriginal Australians" (Eds G. E. Kearney, P. R. de Lacey and G. R. Davidson), pp. 16–25. Wiley, Sydney.
Kelly, M. R. (1970). *T.P.N.G. J. of Educ.*, 55–60.
Kilbride, J. E. and Kilbride, P. L. (1975). *J. Cross-cult. Psychol.* **6**, 88–107.
Konner, M. J. (1972). *In* "Ethological studies of child behaviour." (Ed. N. Blurton-Jones), pp. 285–304. Cambridge University Press, London.
Lefebvre, M. and Pinard, A. (1972). *Rev. Can. Sci. Comp.* **4**, 1–12.
Lefèvre, A. (1970). *Perspectives psychiatriques* **30**, 39–56.
Levine, R. A. (1970). *In* "Carmichael's Manual of Child Psychology." (Ed. P. H. Mussen), Vol. II, pp. 559–612. Wiley, New York.
Levine, R. A. and Price-Williams, D. R. (1974). *Ethnology* **13**, 25–44.
Lewis, M. and Johnson, N. (1971). *Child Dev.* **42**, 1053–1055.
Lézine, I., Stambak, M. and Casati, I. (1969). "Les étapes de l'intelligence sensori-motrice. Monographie no. 1." Centre de Psychologie Appliquée, Paris.
Lloyd, B. B. (1972). "Perception and cognition from a cross-cultural perspective." Penguin Books, Harmondsworth, Middlesex.
Lovell, K. (1961). *Br. J. educ. Psychol.* **52**, 143–154.
Modgil, S. (1974). "Piagetian research: a handbook of recent studies." N.F.E.R., Windsor, Berks.
Mohseni, N. (1966). "La comparaison des réactions aux épreuves d'intelligence en Iran et en Europe." Thèse inédite, Université de Paris.
Opper, S. (1971). "Intellectual development in Thai children." Unpublished PhD thesis, Cornell University, Ithaca, New York.
Paraskevopoulos, J. and Hunt, J. McV. (1971). *J. Genet. Psychol.* **119**, 301–321.
Piaget, J. (1936). "La naissance de l'intelligence chez l'enfant." Delachaux and Niestlé, Neuchâtel. ("The origins of intelligence in the child." Routledge and Kegan Paul, London, 1953.)
Piaget, J. (1937). "La construction du réel chez l'enfant." Delachaux and Niestlé, Neuchâtel. ("The child's construction of reality." Routledge and Kegan Paul, London, 1955.)
Piaget, J. (1965). "Etudes sociologiques." Droz, Genève.
Piaget, J. (1972). *Hum. Devel.* **15**, 1–12.
Piaget, J. and Inhelder, B. (1941). "Le développement des quantités chez l'enfant. Conservation et atomisme." Delachaux and Niestlé, Neuchâtel. ("The Child's Construction of Quantity." Routledge and Kegan Paul, London, 1974.)
Piaget, J. and Inhelder, B. (1948). "La représentation de l'espace chez l'enfant." P.U.F., Paris. ("The child's conception of space." Routledge and Kegan Paul, London, 1956.)
Piaget, J. and Inhelder, B. (1963). *In* "Traité de Psychologie Expérimentale, Vol. VII, l'Intelligence" (Eds P. Fraisse and J. Piaget), pp. 109–155. P.U.F., Paris.
Pinard, A., Morin, C. and Lefebvre, M. (1973). *Int. J. Psychol.* **8**, 15–24.
Price-Williams, D. R. (1961). *Acta psychol.* **18**, 293–305.
Price-Williams, D. R., Hammond, D. W. and Egerton, C. (1976). *In* "Piagetian Psychology: Cross-Cultural Contributions" (Ed. P. R. Dasen). Gardner Press (Halsted, Wiley), New York. In press.
Prince, J. R. (1969). "Science Concepts in a Pacific Culture." Angus and Robertson, Sydney.
Super, C. M. (1973). Infant care and motor development in rural Kenya: some preliminary data on precocity and deficit. Paper presented at the 1st IACCP conference in Africa, Ibadan, Nigeria.

Uzgiris, I. C. and Hunt, J. McV. (1975). "Assessment in infancy." University of Illinois Press, Urbana.
Valantin, S. (1970). "Le développement de la fonction manipulatoire chez l'enfant Sénégalais au cours des deux premières années de la vie." Thèse de doctorat inédite, Université de Paris.
Wachs, T. D., Uzgiris, I. C. and Hunt, J. McV. (1971). *Merrill Palmer Quarterly* **17**, 183–217.
Warren, N. (1972). *Psychol. Bull.* **78**, 353–367.
Werner, E. E. (1972). *J. Cross-cult. Psychol.* **3**, 111–134.
Za'rour, G. I. (1971). *J. Cross-cult. Psychol.* **2**, 165–172.
Zempléni, J. (1970). *Revue Neuropsychiat. infant.* **18**, 785–798.
Zempléni, A. and Zempléni, J. (1972). *In* "Milieu et Développement" (Eds F. Duyckaerts, C. B. Hindley, I. Lézine, M. Reuchlin and A. Zempléni), pp. 151–213. P.U.F., Paris.

Author Index

The numbers in italics are those pages where References are listed in full

A

Adler, P., 145, *151*
Ainsworth, M. D., 160, *198*
Alcalde, E., 93, 94, *117*
Allen, M. G., 77, *86*
Amézquita, A., 93, 94, 95, 97, 98, *119*
Anglin, J., 26, 38, *47*
Annis, R. C., 143, *152*
Anthony, A., 59, 73, *90*
Argyle, M., 137, *151*
Attneave, F., 21, *47*
Axelrad, S., 81, *86*

B

Babayan, S., 93, 94, *117*
Bacon, M. K., 76, 77, *86, 87*
Bahnson, C. B., 140, *153*
Bailey, D. E., 133, *153*
Bakan, D., 54, *87*
Baldizón, G. C., 95, *119*
Barry, H., 76, 77, *86, 87*
Bar-Yosef, R., 128, 151
Battig, W. F., 23, *47*
Bayley, N., 97, *117*
Beach, L. R., 29, *47*
Bear, R. M., 98, *118*
Béhar, M., 93, *117*
Beit-Hallahmi, B., 135, *152*
Bell, S. M., 157, *198*
Beller, H. K., 14, 15, *47*
Bem, D. J., 130, 151
Bennett, J. W., 122, 151
Berger, P. L., 127, 128, 129, *151*
Berkley-Hill, O., 80, *87*
Berlin, B., 4, 5, 13, 31, 32, 33, 39, 41, 44, *47*

Berry, J. W., 95, 96, *117*, 143, *152*, 156, 184, 185, 186, 195, 197, *198*
Bettelheim, G., 122, 129, *152*
Bevan, W., 28, 41, *49*
Biesheuvel, S., 96, *117*
Birch, H. G., 91, 93, 94, 95, 96, *117, 118*
Birns, B., 158, *199*
Boas, F., 61, *87*
Bochner, S., 122, *152*
Bossio, V., 98, *119*
Botha-Antoun, E., 93, 94, *117*
Bourne, L. E., 18, 27, *47*
Boutourline, E., 93, 94, 97, *117*
Boutourline-Young, H., 93, 94, 97, *117*
Bovet, M. C., 156, 157, 160, 161, 164, 167, 171, 173, 176, 193, *198, 199*
Bower, T. G. R., 157, *198*
Bowlby, J., 77, 79, *87*
Boyes-Braem, P., 31, 34, 37, 38, 39, *49*
Bransford, J. D., 21, *47*
Breedlove, D. E., 31, *47*
Brein, M., 124, 131, 141, 142, *152*
Brim, O. G., 122, 128, *152*
Brockman, L. M., 93, 97, *118*
Brody, E. G., 141, *152*
Brophy, J. E., 98, *118*
Brown, R., 4, 38, *47*
Bruner, J. S., 16, 33, 38, *47*, 177, 183, 184, *198*
Brunswik, E., 29, *47*
Bulmer, R., 31, *47*

C

Cabak, V., 93, 94, 96, *118*
Campbell, D. T., 8, *49*, 57, 58, 59, 60, *87*, 132, *152*, 186, *198*
Canosa, C. A., 95, 102, *118*

Carlson, J., 156, *198*
Carringer. D. C., 145, *152*
Carstairs, G. M., 70, *87*
Casati, I., 158. 159, 160, 161, 163, 164, *198, 200*
Castaneda, C., 129, *152*
Castro, L., 93, 94, 95, 97, 98, *119*
Castro, O. R. P., 95, *119*
Catford, J. C., 135, *152*
Catlin, J., 13, *48*
Cattell, R. B., 60, 64, 65, 66, 67, 68, *87*
Champakam, S., 93, 95, 96, *118*
Chase, H. P., 93, 94, 95, 98, *118*
Chávez, A., 93, 94, 95, 97, 98, *118*
Chemers, M. M., 122, *152*
Child, I. L., 57, 59, 72, 73, 75, 76, 77, *86, 87, 90*
Childs, C., 184, *199*
Christiansen, J., 93, 94, 95, 97, 98, *119*
Clark, E. V., 41, *47*
Clement-Murphy, J., 93, 94, 95, 97, 98, *119*
Cobos, L. F., 93. 94, 95. 97. 98, *119*
Coelho, G. C., 141, *152*
Cohen, R., 60. *89*
Cole, M., 7, 28, 41, *47*, 95, *119*, 155, 156. 169, 177, 183, 184, *198*
Collins, A. M., 23, *47*
Conant, J. B., 52, *87*
Cooley, R. E., 135, *152*
Cooper, L. A., 36, *47*
Coover, G. D., 140, *153*
Corman, H. H., 158, *198*
Coulter, F., 122, *152*
Craddock, L. J., 93, 95, 96, *118*
Cravioto, J., 93. 94. 95, 97, 98, *117, 118*
Cremer. H. D., 93, 94, 95, 97, 98, *119*
Cronbach, L. J., 64, 67, 68, *87*
Curle, A., 122, 129, *152*

                        D

D'Andrade, R. G., 75, *89*
Dasen, P. R., 156, 157, 160, 161, 164, 168, 169, 171, 175, 179, 180, 181, 182, 186, 190, 195, *198, 199*
David, K. H., 124, 131, 141, 142, 149, *152*

Davidson, A. R., 131, *153*
Davidson, G., 132, *152*
Décarie, T., 157, *199*
De Léon, R., 95, 102, *118*
Delgado, H., 106, *118, 119*
De Licardie, E. R., 93, 94, 95, *118*
Denney, N. W., 38, *47*
Deregowski, J. B., 70, *87*
De Sola Pool, I., 122, 142, *152*
Deutsch, M., 98, *119*
De Valois, R. L., 12, *47*
Devereux, G., 80, *87*
De Vos, G. A., 142, *152*
Dignam, M. H., 124, *152*
Donaldson, W., 19, 42, *49*
Dornbusch, S. M., 122, *152*
Dowel, W., 172, 177, *199*
Dragastin, S., 93, 94, 95, 97, 98, *119*
Droz, R., 156, *199*
Du Bois, C., 62, 69, *87*
Dull, C. Y., 135, *152*

                        E

Easley, J. A. Jr., 164, 168, 181, 182, 190, *199*
Edwards, L. D., 93, 95, 96, *118*
Egerton, C., 184, *200*
Eisenstadt, S., 128, *152*
Ekman, P., 16, *47*
El Amouri, T., 93, 94, 97, *117*
Elias. M. F., 93, 94, 95, 97. 98. *119*
Engle, P. L., 96, 102, 103, 106, *118, 119*
Escalona, S. K., 158, *198*
Evans, D. E., 93, 95, 96, 98, *118*
Eysenck, H. J., 51, 53, 68, 69, *87*

                        F

Fairbairn, W. R. D., 52, 79, *87*
Farrell, B. A., 52, *87*
Feiden, C., 95, *118*
Fenichel, O., 79, *87*
Flavell, J. H., 156, 157, 166, 169, 176, 177, *199*
Foa, U. G., 122, *152*

Fodor, J. A., 24, *47*
Foner, A., 122, *153*
Frake, C. O., *47*
Frankl, V., 143, *152*
Frankling, D., 93, 94, 95, 97, 98, *119*
Franks, J. J., 21, *47*
Freedman, D. G., 100, *118*
Freedman, N. C., 100, *118*
Freeman, H. E., 98, 102, 103, *118*
Freud, S., 55, 63, 72, 83, *87, 88*
Furth, H. G., 156, *199*

G

Gajdusek, D. C., 124, *152*
Galanter, E., 136, *153*
Garabedian, P. C., 122, *152*
Garner, W. R., 19, 27, 28, *47, 48*
Gattás, V., 93, 95, 98, *119*
Gay, J., 155, 177, *198*
Gergen, K. J., 145, *152*
Gilbert, O., 95, 102, *118*
Gill, M. M., 53, *89*
Ginsburg, H., 156, *199*
Giok, L. T., 93, 95, 96, *119*
Gladwin, T., 184, *199*
Glick, J., 155, 177, *198*
Glover, E., 77, *88*
Gluckman, M., 57, *88*
Goffman, E., 122, 129, *152*
Goldberg, S., 158, *199*
Golden, M., 158, *199*
Goldman, L., 140, *153*
Goldsmith, R., 21, *48*
Gopalan, C., 93, 95, 96, *118*
Gorer, G., 80, *88*
Graburn, N. H. H., 187, *199*
Granoff, D., 93, 95, 97, *119*
Gray, W., 31, 34, 37, 38, 39, *49*
Greenfield, P., 184, 197, *199*
Greenfield, P. M., 33, 38, *47*, 156, 168, 171, *199*
Grygier, T. G., 68, *88*
Guerry, V., 160, *199*
Guilford, J. P., 71, *88*
Guiora, A. Z., 135, *152*
Guthrie, G., 122, 140, *152*

H

Habicht, J.-P., 98, 102, 103, 106, *118, 119*
Hall, C. S., 82, *88*
Hammond, D. W., 184, *200*
Hampson, S., 71, *88*
Handel, S., 27, 28, *47, 48*
Hansen, J. D. L., 93, 95, 96, 98, *118*
Harfouche, J. K., 93, 94, *117*
Harrington, C., 74, 75, *88*
Hartley, R., 126, *152*
Heider, E. R., 9, 10, 13, 41, *48*
Heider, K. G., 9, *48*
Hering, E., 12, *48*
Heron, A., 172, 177, 178, *199*
Herrera, M. G., 93, 94, 95, 97, 98, *119*
Herskovitz, M. J., 8, *49*
Hertzig, M. E., 93, 95, 96, *118*
Hess, B., 122, *153*
Hess, R. D., 98, *118*
Hie, T. T., 93, 95, 96, *119*
Hippler, A. E., 142, *152*
Holley, J. W., 71, *88*
Horowitz, F. D., 100, *118*
Horton, R., 1, *48*, 80, *88*
Huang, I., 28, *48*
Hudson, W., 70, *88*
Hunn, E., 37, *48*
Hunt, J. McV., 158, 163, *200, 201*
Hyde, D. M. G., 171, *199*
Hyman, M., 140, *153*

I

Imai, S., 27, 28, *47, 48*
Inhelder, B., 20, *48*, 101, *119*, 157, 160, 161, 164, 171, 176, 180, 186, 197, *198, 199, 200*
Inkeles, A., 122, *152*
Irwin, M., 95, 96, 103, *118*
Istomina, Z. M., 41, *48*

J

Jacobs, G. H., 12, *47*
Jacobson, A., 135, *153*

Jan, O. H., 93, 95, 96, *119*
Jelliffe, D. G., 92, *118*
Johnson, D., 31, 34, 37, 38, 39, *49*
Johnson, N., 160, *200*
Jones, E., 54, 78, *88*

K

Kagan, J., 98, 103, *118*
Kamara, A., 164, 168, 181, 182, 190, *199*
Kaplan, B., *89*
Kardiner, A., 78, *88*
Katz, J. J., 19, 24, *47, 48*
Kay, P., 4, 5, 13, 20, 41, *47, 48*
Kearney, G. E., 169, *199*
Keele, S. W., 21, *48*
Kelly, M. R., 171. *200*
Kelvin, P.. 127, 131, 137, *152*
Kerlinger, F. N., 81, *88*
Kilbride, J. E., 157, *200*
Kilbride, P. L., 70, *88*, 157, 200
Kimball, S. T., 122, 140, 141, *152*
Klein, R. E., 91, 95, 96, 98, 102, 103, 106, *118, 119*
Kline, P., 52, 53, 60, 64, 68, 70, 71, 82, 84, *87, 88*
Kluckhohn, H., 59, 73, *90*
Konner, M. J., 160, *200*
Krauss, R. M., 4, *48*
Kuper, A., 78, *88*

L

La Barre, W., 80, *88*
Lacey, P. R. de, 171, 181, 182, 189, *199*
Lakoff, G., 25, *48*
Lambert, W. E., 144, 145, *153*
Lambert, W. W., 75, *88*
Lasky, R. E., 106, *118, 119*
Latham, M. C., 91, *118*
Leach, E., 2, *48*
Lechtig, A., 106, *118, 119*
Lee, S. G., 64, 70, 82, 83, 86, *88*
Lefebvre, M., 171, 173, 175, *200*
Lefévre, A., 183, *200*
Lemos, M. M. de, 168, 171, 172, *199*
Lenneberg, E., 4, *47*
Levine, R. A., 8, *48*, 156, 184, *200*

Levine, S., 140, *153*
Levy-Bruhl, L., 41, *48*
Lewis, M., 160, *200*
Lézine, I., 158, 159, 160, 161, 163, 164, *198, 200*
Liang, P. H., 93, 95, 96, *119*
Lincoln, T. S., 81, *88*
Lindzey, G., 64, 69, 70, *88*
Lloyd, B. B., 156, *200*
Loeb, M. B., 135, *153*
Loftus, E. F., 23, *47*
Louyot, P., 93, 94, 97, *117*
Lovell, K., 197, *200*
Luckmann, T., 127, 128, 129, *151*

M

MacCannell, D., 122, *153*
McClaren Stefflre, M., 25, *49*
McDaniel, C. K., 13, *48*
McKay, A. C., 93, 94, 95, 97, *119*
McKay, H. E., 93, 94, 95, 97, *119*
McKnight, R. K., 122, *151*
Malinowski, B., 55, *88*
Manza, B., 93, 94, 97, *117*
Malpass, R. J., 131, 133, *153*
Marolla, F., 93, 97, 98, *119*
Martin, H. P., 93, 94, 95, 98, *118*
Martin, M., 53, *88*
Martinez, C., 93, 94, 95, 97, 98, *118*
Martorell. R.. 106, *118*
Menninger, W. C., 63, *88*
Mervis, C. B., 13, 22, 31, 34, 35, 37, 38, 39, *48, 49*
Miller, G. A., 136, *153*
Miller, R. S., 23, 24, 31, 34, 36, 37, 38, 39, *49*
Millett, R.. 102, *118*
Minturn, L.. 84, *88*
Mitchell, R. F., 14, *48*
Modgil, S., 156, *200*
Mohan, J., 67, 68, 82, *88*
Mohseni, N., 171, *200*
Mönckeberg, F., 93, 95, 98, *119*
Montague, W. E., 23, *47*
Montelli, T. B.. 93, 95, 97, *119*
Moodie, A. D., 93, 95, 96, 98, *118*
Mora, J. O., 93, 94, 95, 97, 98, *119*

Morgenthaler, F., 62, *89*
Morin, C., 171, 173, *200*
Mosak, H. R., 84, *89*
Muensterberger, W., 79, *89*
Mullen, F. G., 84, *89*
Munroe, R. H., 75, 76, *89*
Munroe, R. L., 75, 76, *89*
Munsell Color Company, 5, 13, *48*
Murdock, G. P., 59, 73, *89*
Murphy, H. B. M., 141, *153*

N

Najdanvic, R., 93, 94, 96, *118*
Naroll, R., 57, 58, 59, 60, 87, *89*
Neisser, U., 19, *48*
Nelson, K., 33, *48*
Nerlove, S., 96, 102, 103, *118, 119*
Newcomb, T. M., 122, 126, *153*
Newson, E., 58, *89*
Newson, J., 58, *89*

O

Oberg, K., 139, 142, *153*
Oldfield, R. C., 21, *48*
Olivier, D. C., 9, *48*
Olver, R. R., 33, 38, *47*
Opper, S., 156, 171, *199, 200*
Ortiz, N., 93, 94, 95, 97, 98, *119*

P

Paivio, A., 36, *48*
Paluszny, M., 135, *152*
Paraskevopoulos, J., 158, *200*
Pardo, F., 93, 94, 95, 97, 98, *119*
Paredes, B. de, 93, 94, 95, 97, 98, *119*
Parin, P., 62, *89*
Parry, J. B., 65, *89*
Parsons, A., 78, 79, *89*
Passin, H., *151*
Patel, B. D., 93, 95, 98, *119*
Paterson, J. G., 157, *198*

Peal, E., 145, *153*
Phillips, H. P., 70, *89*
Piaget, J., 20, 33, *48*, 101, *119*, 157, 162, 164, 171, 180, 186, 197, *199, 200*
Pinard, A., 171, 173, 175, *200*
Piñeiro, C., 93, 94, *117*
Pollit, E., 93, 95, 97, *119*
Popper, K., 51, *89*
Posner, M. I., 14, 21, *48*
Postal, P. M., 19, *48*
Preusser, D., 28, *48*
Pribram, K. H., 136, *153*
Price-Williams, D. R., 75, 86, *89*, 171, 184, *200*
Prince, J. R., 171, *200*
Pylyshyn, Z. W., 36, *48*

R

Radcliffe-Browne, A. R., 57, 63, *89*
Rahmy, M., 156, *199*
Ramos, C., 93, 94, 95, 97, 98, *119*
Rapaport, D., 53, *89*
Raven, P. H., 31, *47*
Read, M. S., 91, *119*
Reed, S. K., 21, 29, 36, *49*
Redjeb, H., 93, 94, 97, *117*
Reich, P., 25, *49*
Ribeiro, M., 93, 95, 97, *119*
Ribeiro, M. A. C., 93, 95, 97, *119*
Ricciuti, H. N., 93, 97, *118*
Richardson, A., 141, 147, *153*
Richardson, S. A., 93, 95, 96, *118*
Riley, M. W., 122, *153*
Riley, R., 93, 94, 95, 97, 98, *119*
Rips, L. J., 22, 23, *49*
Roberts, J. M., 102, *119*
Robbins, M. C., 70, *88*
Robles, B., 93, 94, 95, 97, 98, *118*
Rodriguez, H., 93, 94, 95, 97, 98, *119*
Rogers, E., 122, *153*
Roheim, G., 62, 63, 78, 81, *89*
Romero, E. R., 98, *119*
Rootman, I., 122, *153*
Rosaldo, M. Z., 31, *49*
Rosch, E., 4, 10, 13, 14, 15, 16, 22, 23, 24, 25, 26, 31, 34, 35, 36, 38, 39, *48, 49*
Ruesch, J., 135, *153*

S

Saenger, G., 93, 97, 98, *119*
Sarbin, T. R., 133, *153*
Sanford, R. N., 126, *153*
Scarr-Salapatek, S., 100, *119*
Schafer, G., 95, *118*
Schein, E. H., 122, 129, *153*
Schlenker, J. D., 98, *119*
Schutz, A., 124, 140, *153*
Scribner, S., 7, 28, 41, *47, 49,* 95, *119,*
  155, 156, 169, 177, *198*
Seagrim, G. N., 171, 181, *198*
Segall, M. H., 8, *49*
Seligman, C. G., 81, *89*
Semeonoff, B., 69, *89*
Serpell, R., 28. 41, *49*
Sharp, D. W., 155, 177, *198*
Shepard, R. N., 19, 36, *47, 49*
Shipman, V. C., 98, *118*
Shoben, E. J., 22, 23, *49*
Shouksmith, G., 65, *89*
Simonsson, M., 178, *199*
Simpson, C., 23, 24, 36, *49*
Sinclair, H., 176, *199*
Sinisterra, L., 93, 94, 95, 97, *119*
Smith, D. H., 122, *152*
Smith, E. E., 22, 23, *49*
Smythe, P. M., 93, 94, 95, 96, 98, *119*
Spain, D. H., 66, 69, 70, *89*
Spiro, M. E., 61, 63, 75, 76, *89,* 142, *153*
Srikantia, S. G., 93, 95, 96, *118*
Stambak, M., 160, 161, 163, 164, *200*
Stare, F. J., 93, 94, 95, 97, 98, *119*
Stefflre, V., 25, *49*
Stein, Z., 93, 97, 98, *119*
Stephens, W. N., 73, *89*
Stoch, M. B., 93, 94, 95, 96, 98, *119*
Suchman, R. G., 28, *49*
Super, C. M., 157, 165, *200*
Susser, M., 93, 97, 98, *119*

T

Taft, R., 122, 125, 128, 130, 133, 142,
  144, 147, 149, *152, 153*
Tagiuri, R., 16, *47*
Tesi, G., 93, 94, 97, *117*

Tisler, S., 93, 95, 98, *119*
Tizard, J., 93, 95, 96, *118*
Toby, M. L., 122, *153*
Toca, T., 93, 94, *117*
Toro, S., 93, 95, 98, *119*
Trabasso, T., 28, *49*
Triandis, L., 75, *88*
Triandis, H. C., 131, *153*
Trist, E. L., 129, *152*
Tulving, E., 19, 42, *49*
Tyler, M. J., 31, *47*
Tyler, S. A., 20, *47, 49*

U

Umaña, R., 95, *119*
Uzgiris, I. C., 158, 163, *200, 201*

V

Valantin, S., 162, *200*
Vega, L., 93, 95, 98, *119*
Vernon, P. E., 56, 65, 67, 69, *89*
Vuori-Christiansen, L., 93, 94, 95, 97,
  98, *119*
Vygotsky, L. S., 38, *49*

W

Wachs, T. D., 158, *201*
Wagner, M., 93, 94, 95, 97, 98, *119*
Warburton, F. W., 68, *87*
Wardell, W. I., 140, *153*
Warren, N., 91, *119,* 157, 161, *201*
Watson, J. B., 122, 140, 141, *152*
Welton, K. E., 21, *48*
Werner, E. E., 157, *201*
Wertheimer, M., 14, *49*
Wheeler, S., 122, 128, *152*
Whiteman, M., 98, *119*
Whiting, 58, 60, —
Whiting, B., 74, 78, *89*
Whiting, J. W. M., 57, 59, 72, 73, 75, 77,
  88, 89, 90

Whorf, B. L., 4, 41, *49*
Wick, J. A., 122, *153*
Wicks, P., 122, *152*
Williams, M. L., 100, *119*
Wilson, G. D., 53, *87*
Wing, H., 28, 41, *49*
Witkop, C. J., 95, *119*
Wober, M., 70, *90*
Wohlwill, J. F., 157, 166, 169, 176, 177, *199*
Wolf, M., 75, *88*
Wood, M. M., 140, *153*

Y

Yarbrough, C., 96, 98, 102, 103, 106, *118, 119*
Yoschine, T., 93, 94, 95, 97, 98, *118*

Z

Za'rour, G. I., 171, *201*
Zempléni, A., 157, *201*
Zempléni, J., 157, 162, *201*

Subject Index

A

Acculturation, 130–139, 178–184
Analog nature of categories, 2–3, 15, 18, 20–27

B

Basic objects, basic level objects, 30–35, 37, 38, 39, 40, 43, 44, 45
Bi-culturalism, 143–146

C

Categorization, *see* Human categorization
Colour, colour categories, colour terms, 3–15
Competence/performance distinction, 172–178, 183
Concrete operations, 166–197
Conservation, 166–197
Coping with unfamiliar cultures, 121–153
Couvade, 76
Cross-cultural psychology, logic and method of, xiv, 1, 6–8, 10, 13, 40–42, 53–56
Culture and personality, xiv, 61–64
Culture shock, 139–143

D

Dani, 7, 9–13, 16–17, 25
Digital representations of categories, 18–20
Dreams, 64, 81–84

E

Ecological demands, 184–196
Emotional expressions, 16–17
Enculturation, 130–139, 178–184
Ethnobiology, 31, 39, 44, 46

F

Freud, Freudian theory, *see* Psychoanalysis
Form categories, 16, 22, 27, 28, 35, 41
Formal operations, 197

G

Galton's problem, 60

H

History of cross-cultural psychology, xiii–xiv
Hologeistic studies, 57–61, 72–78
Human categorization, 1–46

I

Immigrants, 122–124, 125, 141, 146–151
INCAP study, 98–117
Interview data, 65
IQ, 94–96

K

Kwashiorkor, 92–93

M

Malnutrition and mental development, 91–119
Marasmus, 92–93
Multi-culturalism, 143–146

N

Nutrition, *see* Malnutrition

O

Objective tests, 68–69
Oedipus complex, 73–74, 78–79

P

Performance/competence distinction, 172–178, 183
Personality, *see* Culture and personality
Personality tests, 64–71
Piagetian theory and research, xvi, 155–201
Precocity, African infant, 157, 165
Projective tests, 68–71
Prototypes of categories, 14–18, 20–27, 35–37
Psychic unity of mankind, xvi; *see also* Universals
Psychoanalysis, psychoanalytic theory, xiv, 51–90

Psychological universals, *see* Universals
Psychometrics, *see* Tests

R

Rating scales, 65–66
Reculturation, 130–139
Resocialization, 127–130

S

Sampling, 66, 67–68
Schema, 20–21
Sensori-motor intelligence, 157–165, 196
Social anthropology, 57, 78
Socialization, 127–130

T

Tests, psychological tests, 64–71, 94–96, 100–103

U

Universals, xvi, 6, 9, 16–17, 40, 42, 54–55, 155–156, 163–167, 177, 196–197